Praise for Behind

'This is a blissful book, lovingly and stylishly written'

Daily Telegraph

'A fascinating documentary of post-Communist Eastern Europe . . . a compelling read. That Wilson writes with humour and charm makes it all the more engaging'   Independent

'Wilson captures the essence and the magic that Eastern European football has brought to European soccer as a whole, while documenting the heartache, corruption and decay that now degrade a once noble past. If you love the romance and the history of the beautiful game and have a passing interest in the complex geo-politics of the former Eastern bloc, then the cover price is a mere bagatelle in comparison to the pleasure you will derive from reading and owning Behind the Curtain'   Tribune

'Wilson writes captivatingly with humour . . . anyone with an interest in Eastern European sport will be consulting this book for years to come'   Financial Times

'Intriguing, entertaining history-cum-sports-travelogue of post-war Eastern Europe through the lens of the beautiful game'   Metro London

'Terrific'   Daily Telegraph

'Jonathan Wilson brilliantly plugs the gaps in our knowledge . . . Wilson is an observant and witty guide to life in Eastern Europe as seen through the lens of the beautiful game'

Waterstone's Books Quarterly

'A painstakingly researched and skilfully told journey into previously uncharted territory, which sheds much light onto a fascinating topic'   FourFourTwo

'In this part-travelogue, part-history Jonathan Wilson captures the contemporary chaos of the region'   Observer Sport Monthly

As a youngster Jonathan Wilson holidayed in the former Yugoslavia; as a young journalist for onefootball.com and the football correspondent for the *Financial Times*, his obsession with the region took root. He has lived in a Tibetian monastery in India, but nowadays is a regular contributor to *FourFourTwo*, *Champions* magazine and the *Independent on Sunday*.

By Jonathan Wilson

BEHIND THE CURTAIN

TRAVELS IN EASTERN EUROPEAN FOOTBALL

Jonathan Wilson

An Orion paperback

First published in Great Britain in 2006
by Orion
This paperback edition published in 2006
by Orion Books Ltd,
Orion House, 5 Upper St Martin's Lane
London WC2H 9EA

An Hachette UK company

5 7 9 10 8 6

A CIP catalogue record for this book is
available from the British Library.

Typeset by Deltatype Ltd, Birkenhead, Merseyside

ISBN 978-0-7528-7945-1

Printed and bound in the UK by
CPI Mackays, Chatham ME5 8TD

The Orion Publishing Group's policy is to use papers
that are natural, renewable and recyclable products and
made from wood grown in sustainable forests. The logging
and manufacturing processes are expected to conform to
the environmental regulations of the country of origin.

www.orionbooks.co.uk

CONTENTS

This book could not have been written without Sorin Dumitrescu, Stoyan Georgiev, Nedim Hasić, Taras Hordiyenko, Maciej Iwanski, Sándor Laczkó, Armen Nikoghosyan, Milena and Ljiljana Ruzić, Aleš Selan, Vladimir Soldatkin and Zaza and Natya Tsuladze, all of whom devoted huge amounts of time and effort to helping with research, translation and logistics. To them I am hugely grateful. I must also acknowledge the input of Philippe Auclair, Slaven Bilić, Neil Billingham, Duncan Castles, Marcus Christenson, Fuad Dargakhly, Gamid Gamidov, Luke Gosset, Elvir Islamović, Dennis Kopylov, Yevhen Kravs, Simon Kuper, Ben Lyttleton, Toma Mihajlović, Boris Navasardian, Dejan Nikolić, Vladimir Novak, Gunna Persson, Zdravko Reić, Kristian Sotiroff, Matt Spiro, Radu Timofte, Sergey Tsimmerman, Axel Vartanyan, Duncan White, Rafał Zaremba and Yuliya in Baku, all of whom were generous with assistance, information and advice.

Thanks also to my agent David Luxton for managing to interest anybody in a book on such a recondite theme; thanks to my editor Ian Preece at Orion for his support and suggestions; thanks to Mat Snow and Hugh Sleight at FourFour Two and Paul Simpson at Champions for publishing my pieces on eastern Europe with such bewildering regularity and so providing the seeds from which this book grew; thanks to onefootball, for handing me such a brilliant start in journalism, teaching me the value of distrust, and introducing me to so many wonderful people; thanks to Marcus Christenson, Dan Magnowski and Mithran Samuel for reading the manuscript and making criticisms and corrections; thanks to the Financial Times, for employing me long enough to have the resources to research the book, and for terminating my contract in time to write it; thanks to Emma, Dom, Cath, PJ, Jon, Bic and Sas for at various times putting up with my books, papers and supposed grumpiness; thanks to Rachel, for convincing me it was worth writing a proposal and for introducing me to David in the first place; thanks to Kevin McCarra, for underwriting the project to the tune of 30 Złotys; and thanks, finally, to my parents, for pretty much everything.

PHOTO CREDITS

p. 1 Shakhtar Donetsk
p. 2 Shakhtar Donetsk
p. 3 E. Shainskyi
p. 4 E. Shainskyi; Football Federation of Ukraine
p. 5 E. Shainskyi
p. 6 Empics
p. 7 Empics
p. 8 Empics
p. 9 Toma Mihajlović
p.10 Toma Mihajlović
p.11 Igor Zaplatil
p.12 Toma Mihajlović
p.13 Jonathan Wilson
p.14 Jonathan Wilson
p.15 Jonathan Wilson; Fuad Dargakhly
p.16 Fuad Dargakhly; Pavel Yeriklintsev

The creatures outside looked from pig to man, and from man to pig, and from pig to man again; but already it was impossible to say which was which.

George Orwell, Animal Farm

PROLOGUE

It is a little after six when the train pulls into Belgrade. After the overwhelming heat of the previous day, it is refreshingly cool as I stumble out of my compartment. An early-morning mist hangs over the station, mingling with the smoke and fumes of the trains to form a haze that is tinted yellow by the sun as it slants through the iron-girdered roof. A Serbian folk song, piped through the loudspeakers, plays in the background. As I peer up an almost deserted platform, indistinct figures scurry in the distance. The fact of the railway aside, there is nothing by which to date the scene; I could be stepping off the train at any time from about 1920 onwards. It is probably the music that gives the moment a filmic feel, but I almost expect a mysterious figure to appear at my elbow furling an umbrella and commenting meaningfully on the daffodils in Moscow this spring.

As it is, the first person I speak to that morning is a taxi driver. I don't need a taxi – I've already arranged to meet two journalist friends in the station restaurant at nine – but I know he will know a backstreet money changer. It turns out he's in that line of business himself, and so, after a brief haggle conducted in the dust on the bonnet of his car, I change my Slovenian tolar into Serbia-Montenegrin dinar at a rate significantly higher than that offered by the station *bureau de change*, which is closed anyway. I return to the ticket office, and book myself on a train departing for Budapest that evening, then make for the restaurant. It occurs to me as I sit there drinking coffee after coffee and eating small, bitter sausages, killing time until Milena and Ljiljana, my two

Serbian friends, turn up, that mornings like this are exactly why I like eastern Europe so much.

It's the question people always ask when I mention that I'm heading off to Romania or Ukraine or wherever for a holiday that doubles as a research trip – why there? I'm not sure there is an easy answer. There are the obvious pragmatic reasons, of course. It's cheap, for one, which is a major bonus for a freelance. There is, at least compared to Africa or Italy or South America, very little competition. And, given the widespread corruption, there are stories in abundance. Plus, there is the fact that when I worked for onefootball.com, I developed a range of contacts across the region. In many cases, they are now friends.

But it's also true that something in me warms to eastern Europe, and I rather suspect it's related to my affection for the classic thrillers of post-war espionage. There is, to my mind at least, just something plain romantic about taking a rattling old night-train from Ljubljana through Zagreb to Belgrade, about sipping thick Russian coffee in a St Petersburg café watching ice floes drift down the Neva, about buying raspberries wrapped in newspaper from an Armenian peasant on a mountain pass in the Caucasus. There is a magic even in the names: Odessa, Tbilisi, Szombathely. I fear that sounds frivolous, almost condescending: I hope not. I hope there is a Serb version of me, delighting in his journeys from London to Ipswich to Blackburn, smacking his lips at the thought of another lukewarm station pasty and revelling in the poetry of the Tyne-Wear Metro as it ploughs through Brockley Whins, East Boldon and Seaburn before finally pulling into Stadium of Light. At heart, for me, it's probably little more than nostalgia for a world I've seen only in films. Certainly Belgrade that morning had the feel of a novel by Greene or Le Carré.

Such is the spy-novel theory. My parents, I suppose, should also take some of the blame. Until I was seven we took every summer holiday at Patterdale in the Lake District. Then we started going to Slovenia, which is probably as close as abroad

gets to Ullswater. There were differences, though. Very few
Keswick tea shops, in those days, had pictures of Marshal Tito
on the wall. And then there were borders, and dinars, and
breakfasts of black bread and cheese – all fine, enticing things.
I'm not saying that if I hadn't gone to Bohinj in 1984 I'd now
be writing a history of football in the Lake District, but there's
no question that those holidays made me far more aware
of Communism, and particularly of Yugoslavia. Certainly I
was the only person in my class who wanted Red Star to win
the 1991 European Cup final against Marseille, with
their Sunderland-supporting former Newcastle winger Chris
Waddle.

And then there is the style of football played in eastern
Europe. I'm not sure there is any particularly good reason for
this, but I just prefer precise, technical football. If I'd been a
decade older I'd probably be one of the many Dutchophiles
who grew up on Johan Cruyff and Rinus Michels. As it is, my
benchmarks were Valeriy Lobanovskyi and Dragan Stojković. I
suppose, my brain having always been more adept than my
body, I naturally look to those who try to make football a
cerebral pursuit. In October 2002 I saw Vojvodina beat Sartid
Smederevo 5–1 in Novi Sad with some wonderfully fluent
pass-and-move football. After the match their coach asked me
what division Vojvodina would be in if they were an English
side. Technically, I said, they were as good as pretty much
anybody in the Premiership; physically they would be
destroyed by even an average first division side. The emphasis
is just on a wholly different part of the game.

I am also, I confess, largely a pragmatist when it comes to
sport. I may condemn it, but deep down I quite admire
cynicism, and there will never be a greater blend of cynicism
and sublime skill than that Red Star European Cup-winning
side of 1991. I'm not sure I will ever love a side as much as I
loved that one. If you can, get a video of their 2–1 victory
away to Bayern Munich in the first leg of the '91 semi-final.
FIFA clearly deserve praise for the way they have made

football more open in the past decade by doing away with the tackle from behind and the backpass, but that game shows how beauty could flourish despite the brutality, and how, being harder earned, it was somehow worth more. If Dejan Savićević and Brian Laudrup were that good then, with defenders hacking at their every stride, they would be truly extraordinary players today.

And so, predisposed to eastern European football, I joined onefootball.com, where I was given the chance to do something about it. What had been an interest became a passion, if only because it is far more stimulating to write pieces involving match-fixing, prostitutes and assassinations, than yet another transfer rumour concerning Mario Jardel.

And if it sounds self-centred and flippant to take to a country because it does good scandal, the other side of the coin is that there is just a chance that my publishing a story in Britain about corruption in, for instance, Romania may make some impression on the ground in Bucharest. And however meagre that impact is, writing that kind of article still seems far more worthwhile than the 'St Mirren full-back strains hamstring' sort of story. Maybe that's just the guilt of an easy-living football journalist talking.

This, then, is the book of my work covering eastern European football, first for the late onefootball.com, and then as a freelance. It isn't a history of eastern Europe, or even of eastern European football. In some ways, it isn't even about football *per se* – at least not in the sense of goals and bookings and corners – even if football is at the same time the ostensible purpose of my travels, the lens through which events are viewed, and the agent that binds the whole thing together. It is a personal book, a record of my trips to eastern Europe, of the people I met there, and of the tales they told. In that sense, it is a testament to the extraordinary cultural fact of football, its universality, its ability to draw together people from utterly different backgrounds.

Primarily, though, it is the story of how eastern Europe has changed since the Berlin Wall came down – told through football. Vestiges of the old system coexist uneasily with the new, and the result isn't working: whatever else has changed for the better, the football – with the possible exception of the game in Russia – has grown immeasurably worse. So inevitably, this is also, in an indirect way, the story of capitalism, and its effect on the socialist economies of the east, the story of how football has dealt with the new ideology and its new set of masters.

1 UKRAINE

Playing the System

Stark and black, a statue of Lenin strides along Artema, the main street of Donetsk. Stand in front of him, beside the fountains in the square, and it is as though nothing has changed since the city – noticing about eight years too late the way the wind was blowing – abandoned the name Stalino in 1961.

Walk behind Lenin, though, and the perspective changes. Incongruously, he now appears to be marching straight towards the McDonald's. Perhaps he intends to give them a piece of his mind, to overturn the tills and the deep fat fryers as Christ slung the money changers from the temple, but a glance around would tell him he is fighting a losing battle. To his left is a German bank, to his right an Irish pub, and straight ahead, just over the road from the McDonald's, is the Donbass Palace, a luxury hotel with rooms costing between $250 and

$2,500 a night. And this on a street named after a hero of the 1917 Revolution.

Everywhere you go in Donetsk there is building work, and most of it, at least in the centre of town, seems to involve neon lights. Having watched Shakhtar Donetsk reserves draw 0–0 with Chornomorets Odessa reserves one Tuesday, I headed out for a couple of quiet beers, but my conservative soul was soon driven back. Even in the middle of the week, the nightlife throbs. There is a disconcerting brazenness to it, but there is also a great energy, a palpable sense of a region on the up – even if there are persistent concerns about the traditional heavy industries. Again and again people say to me with a shake of the head, 'Ah, but you should have seen it two years ago . . .', should have seen it, in other words, back in the old days, back before the boom.

Back then, Donetsk was little different from how it had been in Soviet times, just another grimy industrial city churning out coal and steel to further the socialist dream. So rooted was it in industry that, until Stalin had it renamed in 1924, the city was known as Yuzovka, after John Hughes, the Welshman who established the first ironworks in the area in the late nineteenth century. When a football team was established in the city in 1936, it was called Ugolshchiki – or 'Coal-workers' – but by the summer it had been renamed Stakhanovets in honour of Aleksey Stakhanov, the local miner who produced such prodigious quantities of coal that he was lionised by the Soviet regime as an example to other workers. For years Shakhtar ('Miner'), as they finally became known in 1946, were just another Ukrainian team, chugging along in the wake of Dynamo Kyiv, winning four Soviet Cups but little else. All that, though, is in the past: the team is as upwardly mobile as the town and the face of Ukrainian football is changing. 'When I came to Shakhtar,' as their captain Anatoliy Tymoschuk put it, 'I dreamed of being champion; now I want to be champion of champions.'

I went to see Shakhtar play Dynamo in Kyiv on the opening

day of the Ukrainian season in 2004. It was July, but the
weather was hideous, a stiff wind driving across the Valeriy
Lobanovskyi Stadium and drawing with it grim curtains of
rain. None of the ground was under cover, so I huddled in the
press box under half an umbrella. Under the other half was
Taras Hordiyenko, who was once onefootball's correspondent
in Ukraine and on that trip was acting as my fixer. He learned
his English from technical manuals, and, at least when he's
detailing plans, it shows. 'What we shall do today is the
following,' he said when he turned up at my hotel that
morning. 'Number one: make some phone calls. Number
two: leave the hotel. Number three: buy our rail tickets to
Lviv. Number four: have breakfast . . .' The effect is rather like
Orwell's instructions for making a cup of tea, or perhaps the
catechism: it may sound a bit stilted, but at least you know
where you stand.

On the way to the ground Taras had insisted on making a
detour into an expensive ladies' clothes shop to buy a carrier
bag each. We could, clearly, have popped into a supermarket
and picked up bags for far less than the one hryvna (12p.) we
ended up paying, but in Ukraine carrier bags are a symbol of
status. It is very rare, for instance, to see a Ukrainian on a
night-train who is not clutching a Hugo Boss carrier bag.
'What we shall do with the bag is the following,' Taras said.
'Number one: place it on the seat. Number two: sit on it.' A
fine plan, which at least meant I was never getting wet from
underneath, but with the rain dancing and swirling beneath
the defences of the umbrella I was nonetheless soon drenched.
With the possible exception of a Sunderland game at Grimsby
when I stood out in the sleet for two hours selling the fanzine,
only for the game to be abandoned after seven minutes (a day
that was so cold that my mate Iain, after a quick dash to the
toilet, couldn't get his fly buttoned again), I'm not sure I've
ever been so miserable in a football ground. It's one thing to
get soaked on the open terrace at the Roker End as a teenager,
revelling in some half-baked notion of suffering for the team

and knowing that within a couple of hours you'll be back in the warmth of your gran's front room drinking coffee and eating ginger biscuits, quite another to do so a decade later in a press box in Kyiv with only the nebulous thought of a book to write for consolation.

At the same time I was aware that what was happening on the pitch was, at least in terms of Ukrainian football, of seismic importance. Shakhtar gave Dynamo a pasting. Admittedly they only wrapped the game up when Igor Duljaj made it 2–0 nine minutes from the end, and Dynamo did have the odd chance to equalise early in the second half; but Shakhtar, as their coach Mircea Lucescu said afterwards, could easily have been three up by half time. No matter, the result was significant enough: Dynamo had never previously lost a home league game in the Ukrainian championship by more than one goal.

Dynamo, naturally, attempted to play down the defeat. 'The way our team is prepared in the summer means we are not in peak physical form at the beginning of the season,' their midfielder Andriy Husyn explained. 'We have certain problems because of that, but if you look at the past few seasons, the evidence is that the system is correct.' The belief in systems is characteristically Ukrainian, and there is an element of truth in what he says: Dynamo have made a habit of late-season surges (and Shakhtar of late-season collapses). There appeared more to this defeat, though, than early-season teething. For much of the game, Shakhtar were utterly dominant, and only when the thought that they might actually beat Dynamo occurred to them did they begin to look vulnerable. For half a century Dynamo reigned supreme in Ukrainian football, and everybody else still lives in their shadow.

'In the Soviet period, Dynamo were almost sure of beating other Ukrainian teams,' József Szabo, a former Dynamo player who was appointed coach for a second time shortly after the defeat to Shakhtar, explained. 'It was like a pyramid in

Ukraine with Dynamo at the top.' Crucially, the patron of the club through the seventies and eighties was Volodymyr Scherbytskyi, the leader of the Ukrainian Communist Party. 'He was a great football fan,' Szabo said, 'and if there was a good player at Dnipro or Shakhtar or some other Ukrainian club he would make one phone call and the player would be in Kyiv – no money, or anything like that.'

It would be difficult to overestimate the extent to which Dynamo dominate the psychological landscape of Ukrainian football. In Soviet times, they effectively represented the whole of the republic, and fans from across Ukraine rejoiced when they got one over on central authority, as represented, however tenuously, by the Moscow clubs. That gave them a significant advantage, because the Moscow clubs, as well as being hated by teams from outside Russia, all squabbled among themselves, whereas the likes of Shakhtar and Dnipro Dnipropetrovsk had a tendency to roll over for Dynamo. The major clubs in other republics – Ararat Yerevan in Armenia, for instance, or Dinamo Minsk in Belarus – had a similar function as national symbols.

'In Soviet times,' the former Dynamo and USSR defender Andriy Bal told me, 'one of the ways each republic presented its face was through its best football team. Every team had its own way of playing. The Caucasus states and Uzbekistan could be recognised by their technical ability, the way they kept possession of the ball and their movement – just like the South Americans. Latvians, Lithuanians and Belarusians played like Germans. Moldova was similar to Romania. Ukrainian and Russian sides combined Western features and technical ability.' Dynamo, though, had a particular emotional hold because of events during the Nazi occupation.

Just on the right as you come out of the main door of Dynamo's stadium is a curious sculpture, a blockish structure bearing in relief the images of four footballers. You wouldn't know unless somebody told you, but it commemorates the Dynamo players killed after the notorious 'death match'. Its subtlety is appropriate: no game has ever been so submerged in myth and counter-myth. After the Second World War, the match became the stuff of Communist legend, the 'official' version claiming that the Luftwaffe challenged Dynamo to a match, and responded to losing by having every Ukrainian player summarily shot at the final whistle. Various embellishments were added, the wildest of which had German soldiers shooting at Dynamo players during the game. As inconsistencies in the various accounts were exposed, and the issue of whether the players were in some way collaborators was raised, there were even those who claimed the match had never happened at all.

The truth, as Andy Dougan sets it out in *Dynamo: Defending the Honour of Kyiv*, is rather more complex, but hardly less tragic. Several Dynamo players, and three from Lokomotiv Kyiv, ended up working in the same bakery during the occupation, and they entered a re-established Kyivan league as FC Start in 1942. They won every match, beating, among others, Hungarian and Romanian garrison sides. Flakelf, a team representing the Luftwaffe, then challenged them to a game, which Start won 5–0. A rematch, with an SS referee, was hastily arranged, but despite some brutal tackling from the Germans, Start won 5–3, Flakelf's humiliation being compounded when Oleksiy Klymenko, a young defender, rounded the keeper, dribbled to the line, then, rather than score, ran beyond the ball and hoofed it back towards the middle of the pitch.

Gradually, after the game, the eleven Start players were rounded up for interrogation. Mykola Korotkykh, who had served in the NKVD (the forerunner of the KGB), died after twenty days of torture, while the other ten were sent to the prison camp at Syrets, near Babi Yar, the ravine where thousands of Jews and others undesirable to the Third Reich were massacred. Being physically fit, the players survived atrocious conditions for six months, until, in reprisal for an attack on a plant that repaired motorised sleighs, Paul

Radomsky, the camp commandant, had one in three prisoners executed. Klymenko, Ivan Kuzmenko, the huge centre-forward, and Mykola Trusevych, who still wore his goalkeeping jersey, were shot in quick succession. Another player, Pavlo Komarov, who is believed to have collaborated, simply disappeared. The myth may have been better known than the truth, but the effect was the same: Dynamo became a rallying point in the darkest days of occupation, and, at least until fragmentation, retained a patriotic value as the team of all Ukraine.

A little further away from the stadium is another statue. If the first is difficult to decipher, there is no mistaking the second. Perched on the end of a bench, chin propped on hand, it is emphatically Valeriy Lobanovskyi – the Colonel – Dynamo's greatest manager and the man who, appealing to nationalist sentiment three decades after the death match, gave Dougan his subtitle. It is a remarkable work, its sharp angles, surprisingly redolent of the young Brian Clough, hinting at the revolutionary energy of Lobanovskyi's early managerial self. Even the yellowish bronze in which it is cast seems to recall the gingery tinge of his hair.

Bizarrely, the day after the Shakhtar match I was asked to ape the pose for Ukrainian national TV news, not on the bronze replica outside, but on the actual blue plastic bench inside the stadium. Not for the first time in eastern Europe, I found locals bemused that a British journalist should have come to watch one of their league games. I still treasure a small clipping from a Serbian sports paper topped with the implausibly dull headline: WILSON WILL REPORT (perhaps in Serbian it's a clever pun) after I'd gone to Belgrade to see a Red Star–Partizan derby. Nonetheless, I'd never been the subject of a TV news report before, so I unhesitatingly acceded to the crew's demands that I wander around the stadium gazing whimsically into the middle distance, as though the concrete bowl itself shimmered with the ghosts of Blokhin and Belanov, and then fold myself into Lobanovskyi's place in the dugout. Only later did it occur to me that I might have been the victim of some weird candid camera programme in which unsuspecting foreigners are gulled into impersonating famous Ukrainians, but if I were, nobody ever told me.

Lobanovskyi died in 2002, but his genius still presides over Ukrainian football. I met him only once, at a Champions League game eight months before his death, when the ravages of time and cognac had left him white-haired and red-faced; overweight and wheezing. He was sixty-three when he died, but he looked twenty years older. After that 2–1 defeat to Liverpool, though, even as he slumped behind a press-conference desk, answering questions with a splenetic reluctance that made clear he was there only because UEFA demanded he should be, his authority – the unthinking deference with which he was treated by Ukrainian journalists – was obvious.

In a coaching career that lasted thirty-three years, he won eight Soviet titles, six Soviet Cups, five Ukrainian titles, three Ukrainian Cups and two European Cup-Winners' Cups. But, more than that, Lobanovskyi defined Ukrainian football. If one goal can encapsulate a philosophy, Dynamo's moment of self-expression came in Lyon in 1986. With five minutes remaining in the Cup-Winners' Cup final, and Dynamo leading Atlético Madrid 1–0, Vasyl Rats advanced down the left, drew two men, and played the ball inside to Ihor Belanov. Belanov took two touches, and, as the centre-back moved across to close him down, he, without so much as a glance, laid the ball right for Vadym Yevtushenko. He moved one pace forward, forcing the full-back inside to close him down, then instinctively flicked the ball right for the overlapping Oleh Blokhin, who ran on to his pass, and, as the goalkeeper came off his line, lofted the ball over him to make it 2–0. Three minutes later Yevtushenko added a third, and Dynamo had their second Cup-Winners' Cup.

It is the second goal, though, that has become the image of

that final. It was quick, instinctive, and utterly clinical; once Rats had initiated the move, there was something almost inevitable about its conclusion. It was a goal conceived in the laboratory, and practised relentlessly on the training pitch, until, when the opportunity arose at the highest level, it could be executed without a thought. It was Lobanovskyi's scientific football in its purest form.

To speak of scientific football in Britain can be misleading. It was a supposedly scientific approach with which the former FA technical director Charles Hughes and Wing Commander Charles Reep tried to convince us that football is at its most efficient when it consists of whacking endless long balls into Positions of Maximum Opportunity, the damaging theory that became orthodoxy at the FA in the eighties. Lobanovskyi's conception was far more subtle and lethal than that.

It is overly simplistic to claim that Lobanovskyi and the prevailing ideology turned players into little more than cogs in a machine, but there is no denying that his Dynamo were a discernibly Soviet side and it is probably not inaccurate to say that they played a Communist version of the Total Football of Rinus Michels and Johan Cruyff, which emerged in the West at roughly the same time. The key difference, I would suggest, was less in the philosophy itself than in how it developed: Lobanovskyi thought up his systems and imposed them on players, whereas the Dutch model was more organic, growing out of the happy accident that several of that Ajax side had played together for years, having grown up in the same district of Amsterdam.

The tenets, in essence, were the same: hard pressing when out of possession, rapid movement of the ball and interchange of players while in. Control of space was still the key, but whereas the Dutch had great individual skills, and in Cruyff a brilliant, charismatic leader, the prime asset of Dynamo was their fitness. 'Since Lobanovskyi's time,' Szabo said, 'we have used the same training programme, which was produced from a special laboratory that we developed. In former years when our players were lacking technical skills compared to western European players, the feature we had was our ability to run a lot.' Although not, if Husyn is to be believed, early on in the season.

The idea recurred whenever I asked what was distinctive or unique about Ukrainian football, yet strangely a number of the Ukrainians who have moved west have been notorious for their laziness. The former Rangers manager Walter Smith once dismissed a question about Oleksiy Mykhailychenko's lack of work-rate by referring archly to his 'economy of movement', while Serhiy Yuran at Millwall became a byword for the flabby foreign star, picking up his wages and lapping up the lifestyle while contributing little or nothing to the club. In fact, only Andriy Shevchenko could truly be said to have prospered having left the Lobanovskyi fold. Oleksandr Zavarov was a flop at Juventus; Serhiy Rebrov did nothing at Tottenham (although he is not alone in that); while Belanov's form over his first two seasons in Germany was so bad that, when his wife was caught shoplifting, Borussia Mönchengladbach offloaded him to Eintracht Braunschweig of the third division.

For all their fitness, though, Dynamo were not, as the Western press liked to portray them, a machine. Yes, they practised set moves, but as Professor Anatoliy Zelentsov, Lobanovskyi's great collaborator, has always been at pains to make clear, more in the manner of chess players, ready to adapt to circumstance, than of robots. And while they may not have had a leader as overt as Cruyff, constantly marshalling and cajoling, it would be nonsense to suggest they were little more than a clockwork model programmed to do Lobanovskyi's bidding. 'Have you seen how bees fly?' Zelentsov once said. 'A hive is in the air, and there is a leader. The leader turns right and all the hive turns right. It turns left and all the hive turn left. It is the same in football. There is a leader who takes a decision to move, say, here. The rest need to correct their motion to follow the leader. Every team has players which link "coalitions"; every team has players which destroy them. The first are called on to create on the field, the latter to destroy the team actions of the opponent.'

In such a system discipline is paramount, yet Lobanovskyi the player was the image of the dilettante left-winger, taller than most, and slower, but blessed with sublime close control and one of the best left feet the Soviet game has known. In the Moscow press, they called him 'Cord', because of the way the ball at times appeared to be tied to his boot laces. He was innovative as well, studying the great Brazilians of the late fifties and developing his own version of Didi's 'falling leaf', a means of imparting backspin on to the ball such that it loses pace mid-flight and drops. Talk to older supporters and they recall how they used to go to Dynamo matches to watch Lobanovskyi take corners. Dynamo won the Soviet title in 1961 and the Cup three years later, but although Lobanovskyi was popular with the fans, he never got on with Viktor Maslov, who took over as coach in 1964. Yet Maslov was effectively Lobanovskyi's precursor, a fearsome disciplinarian who introduced the notion of a tight pressing game to the Soviet Union. After early opposition – one newspaper printed a picture of four Dynamo players closing down an opponent with the caption 'We don't need this kind of football' – he led Dynamo to three successive titles between 1966 and 1968. By then, though, Lobanovskyi had gone.

'As a player, Lobanovskyi could do almost anything on the pitch,' his Dynamo team-mate Viktor Serebrennykov said. 'But he didn't like to fulfil the routine work, and he was very clever and keen on tactics; that was why he fell out with Maslov. But this difference of opinion forced Lobanovskyi to re-evaluate his conception of football, and that was what made him the great coach he became.'

Lobanovskyi played just nine times in the Cup-winning season of 1964, and the following year moved to the comparative backwater of Chornomorets Odessa. After two years there, he joined Shakhtar. In 1968, as Maslov won his third straight title with Dynamo, Lobanovskyi finished four-teenth. At the age of twenty-nine, utterly disillusioned, he retired from football. 'That's it,' he told club directors. 'I'm leaving. I'm sick of playing anti-soccer.' Again it is easy to see the similarity with Clough. He too was a brash and brilliant forward whose playing career ended at the age of twenty-nine. He too developed a style of play so distinctive that when players left it they tended to struggle, and he too had his battles with alcohol.

Lobanovskyi could have drifted out of football, but later that year he met Zelentsov, in those days a young academic brimming with enthusiasm for the statistical methods he believed could be employed to improve standards of coaching. Lobanovskyi quickly warmed to the idea. He was a qualified plumber, but he had been a talented mathematician himself, graduating from high school with a gold medal, and even after joining Dynamo Kyiv as a nineteen-year-old, he continued his education at the Kyiv Polytechnic Institute. 'All life,' he once said, 'is a number.'

Zelentsov, with his chunky jumpers and faintly absurd Michael-Caine-as-Harry-Palmer-style glasses, is almost a stereotypical academic, but even in 2005 he was presiding over Dynamo's laboratory. 'Lobanovskyi and I became really inseparable,' he said. 'He once told me in public at a party: "You know, if not for you, I might not have come off as a coach. I owe you my formation, my knowledge, skills, understanding and realisation of football." '

Lobanovskyi took charge of Dnipro Dnipropetrovsk, then in one of the four parallel second divisions, in 1969, and immediately set about applying his new methods. 'If you want to be a good coach, forget the player you were,' he said. 'My relationship with Maslov didn't turn out well, but that's not important. He was a great tactician who taught his players how to play football.' Lobanovskyi, the man who as a player had called himself an artist and demanded the artisans did his running for him, came out in favour of a hard pressing game.

'To attack,' he said, 'it is necessary to deprive the opponent of the ball. When is it easier to do that – with five players or with all eleven? The most important thing in football is what a player is doing on a pitch when he's not in possession of the ball, not vice-versa. So when we say that we have an excellent player, that comes from the principle of one per cent talent and ninety-nine per cent hard work.'

Dnipro won promotion in 1971, and, two years later, Lobanovskyi returned in triumph to Kyiv, winning the league and cup double in his first season. Then, in 1975, Dynamo became the first Soviet side to win a European club competition, beating Ferencváros of Hungary in the Cup-Winners' Cup final.

There were, though, flaws to his method, which were highlighted at international level. 'I don't want a team of stars,' he always maintained. 'I want to create a star team.' He had that at Dynamo, but, in the limited time international managers are given to work with their players, he found it impossible to create the same fluency or understanding with the USSR. There was an obvious solution, and Lobanovskyi took it in April 1975, sending the USSR out for the 200th international in their history – a European championship qualifier against Turkey – with a team comprising eleven Dynamo Kyiv players. The Soviets won 3–0, but Lobanovskyi, mindful of the potential political dangers if a team of Ukrainians was seen to let down the USSR, repeated the experiment only once – in a 2–1 win over the Republic of Ireland the following month. When he tried to impose his regimen on players from other clubs, though, they resisted, and his first spell in charge of the USSR ended after players went on strike following defeat to East Germany in the semi-finals of the 1976 Olympic Games, in protest at his exhausting training methods. The closest he came to international glory was in the 1988 European Championship in Germany, when the USSR, having beaten Holland in the group stage, lost to them in the final, missing a penalty and suffering that ludicrous Marco van Basten volley as they did so. Football is full of what-might-have-beens, but there is no doubt that the USSR struggled without their sweeper Oleh Kuznetsov, who was suspended for the final; as Zelentsov says, without its leader, the hive cannot fly.

At club level, though, the success never ended. Lobanovskyi's genius was to continue developing his system as the game evolved, and he also proved remarkably adept at adapting to the changing political climate in the late eighties. In Soviet times Dynamo, like all clubs with the name, were the team of the secret police, and so were run by the Ministry of the Interior. As glasnost took hold, though, Lobanovskyi saw huge advantages in turning professional, in becoming a proper, commercial enterprise. If he could achieve the success he had with a group of Ukrainians who were technically still amateur, what would he be able to do if he could buy players from abroad and pump even more money into developing the laboratory? And how much more expensive Armenian cognac would he be able to buy?

Lobanovskyi lobbied Scherbytskyi, for whom Dynamo had built a five-storey underground palace, and he pulled strings until the politburo gave Dynamo permission to privatise. Given that sports clubs were exempt from taxation, that proved hugely profitable, as Dynamo set up joint ventures with Western companies and began what was effectively an import–export business. They had licences to deal in gold, platinum and parts for nuclear missiles; and those were not obtained without the involvement, or at least the blessing, of organised crime. Nobody who made a profit when the USSR fragmented did so entirely legally, but there were constant rumours – many, admittedly, emanating from Russia – that Dynamo were the team of the Ukrainian mafia.

After a poor World Cup in 1990, Lobanovskyi left Ukraine for the UAE, but he was persuaded to return in 1996. As other eastern European teams, deprived of state subsidies, crumbled, Dynamo thrived. 'We were fortunate that three things came together,' Serhiy Polkhovskyi, their urbane vice-president, told me. 'We had the generation of Shevchenko, Luzhny and Rebrov, we had rich investors, and we were able to persuade Lobanovskyi to come back. Of course the fact we had rich investors persuaded the generation of Shevchenko, Luzhny and Rebrov to stay, and the fact we had that generation and rich investors persuaded Lobanovskyi to come back.' So in the end, it all came down to the money – often, it was felt, rather too directly. In 1995, Dynamo were banned from European competition for three years after an attempt to pay off the Spanish referee Lopez Nieto ahead of a Champions League game against Panathinaikos. The ban, though, was lifted after a year because UEFA decided that suspending Dynamo was hampering the development of Ukrainian football; that is how dominant Dynamo were.

With Shevchenko, Luzhny and Rebrov, Dynamo reached the semi-finals of the Champions League in 1999, and it would have been they rather than Bayern Munich who met Manchester United in the final had they not squandered 2–0 and 3–1 leads in the first leg. Quarter of a century after he had first become coach at the club, Lobanovskyi was still performing miracles. Polkhovskyi, though, believes that it was not long after that that the warning signs began to emerge.

I first met Polkhovskyi at Dynamo's Champions League game against Liverpool in October 2001. Gérard Houllier, then Liverpool's manager, was in hospital after collapsing with a ruptured aorta at a league game against Leeds the previous Saturday, and, given that Lobanovskyi had recently had heart surgery, it seemed not unreasonable that he might offer a few words of sympathy and support. Most managers would leap at such an easy opportunity to satisfy the press, but Lobanovskyi didn't turn up at the pre-match press conference, sending instead the Serbian sweeper Goran Gavrancić, who had neither had cardiac problems nor been heard of in England. So I asked Polkhovskyi if he could perhaps phone

Lobanovskyi for a quote. Absolutely not, he said, with a weary resignation that bordered on the apologetic.

These days, Polkhovskyi admits that working with Lobanovskyi was a nightmare. 'He was like Kha from the *Jungle Book*,' he said. 'You never knew what he was thinking, and he was always ready to pounce.' Bolstered by his statistics, Lobanovskyi was notoriously dogmatic and authoritarian. 'When I was a player it was difficult to evaluate players,' Lobanovskyi said. 'The coach could say that a player wasn't in the right place at the right moment, and the player could simply disagree. There were no real methods of analysis, but today the players cannot object. They know that the morning after the game a sheet of paper will be pinned up showing all the figures characterising their play. If a midfielder has fulfilled sixty technical and tactical actions in the course of the match, then he has not pulled his weight. He is obliged to do a hundred or more.'

Inevitably his attitude led to conflict. Oleksandr Khapsalys, who played for Dynamo in the late seventies and early eighties, recalled how Lobanovskyi would simply shout down any perceived criticism. 'It was better not to joke with Lobanovskyi,' he said. 'If he gave an instruction, and the player said: "But I think . . .", Lobanovskyi would look at him and scream: "Don't think! I do the thinking for you. Play!" '

Oleh Blokhin, the star of the 1975 side, never enjoyed the warmest of relationships with his coach and neither did Ihor Belanov, who won the European Player of the Year award in 1986. 'My relationship with Lobanovskyi wasn't hostile, but it wasn't friendly either,' he said. 'It was simply professional. But he did a lot for me. He invited me to Dynamo and persuaded me to play his way. We had quarrels, but we were aware that we were doing a great thing.' As if to prove there were no hard feelings, Belanov named his son Valeriy.

As the world moved on, though, the distance between Lobanovskyi and his players grew. The age difference didn't help, but the problem was more the difficulty of having increasingly to deal with players who had not been brought up in a Communist society. 'He had internal torments,' Polkhovskyi said. 'Previously, a word or a glance was enough to assert his authority and explain what he wanted. Maybe it was typical of the Communist system, but now players have a greater freedom and an individuality. They become stars – like Beckham, what is Beckham? A pop star? – and so they do not put the team first.' In other words, Lobanovskyi, a product of socialism, struggled to come to terms with the advances of capitalism. In that, he is far from unique.

For all their off-field activities, on the pitch Dynamo continue to play the socialist football Lobanovskyi and Zelentsov developed in their laboratory. I remember the bewilderment in the press box at Highbury during a Champions League game between Arsenal and Dynamo as we tried to identify the blond bloke who'd just put in a cross from the left. 'Georgi Peev?' somebody suggested, reading his shirt number from the replay on the TV screen and checking it against the team-sheet. 'Can't be – he's the right-back,' came a dismissive shout, but it was: at its best, their movement can still delight. Football, though, has moved on from the days when teams would be mesmerised by protean opponents.

When Lobanovskyi died in May 2002, Oleksiy Mykhaily-chenko, who had been his assistant since 1997, took over and Shakhtar promptly won their first Ukrainian title. Dynamo won the next two championships, but nobody ever seemed convinced by Mykhailychenko. He was, in fairness, in an impossible position. How, after all, do you replace a national icon; a man so popular that over a million Ukrainians flooded the streets on the day of his funeral to pay their last respects? When Bill Shankly resigned from Liverpool in 1974, Bob Paisley, feeling his authority undermined by his predecessor's continued presence, had to ban him from the training ground. Ghosts, though, are not so easily banished. Lobanovskyi's genius was to keep the club in a state of perpetual evolution, but any change Mykhailychenko made became a major risk, fraught with the possibility of a failure that would be seen as a betrayal of Lobanovskyi's tradition. And so Dynamo stagnated.

After the defeat to Shakhtar, Mykhailychenko was downbeat to the point of moroseness. 'Don't blame the players,' he said. 'Blame me.' Dynamo did, and after a Champions League defeat to Trabzonspor a month later, he was sacked. The laboratory, though, will go on; Szabo, the man who replaced him, had been acting as vice-president with a responsibility for football and had coached the club between Lobanovskyi's second and third stints as manager.

When I met him in his office in the Valeriy Lobanovskyi Stadium, he was quite open about the fact that in his first spell in charge he remained in the great man's shadow. 'The laboratory would develop some plan and would propose it to Lobanovskyi,' he explained. 'He would look at it and then change it according to his opinion. It was the same for me. I took something from the lab and we introduced some changes according to what I thought. But I knew what Lobanovskyi would think, and tried to do the same.' And now? 'It seems that times have changed, and so it may be necessary to introduce some changes to our playing style.' Their socialist football has been superseded by Shakhtar, the thrusting capitalists from the home of Ukrainian socialism. Polkhovskyi, ever a man for a literary allusion, compared them to Rastignac, the ambitious youth created by Balzac who first appears in *Père Goriot*.

I arrived in Donetsk at lunchtime four days after Shakhtar's victory in Kyiv, having taken an early-morning train from Dnipropetrovsk. Having expected the industrial heartland to resemble a bleak Beamish – all grim terraces huddling in the drizzle – I confess I was slightly disappointed by its modernity. There wasn't even any miserable Dickensian weather, just a baking sun that had pounded relentlessly through the train window leaving me in desperate need of a shower. 'The things we shall do today are the following,' said

Taras. 'Number one: go to the hotel. Number two: take a room. Number three: you will take a shower. Number four: meet Mark Levytsky . . .'

In fact, we had barely had time to complete numbers one and two when Levytsky turned up at the hotel. He was an imposing bear of a man, who, with his pale linen suit, neat grey moustache and gigantic spectacles, could have been a Greek shipping magnate, but was actually a vice-president of Shakhtar, a post he took after an illustrious career as a sports journalist. He immediately offered a tour of the training base. These are normally necessary evils, diplomatic plods round empty fields while a painfully enthusiastic groundsman lists the 'x' pitches, 'y' of which have undersoil heating, and 'z' of which floodlighting, but Levytsky's tour was different. For one thing, he gave me a lift in a vast chauffeur-driven car with blacked-out windows; for another, even through the medium of a translator, Levytsky was outrageously funny. He had an aura of gravitas, but seemed to revel in puncturing it with conspiratorial stage whispers (the serious leather-bound notebook in which he made regular jottings, I noticed, was decorated with pictures of Britney Spears). And for another, Shakhtar's training base was like no other I had ever seen.

The pitches were immaculate, the weights room modern and spotless, the players' quarters spacious and comfortable, but it was the extras that were extraordinary. There was, for instance, an aviary. 'Some of the players and a couple of the coaches,' Levytsky explained, 'like birds.' It is easy to imagine a director in England uttering the words with dread, but Levytsky's meaning was entirely ornithological. Players have a stressful job, they need to relax, and so the club has provided the means for them to do so. And if the aviary doesn't do it for them, there is also a huge fishing lake, specially stocked with swans, a basketball court and a myriad other distractions. The effect is more five-star resort than boot-camp. Perhaps, though, it needs to be. How else would the club attract players to the blasted industrial east?

These days, barely a summer goes by without Shakhtar smashing the Ukrainian transfer record to sign the likes of the Nigerian striker Julius Aghahowa or the Brazilian midfielder Matuzalem, and they have brought in coaches of the international stature of Nevio Scala and Mircea Lucescu. For much of their history, though, they were just another provincial club, whose sole distinguishing feature was the passion of their support, the local miners turning out in sufficient numbers that Shakhtar regularly won the trophy awarded by the Soviet authorities for having the largest average home gate. Everything changed in October 1995 during a home game against Tavriya Simferopol.

Shakhtar tend to play home games these days at the Olympic Stadium, which is passably modern, but back then their home was the crumbling and faded Shakhtar Stadium, which still hosts reserve games. There is something striking about the scale of the construction and the resolute functionality of the design, but the overriding impression, even on a sunny day, is of drabness. Being there was like viewing everything through a grey wash: there wasn't a bright colour anywhere, apart, that is, from the area immediately around the VIP box, where the plastic seats were new, and screamingly orange.

Tavriya were the first champions of the independent Ukrainian league, but their visit to Donetsk three years later should have been unremarkable. The match, though, was immediately given an edge when Shakhtar's president Oleksandr Bragin (or Alik the Greek, to give him his underworld nickname), having missed a number of games following an attempt on his life, decided he would put aside security concerns and attend. He and his right-hand man, Rinat Akhmetov, went first to the nearby village of Dokuchayevsk to see the reserve side play, then hurried back to Donetsk for the main game. By the time Bragin got there, the match had kicked off, so, deciding not to wait for Akhmetov, who had been held up in traffic, he and his bodyguards rushed straight up the stairs to the VIP enclosure.

'It was a very humid day,' Levytsky told me. 'I was leading the TV broadcast and I was sitting in the commentators' cabin just below the VIP lodge. We saw before the game that Bragin's security people had gone through the place, but I can't remember whether they used sniffer dogs as Akhmetov does now.'

It was pronounced safe, but a few seconds after Bragin had opened the door and entered the passage leading into the box itself, there was an almighty explosion. 'They had recently constructed the roof on the main stand,' Levytsky said, 'and when the bomb went off there was such a sound that I thought one of the girders must have snapped. The game went on for maybe twenty or thirty seconds before the referee realised what had happened and took the players off.'

It was almost a decade after the incident that I spoke to Levystky, but he clearly still found it difficult to discuss, constantly taking his glasses off and rubbing his eyes. 'I stopped commentating and went upstairs to see what had happened,' he said. 'I saw a TV reporter running away and asked him what was going on. He told me not to go into the VIP lodge because it was too terrible to look at. Then I saw Ravil Safiullin who was the brother of Bragin's wife and at the time was Shakhtar's vice-president. We went into the lodge together. There were bits of bodies everywhere. Then Safiullin saw a severed arm, and recognised that the watch around the wrist was the president's, and that was when we knew he was dead.' Four bodyguards were also killed.

In 2004, at a trial in Luhansk, the one surviving member – or so he claimed – of the group that carried out that attack explained how they had tailed Bragin for several days before planting the bomb and detonating it remotely. 'As to who ordered it,' Levytsky said, 'there is no clear answer, but in the early nineties criminal groups were dividing up the territory of the former USSR, and it was rumoured in Donetsk that the assassination was something to do with that.'

A year later, Akhmetov replaced his former mentor as president. Thanks to his metallurgical interests, he is now the richest man in Ukraine. He owns the Donbass Palace Hotel and, quite aside from the redevelopment of the training facilities, has spent in excess of £50million on players. He is, as anybody in Donetsk will tell you, the Ukrainian Abramovich, except that he has invested at home. So emotionally attached to the club is he that in September 2000, after Arsenal had come from two down to beat Shakhtar at Highbury with, of all things, two late Martin Keown goals, he was the last person to leave the ground, slumping in his seat as the lights went out around him. 'He has fallen in love with the club,' said Lucescu. 'Maybe when he was a child he wanted to be a football player. His passion for the club makes me passionate.'

Passion is a word used a lot about Shakhtar. To their fans, that is what separates the miners – the living, breathing blue-collar proletariat – from the bloodless aesthetes in Kyiv. And a part of that, at least in the years before the arrival of Scala and the death of Lobanovskyi coincided to bring them their first league title, was their habit for surging into leads only to fritter them away. In 2001, on a freezing night in Poltava, I saw them play a poor Vorskla side. They took an early lead, hurled everything forward in search of a second, and conceded a sloppy equaliser, allowing Dynamo back into a title race that could have been over by Christmas.

That night, as their coach Viktor Prokopenko, an emotional, charismatic man committed to cavalier football, resigned, I asked a Shakhtar fan if he was frustrated by the way his team persisted in a suicidally attacking approach. He told me that that was the spirit of the club, that they were all about heart and passion, whereas Dynamo, with their scientific ethos, their computer printouts and their laboratory, while they might be winners, were little more than machines. Little wonder what success Shakhtar have had has come in the Cups.

When I relayed Polkhovskyi's description of Shakhtar as a modern Rastignac to Levytsky, he snorted. 'Let them read Balzac,' he growled with a dismissive waft of his arm. 'We will concentrate on football.' Typical Kyivans, he seemed to be suggesting, always over-intellectualising. Even the club song, after eulogising miners completing a shift and going to watch the team, contains a snide reference to the fact that 'not only students with books are waiting for Shakhtar's victory'. Everything at Shakhtar is referred back to the collieries: even their kit of orange shirts and black shorts is supposed to represent the experience of miners leaving the dark of the pit for the bright of the day.

Shakhtar are comfortably the best-supported side in Ukraine, regularly attracting over 20,000 fans to home games, although that is nothing to the figures they got in the eighties. All over Ukraine, clubs are struggling for crowds, partly because the football is poorer and partly because there are simply far more recreational distractions now than there were twenty years ago. Dynamo, curiously, although they pack out the 80,000-capacity Olimpyskyi Stadium for Champions League games, struggle by on an average of under 10,000 in the league.

Akhmetov would have it no other way: when he bought into football, he wanted the whole package, including a backdrop of fervent orange-clad fans. More because of that than for commercial reasons, Shakhtar are desperate to attract more fans to matches, offering free tickets and inviting supporters to training sessions where they can quiz their president. They even offer a VIP package, costing around three times the usual entrance fee, by which fans get a cushion, a copy of the club newspaper and a cardboard lunch box that includes sandwiches, chocolate and (pertinently for anybody who remembers the *Fast Show* sketch about nouveaux middle-class fans in England), a tube of Pringles. However many they attract, though, they will never generate the kind of merchandising revenues possible in Britain, because the fans just aren't rich enough. The major sportswear manufacturers apply a uniform rate across the world, so a replica Adidas shirt, for instance, costs £45 whether you buy it in Donetsk or Doncaster. If it seems expensive in Yorkshire, it is three-quarters of the average Ukrainian monthly wage.

That Shakhtar are now capable of providing a challenge is good for Ukrainian football as a whole, as even Dynamo admit. 'Competition,' Polkhovskyi said with a twinkle, 'can only give more honour to our victories.' It has not, though, made much of a difference to the smaller clubs, who still find themselves banging their heads against a glass ceiling. As far as they are concerned, the only difference is that where once the structures of power were controlled by Dynamo, now they are controlled by both Shakhtar and Dynamo.

Dnipropetrovsk is a sprawling industrial city on the banks of the Dnipro. With its bars and restaurants the waterfront could be idyllic, a Ukrainian equivalent of the Docas in Lisbon, were it not for the lurid green sludge on the surface of the water, and the huge factory on the far bank, on which is written, just in case you hadn't got the message: HOUSE OF STEEL.

In the bar of my hotel, a gloomy, dark-panelled chamber, I met Ihor and Volodymyr, two Dnipro fans with aspirations to hooligan status. They were both convinced that their team was the victim of a national conspiracy. 'You know that Dynamo run the federation and Shakhtar the league?' Ihor asked as soon as our conversation turned to football. At the time, the president of the Ukrainian Football Federation was Hrihoriy Surkis, the brother of the Dynamo president Ihor Surkis, while the president of the league was Ravil Safiullin, the former vice-president of Shakhtar.

To Ihor, it is simply a fact that if Dnipro challenge the duopoly, they will be beaten down. In 1994, for instance, Dynamo only pipped them to the league title in the final match of the season, but then neutered Dnipro as a serious challenger by signing their four best players the following day. Which begs the question of why, if they know their team can finish only third, the likes of Ihor and Volodymyr bother (and, judging by the scars on his arms, Ihor has suffered for his devotion). 'A man can love his wife,' Ihor said, 'even if he knows she does not look like Brigitte Bardot.' True enough, but most fans surely dream that there will come a time, for two brief hours on a Cup final afternoon, when football will enact its magical transformation and she will.

For all Ihor's pessimism, it has happened to Dnipro before. They won the Soviet championship in 1983, famously beating Spartak Moscow 4–2 on the final day of the season to clinch the title, and then again, even more remarkably, five years later, despite losing their two best players, Hennadiy Lytovchenko and Oleh Protasov, to Dynamo on the eve of the season. Their manager for that second triumph was Yevhen Kucherevskyi, and, after a spell in Russia with Arsenal Tula, he has returned to the club. With his battered face and straggly hair – imagine a taller, stockier version of Eric Gates – he is instantly recognisable as one of the old-school football men who no longer exist in English football, or at least not in its upper echelons. He is somehow both enthusiastic and world-weary, as though the cynicism built up by years of frustration cannot quite extinguish his passion for the game. 'To be honest, I didn't think the team would challenge for the title that season,' he recalled. 'During pre-season I said to the players: "I know that some of you were dissatisfied that all the newspapers wrote about Lytovchenko and Protasov, but now they have gone, and you must prove that you are worthy of praise." It was only two nails missing from a whole bench.'

The bench held up remarkably well, but it was only as autumn drew in and Dnipro faced Zenit in St Petersburg (then Leningrad) that Kucherevskyi began to believe his side could win the title. 'Matches against Zenit were always difficult,' he said, 'and the difficulty was increased because it was already cold and they were playing on their artificial pitch. Also, their coach Yury Morozov was a friend of Lobanovskyi, and so because our main rivals were Dynamo we knew it would be a hard game. Before the match I told the players to forget they were playing on an artificial surface and just play as though they were playing on grass. All the players were covered in blood because of friction burns, but we won 1–0, and that was when I knew we would win the league.'

But then came glasnost and fragmentation, and, although Dnipro were the first Soviet club to privatise, financially they have fallen way behind both Dynamo and Shakhtar, and are notable today only for having taken the decision not to sign any foreign players. 'Today, here as in all European countries, money is the decisive factor,' Kucherevskyi said. 'Nowadays, if you have money, you can buy players, you can pay salaries, you can build a training base – everything that is necessary for football. In the USSR, everything was based on order, on being afraid, on discipline. Back then we often had to break the law. We had to find money to motivate the players because footballers earned less than a cleaner did in England. Coaches were not simply coaches: I would wake up in the morning and have to think about everything from the toilet paper for the players to the team bus. I had to go to the authorities to beg them for things. At that time it was normal to say "I have wangled something", rather than just "I have got something".'

His ambivalence is not uncommon. In many cases the supposed freedoms of capitalism are merely theoretical, while corruption continues to blight the system. Certainly that is the general feeling in Taras's home town of Lviv, way out in the west near the border with Poland. We arrived on the night-train from Kyiv and made straight for his flat, where I would have had a shower had there been any hot water. On the plus side, there was breakfast, prepared by Taras's wife, Olenka.

Ukrainians don't do breakfast as we know it. To them it's a meal like any other, and so most days in Ukraine began with a search for a restaurant where I could eat something bland like yoghurt while Taras tucked into a cutlet or a steak. The only concession he made was not to have soup, which apparently is only for lunch. Olenka, with a kindly nod to my Western tastes, laid out a plate of cooked meats and cheeses. And boiled potatoes and a cauliflower, grown in Taras's allotment, battered and fried, which was far nicer than it had any right to be.

It was in Lviv, on 14 July 1894, that Ukrainian football was born (although Lviv was in those days part of the Austro-Hungarian empire). There may have been impromptu games before that, but it was then that the first organised and verifiable match took place, a show put on by the Sokil Sports Club. Part of a whole day of demonstrations of various sports, it was scheduled to run until the first goal was scored, and so lasted only six minutes (or possibly seven, Yaroslav Hrysyo, the president of the Lviv Regional Football Association allows). It was enough, and football took off in the region, although Karpaty, Lviv's major local club, were not founded until 1963 as a civil side, run by a trade union, to match the local army team, SCA.

Karpaty became one of the better Ukrainian teams, no Dynamo Kyiv it is true, but able to hold their own in the second division of the Soviet league, and, between 1971 and 1977, and in 1980, good enough to take their place in the Supreme League. On an extraordinary night in 1969, they even won the Soviet Cup, beating SKA Rostov in the final to become the first winners from outside the top flight.

Volodymyr Paltsun, the editor of *Vilna Ukrayina*, the official Lviv-region newspaper, watched the final on television in his office. It was a warm evening and he had the window open. Early in the second half, with Karpaty desperately chasing an equaliser, he heard a shout from the Regional Communist Party offices across the street, urging the Karpaty captain Ihor Kulchytskyi forwards: 'Kulya, don't give in!' It may not seem like much, but it has become one of the emblematic anecdotes of their triumph. At a time in which a stony face was part of the uniform of political leaders, such an outburst of emotion was remarkable. Later that evening, after the celebrations had burned themselves out, trams left their official routes to carry the relatives of players home, which in Brezhnev's USSR was tantamount to anarchy.

That triumph confirmed Karpaty's place in local hearts, and, with their policy of fielding players from the Lviv and Zakarpattya regions – as opposed to SCA, who conscripted from throughout Ukraine – they became an outlet for western Ukrainian nationalism. That anti-Moscow sentiment was intensified by events in 1977, when they were relegated behind CSKA, who had not merely arranged that their final two away games should end in draws, but had even reneged on that agreement and 'inadvertently' beaten Ararat Yerevan 3–2. Once match-fixers start cheating each other, there is no honour left in football at all.

Karpaty went up again in 1979, but as post-match demonstrations in Lviv, particularly after victories over Moscow sides, became increasingly common, the club became ever more problematic for the local Communist leadership, until finally, in 1981, Viktor Dobryk, the first secretary of the Lviv Region Communist Party, shut them down.

Despite having a USSR international and three players who had played in the USSR side that had won the 1978 Under-21 World Championship in their squad, Karpaty, rent by cliques, were relegated in 1980, and, the following season, weakened by the departure of several key players, finished a disappointing eleventh in the second flight. Dobryk, citing 'problems with trade-union financing', and insisting he was acting 'to strengthen Lviv football by collecting together the best players from both teams' merged the two clubs to form SCA Karpaty. The army were put in control and, although the new entity took Karpaty's place in the second flight, most of their remaining players had left within two years. Interest in the team diminished, but the final straw came in 1985 when SCA

Karpaty were ordered to throw a game against CSKA Moscow. Both sides were battling for promotion, but a decision was taken in Moscow that a military team from the provinces should not be allowed to get in the way of the army's premier club.

Karpaty's story took a turn for the better in 1989, when they re-formed and began the slow process of working their way up from the bottom of the Soviet championship; SCA Karpaty, meanwhile, slowly sank, and now play in the regional leagues under the name Halychyna, having moved to Drohobych, a small town about forty miles south of Lviv.

This, though, is not a story with a happy ending. Karpaty were relegated in 2004, and once again there were widespread accusations that they had been deliberately targeted for having kicked against the system. Most clubs tend to spend most of their existence at least partly convinced that they are being cheated, but in Karpaty's case there was definitely something odd going on.

Karpaty's problems, it seemed, centred on their president Petro Dyminskyi. Most people seemed to agree he is 'difficult', a man who adheres to his principles no matter what, the real trouble being that a rigorous belief in 'fair play' (the English term is used across Europe, and the English, curiously, are seen as its prime exponents) is not necessarily the most useful asset if you're looking to prosper in Ukrainian football.

There are almost constant complaints about referees, while it is generally accepted that, particularly towards the bottom of the table, the practice of 'three-for-three' is commonplace. The scam is practised throughout eastern Europe, and involves a cooperative of sides who agree that when they play each other the team at home will always win – if five teams are involved, for example, each is guaranteed fifteen points. 'In our federation there is a division of honest play,' Oleksandr Bandurko, the vice-president of the Football Federation of Ukraine (FFU), explained to me through his press officer. 'If there are signals that such a thing has happened we refer it to the commission and they try to clear up the situation. We generally use the reports of the referee and the match delegate, which can indicate that the match was played without due sporting struggle, but really it is not easy to prove that the match was arranged in advance. The problem is serious because the only strict proof is to catch somebody red-handed. We realise such a problem exists, as it does in any country, and we are working on it.' Which is no great consolation to Karpaty.

It is refereeing decisions that provide the most direct evidence. One club official claimed to have heard a referee say that he would 'kill Karpaty because they are not paying', while estimates of how many points Dyminskyi's refusal to play along cost Karpaty in the 2003–04 season range from seven to ten. On three occasions the mistakes against Karpaty were so blatant that match officials were subsequently suspended by the FFU. As president of the Lviv Regional Football Association and a member of the FFU's Referees' Committee, Yaroslav Hrysyo has a foot in each camp. I met him in a hotel room in Kyiv where he was staying after attending a FFU congress that had elected the former Dynamo Kyiv supremo Hrihoriy Surkis, unopposed, for another four-year term as president. Hrysyo was adamant that Karpaty were moaning about nothing. 'We considered all the games that were presented to us,' he said. 'The referees were punished for their mistakes. These appeals concerned three matches; the league consists of thirty matches, so I don't think such mistakes can be an excuse for the team's failure. The mistakes were punished so it's impossible to say other agencies were involved.'

The situation has improved immeasurably, he insisted, since his time as a referee, when he was often called upon to take charge of games being played in war zones. He spoke of tanks at a stadium in Azerbaijan, and a blockade at Yerevan airport, but his worst experience came in Fergana, Uzbekistan, refereeing a game between Neftyanik and Kotayk of Armenia.

Neftyanik had an Armenian president, and, as Kotayk were desperate for points to avoid relegation, he was concerned that if Neftyanik lost, he would be accused of throwing the game. Accordingly, he did the exact opposite, and offered Hrysyo a bribe. 'I never agreed to such proposals,' Hrysyo said. 'I heard about it happening several times that something would be promised, but it would remain only a promise.'

At half time, Kotayk led 1–0, and as he left the pitch Hrysyo was greeted at the touchline by the city mayor, who was carrying a gun. 'You can imagine what pressure like that does,' he said. 'You try not to make mistakes against the home team. Anyway, I was lucky; soon after half time Neftyanik scored twice and the game passed off much more peacefully.' Both penalties, perhaps? 'Oh, no,' he said. 'Whenever teams lost away games and there'd been a penalty, they always went home and blamed the referee, so I tried never to give them.' It might not be perfect, but Ukrainian football has at least moved on from those days.

Perhaps not far enough, though, for quite aside from the refereeing, Karpaty felt aggrieved by their 3–2 defeat to Borysfen four games from the end of the season. Borysfen's captain, the former Ukraine midfielder Yuriy Maksymov, was suspended, but played anyway, scoring one and setting up another. Karpaty, not surprisingly, appealed, but the FFU, contrary to all precedent, allowed the result to stand.

I had spoken repeatedly to the club, and they had assured me that they were keen for me to investigate and would give me every assistance. Even the day I left Kyiv on the night-train west, I was told I could talk to players and club officials, and examine the videos of the dubious games myself, but by the time I arrived, something had changed. There was cordiality, but little cooperation. A new general director, Yuriy Dyachuk-Stavytskyi, had been appointed, and, after forty years in the Soviet and post-Soviet game, he was a pragmatist. The president's anti-corruption drive had been tempered, and the logic seemed to be that if Karpaty were to be promoted the following season, the last thing they wanted to do was to antagonise the FFU or the Professional League.

During my conversation with Dyachuk-Stavytskyi, he received a number of phone calls, two of which were of particular interest. One informed him that the tapes of the controversial incidents had arrived, but, presumably reasoning that I would not understand, he ordered them to be taken away again. The other was to tell him that members of the official fan club wanted to arrange a meeting with me; he insisted that I should not be allowed to talk to them. Dyminskyi's war on corruption, it seemed, was over, and a full-scale cover-up was in effect.

That left just one person willing to talk: the remarkable Yevhen Kravs, a local journalist probably related to the general who led the Ukrainian Galician Army through the turmoil of 1918–19. Perhaps because of his glorious ancestry, he holds little truck with the discretion most of those involved in Ukrainian football practise. We arranged to meet at his apartment in central Lviv. He arrived fractionally after me, zipping up in a brightly painted Zaporozhets. Robust and small, the cars – known locally as Horbatyi, or Hunchbacks – were produced in huge quantities in Ukraine in the sixties and developed a reputation for smoky unreliability. Kravs, though, drove a souped-up model that he races with other enthusiasts. That afternoon he should have been covering a tennis tournament, but, because of persistent rain, he had spent the day tinkering under his car. When I first met him, he was covered in oil.

His apartment was large, but sparsely furnished, achingly Bohemian. In one corner of the room, where we chatted, stood a magnificent nineteenth-century boiler, its gleaming white front adorned with a depiction in bronze of the head of a German queen. In another, curled disdainfully in a window box, was a Siamese cat. On the table between us was set a pot of excellent coffee and a bottle of brandy. In Ukraine, he said, it is considered unlucky to stop at two glasses, so we made sure we left that landmark well behind.

The first thing to understand, Kravs told me, was the power wielded by Dynamo and Shakhtar. Under normal circumstances, it would be possible to play one off against the other. In 2002–03, for instance, Volyn Lutsk, one of the smaller sides in Ukraine, persuaded Dynamo to pay them a win bonus if they beat Shakhtar and, having done that, got Shakhtar to pay them a win bonus if they beat Dynamo, which they also did.

With presidential elections scheduled for the autumn, though, circumstances in 2004 were far from normal. Hrihoriy Surkis, the president of the FFU, was a key figure in the Social Democratic Party of Ukraine (United), a political grouping of Kyivan oligarchs. His brother Ihor succeeded him as president of Dynamo, and such was the identification of club and party that in 1998 every player joined the SDPU. Dynamo's badge was regularly used on election literature, and it has even been suggested that the sale of Shevchenko to AC Milan in 1999 was arranged at a time that would do Surkis least political damage. (Although the fact he had just scored three times in a Champions League quarter-final against Real Madrid made it a sensible time to sell anyway.)

Usually, the SDPU would stand in opposition to the so-called Donetsk Clan, which is headed by Akhmetov, but, having no viable candidate of their own, the Surkis brothers, desperate to prevent the reformist Viktor Yushchenko becoming president, were forced to back Viktor Yanukovych, the Donetsk candidate.

Politically, anyway, Dyminskyi was known to oppose Surkis, and it is probably no coincidence that his company found its tax affairs under scrutiny during the 2003–04 season. 'Two or three years ago the clans were enemies,' Kravs said, 'and that might have helped, but now Dynamo and Shakhtar are friendly so they have no interest in a third party, and have ganged up on Dyminskyi. It is now less important for Surkis to win against Shakhtar than to make his man president of Ukraine. For Akhmetov at the moment it is less important to beat Dynamo than to buy the biggest metallurgical organisation. They cannot be at continuous war, and it happens that in the course of the last year they have come to peace. If Dynamo and Shakhtar were at war, then Akhmetov might have helped Karpaty.

'They talked about three matches, but I know about more than three matches. I can point to nine matches where the refereeing has been directed against different teams. You can compare it to chess: the big players are sitting in a room somewhere moving the pieces. Arranged matches and bent referees happen all the time, and Dymynskyi is the first to stand against it. He has suffered for that and I respect him for such a struggle. He is a difficult person with many negative aspects, but I respect him. The problem is that he has got the timing wrong.'

Maybe, but two decades ago Karpaty were run down just as surely. To speak of timing seems merely a consolation, for the truth is that, historically, in Ukraine it hasn't paid for the little man to kick too hard against his betters. Perhaps, though, times are changing, and not just with the rise of Shakhtar. History does not make Ukrainians optimistic, but then few predicted the kind of popular revolution in December 2004 that overturned Yanukovych's flawed election victory, and saw Yushchenko installed as president.

Things, inevitably, will change as a result of the Orange Revolution. The Zakarpattya chairman Volodymyr Paulyo, for instance, was arrested at the club stadium in Uzhhorod, the heartland of SDPU support, having apparently begun to equip a counter-revolutionary force. Some say he intended to fire on demonstrators, others that he planned to disguise himself as a Yushchenko supporter and seize a school in an effort to discredit the protests. He was formally accused of having interfered in mayoral elections in Mukachevo the previous spring, when opposition candidates were attacked, polling stations looted and ballot boxes thrown into a nearby river. The head of the local administration, Ivan Rizak, was also arrested, at which his replacement, Viktor Baloha, decided local government could not finance the club.

As Yushchenko's reforms took hold, Naftohaz Ukrayiny, the state oil and gas company, ended their $4m annual sponsorship of Vorskla Poltava, and demanded the return of the team bus, which, it turned out, belonged to them. In Kharkiv, the Metalist coach Hennadiy Lytovchenko, all his assistants and a group of leading players abandoned the club – which was controlled by the oligarch Oleksiy Yaroslavsky – and went across the city to Arsenal, a division lower, but led by Viktor Chumak, a close ally of the new head of the local administration. In Crimea, Serhiy Kunitsyn, president of the regional football federation, was charged with budgetary irregularities over the construction of a new stadium in Symferapol.

The biggest threat, though, is to the Surkis brothers and their control of Dynamo. Andriy Shevchenko read out a statement on television backing Yanukovych during the demonstrations, but others from the 1999 team have deserted them. Oleh Luzhny spoke out in favour of the revolution, while Serhiy Rebrov wore an orange sweatband in support of Yushchenko at West Ham's Championship victory over Watford. In February 2005, the club's shares were frozen by the state, pending investigations into the club's privatisation and subsequent financial activity.

If the power of the oligarchs really is waning (and they are not simply being replaced by a new cabal), then perhaps there is a chance of free and open competition and there is hope for the likes of Dnipro and Karpaty, and league titles will have the 'honour' Polkhovskyi craves. That, though, is for the future. As I bounced over the grass start to the runway at Donetsk International, on a flight bound for Kyiv, I chatted to the businessman next to me, a trader in aluminium. He liked football he said, and watched AC Milan's games in Serie A because of Shevchenko. And Ukrainian league games, did he ever go to them? 'Oh no,' he said. 'It's too predictable.'

2 POLAND

The Ugly Daughter

It was night, it was snowing on and off, and we had about 250 miles back to Warsaw. Maciej Iwanski, a commentator for TVP and my fixer in Poland, being young and thrusting, was driving quickly. As we zipped around a shallow bend, the front right of the car bucked suddenly, dipping down, and then, with a dreadful thump, jolted upwards. Maciej hit the brakes, and we slithered to a squealing halt in the gravel by the side of the road. The problem wasn't difficult to spot: a large pothole, probably four inches deep, eating across the asphalt. Using his mobile phone as a torch, Maciej checked the wheel. We were lucky, just a crack in the hubcap.

A couple of days later, in an Irish pub in central Warsaw, I met Jerzy Engel, the coach who led Poland to the 2002 World Cup finals. The week he took the national job in early 2000, he told me, a newspaper had run a survey on the state of the nation. Asked what the worst thing about Poland was, most people replied 'the roads'. Coming a close second, though, was the national football team. Given they had failed to qualify for a major tournament since 1986 that, perhaps, was not surprising. The abjection of the national team, whatever the reality, has become a joke as solidly rooted in the Polish comic landscape as England's tennis players or British Rail sandwiches are here. Poland, though, have not always been hubcap-crackingly awful.

Wembley in 1973 was a good place to be the goalkeeper of an unfancied team, and a bad place to be a Leeds United forward. If Jim Montgomery's reflex parry from Peter Lorimer in the FA Cup final was the greatest save Wembley has known, the greatest goalkeeping performance came five months later, as Jan Tomaszewski, having been dismissed as a 'clown' by Brian Clough, produced a series of unorthodox blocks to earn Poland the draw that saw them to the World Cup finals at England's expense. Allan Clarke converted a penalty to equalise midway through the second half, but it is the footage of him – hands on hips, slowly, disbelievingly, shaking his head as he spits and turns away after a close-range header has been brilliantly parried – that endures as the image of Sir Alf Ramsey's final competitive game. It may have been only a draw, but back then, as Tomaszewski said, 'a draw at Wembley was like a win' for away sides, and that result, heralding four successive appearances in World Cup finals, remains the pinnacle of Polish football history.

Clough later apologised to Tomaszewski for the clown jibe, claiming that as he expected to be the next England manager he had wanted to downplay Ramsey's achievements, but the comment remains part of football lore because it was so apt. Brilliant as Tomaszewski was that night, with his dishevelled appearance, his mop of gingery hair held in place by a length of twine, he seemed perpetually on the brink of comic mishap. He looked like a clown, he acted like a clown, but he kept goal like a brick wall.

I met him on a morning of gentle snow in his home town of Łódź, amid the faded opulence of the café at the Grand Hotel. ('You'll easily find it,' he had said. 'In Łódź there is only one real street, and all the buildings that aren't on it are queuing to get on it.') He was in his late fifties by the time I met him, his face ruddied by alcohol and the ginger visible only in a faint haze around his temples. The most striking thing about him, though, was his size, and specifically the enormousness of his hands, which, it is no exaggeration to say, were so big that he must have been able to catch a football quite comfortably with just one of them.

Before Wembley, Poland's only previous appearance in a major tournament finals had come in 1938, when Ernest Wilimowski scored four in a 6–5 extra-time defeat to Brazil in Strasbourg on a pitch so muddy that the Brazilian forward Leônidas briefly experimented with playing in his stockinged feet. Evidently recognising he was much too good for Polish football, Wilimowski defected and later played for West Germany.

Poland won Olympic gold in Munich in 1972, and beat England 2–0 in Chorzów the following May, but to have played just one game in nine previous World Cups left a sense of inferiority, and Tomaszewski spoke of Poland going to Wembley in a state approaching terror. 'It was like Cinderella going to the ball,' he explained. 'It was the first time we'd ever played in a stadium with a roof; with a roof the roar is different. In Poland we had only open stadiums. Wembley was hell.

'Before the game there was a presentation to the queen. The Polish players all stood to attention, but the England players were used to it, and very casual.' He mimed them standing, arms folded, chewing gum. 'I said then I would give five years of my life simply not to be humiliated.'

England had demolished Austria 7–0 there in a friendly three weeks earlier, a result that had done much to reassure people that Chorzów was a one-off aberration. 'The English "knew" they had qualified,' Tomaszewski said. 'It was only a question of how big the defeat would be, and that gave us an internal motivation, like when your apartment is on fire and you rush out with a huge TV. It's energy from the liver, the kind of energy that you produce when you are highly stressed, the power that comes from I don't know where.'

Poland's goal, scored ten minutes after half time, was the result of two mistakes – the first by Norman Hunter as Grzegorz Lato skipped by him on the Polish left, and then by Peter Shilton as Jan Domarski's shot squirmed under his dive – but it remained Tomaszewski's match. 'That night I would have put the mortgage on any horse he had a fancy for,' Mick Channon said. The draw remains one of those landmarks in the perceived decline of English football, the first time England had failed to qualify for a World Cup, but it was not a humbling lesson in the manner of the 6–3 defeat to Hungary in 1953, or even the 3–1 defeat to West Germany in 1972. It was a freak, and even at the time was widely seen as such, although that did not prevent Ramsey being criticised for his negativity. Shilton described Tomaszewski's performance as 'haphazard, wildly eccentric and, at times, downright lucky', and such was the clown's psychological impact, that the myth endures that Poland are a bogey team for England, even though England have not lost to them since.

He was the indisputable hero at the end, but Tomaszewski almost gifted England a goal in the opening minutes. 'Our basic strategy was to play anti-football, to stop England playing, just to keep possession,' he said. 'But because I was so bewildered by the atmosphere, I made a crucial mistake that could have ended everything before it had begun. I was ready to kick the ball clear, and I put it down to run it out to the edge of the box. I hadn't noticed Allan Clarke, and he nipped in to steal the ball from me. I just saw some shadow of a white shirt, so I grabbed at the ball. I got a hand on it, and I was kicked by Clarke. It wasn't a foul, but the referee whistled and gave us a free-kick. That was what woke me up.

'I remember hardly anything from the game. It was so noisy we were going crazy. With 100,000 people screaming for England we couldn't hear our own thoughts, so I only realised, in the dressing room after the game, that something special had happened when the vice-president of the Polish Football Federation (PZPN) ran into the showers fully dressed, came under the water and hugged me.'

The draw at Wembley gave Poland a new belief – 'After Wembley,' Tomaszewski said, 'everything was different' – and they went on to finish third in the 1974 World Cup. They performed creditably in Argentina in 1978, and were third again in 1982. Then, in Mexico in 1986, having drawn with Morocco and beaten Portugal, they lost their final group game to a Gary Lineker hat-trick – creating the (statistically corroborated) impression in Poland that England were their bogey team – and, qualifying only as one of four best third-placed teams, were condemned to meet Zico's Brazil in the second round. Dariusz Dziekanowski and Jan Karas both hit the woodwork with the score at 0–0, but Poland were eventually outclassed and lost 4–0. They did not qualify again for sixteen years.

From nothing, they went to three good World Cups, had a slightly iffy one, and vanished back into nothing again. What happened, then, in the early seventies to prompt those twelve years of plenty? Success is rarely complicated. Polish football is riven by division, but on this issue everybody seemed agreed: a good generation of players nurtured by visionary management. 'Players come and players go,' as a Serbian journalist once told me. 'All you can do is make sure that whatever seeds you have are being cast in fertile soil.'

The man who prepared the ground in the early seventies was Kazimierz Górski, described by Engel as 'a fantastic coach'. Born in Lviv in what is now Ukraine, Górski joined the army when the Second World War began, continuing his football career with Legia Warsaw, the army club, in 1945. There, his speed and nimbleness earned him the nickname

Sarenka – 'the Roe-deer' – but it was when he began coaching the national youth side in 1956 that his genius became apparent. Górski was famed for his modesty, his mildness and his liberal attitude to discipline, but in post-war Poland that in itself was revolutionary.

'You need to understand that before Górski there was a special socialist thing,' Tomaszewski explained. 'It was like the military. The coach was not the same as the team; he was their commanding officer. But Górski created a community. He treated the players as though they were his younger friends. He said that everything is for all people – women, wine and song – but he needed to know where, how much and with whom. We had private lives. We were not like monks, but he was highly respected, so we also knew there were limits. For instance [in the 1974 World Cup] Adam Musiał was twenty minutes late for training before the game against Sweden, and that's why he didn't play in that match. We could have lost the game – Musiał was an important part of the team – but he broke the rule and that was it.'

Górski was famous also for his banal, fatalistic catchphrases, which, in Poland at least, are regarded as nuggets of gnomic profundity: 'You can win, lose or draw'; 'The ball is round and there are two goals'; 'He's a good coach, but he hasn't had good results'. More importantly, he was a gifted motivator, organiser and delegator, and instituted a professional mentality two decades before professionalism was legal.

Janusz Basałaj, a former television commentator who is now president of Wisła Kraków, is a man who takes the opposite view to Tomaszewski on most issues. Characteristically, he preferred to give most of the credit to Jacek Gmoch, the assistant coach, but even he acknowledged Górski's influence. 'It was a good combination,' he said. 'Górski was a very good old man. He got on very well with the players, with his humour and his calmness. Gmoch had a very modern view of football and tactics. Gmoch gathered information about opponents. For example, before the game against

England in Chorzów, he told the forwards that sometimes Bobby Moore did not control the ball well, to press him in possession and that's how Włodimierz Lubanski scored the second goal.' Górski's supporters, of course, would argue the credit is his for having appointed the right man as his assistant.

Gmoch was in charge on his own by 1978, and Antoni Piechniczek was manager in both 1982 and 1986. 'In 1982 Piechniczek had almost the same team,' Tomaszewski said. 'They had the same mentality, and that's why they had success. It wasn't created by him, it was all created by Górski. In 1986 we had a different generation, and we were humiliated.' The advances made by Górski, Tomaszewski said, were lost. As the rest of the world adopted an increasingly professional approach, Poland drifted backwards.

It is not, he insisted, simply an example of football's cyclical nature. Poland continues to produce talented players and their failure to translate that into competitive success, to Tomaszewski, is the result of gross mismanagement at every level from the government downwards, but most particularly at the PZPN. 'At Euro 2004,' he said, 'the best players were mostly born between 1976 and 1978. If you were born in 1976, you would have played at the European Youth Championship in 1993, which Poland won. Where are those players now?' They certainly weren't in Portugal. Youth football, though, is an unpredictable beast. In 1993, Poland also came fourth at the World Youth Championship. If they are complaining about failing to translate that promise into senior success, so too are Nigeria, Ghana and Chile, the three teams who finished ahead of them.

The level of wastage is nonetheless remarkable. Poland were European Under-18 champions again in 2001. 'Where are those players?' Tomaszewski asked. 'In the third division.' That is an exaggeration, but only a small one. The best of that generation was probably Sebastian Mila, who scored a swerving free-kick for Groclin Grodzisk against Manchester City in the UEFA Cup in 2003. He left Groclin to join FK

Austria during the winter break in 2005, but, the morning I spoke to Tomaszewski, having been left out of the side for a couple of games, Mila was splashed over the front of the sports papers vowing to retire from football if he were not handed a regular first-team place within six months. This, for Tomaszewski, was evidence of the moral malaise of the Polish game. 'We need to change the whole structure,' he said, 'because football in Poland is corrupted. It is an illness that has affected the coaches and everybody who is working in football.'

After a brief and unsuccessful stint as coach of ŁKS Łódź, Tomaszewski has become a highly controversial columnist, a gadfly pricking perpetually at the hide of the Polish footballing establishment. For him, it is not only a question of facilities and organisation, but also, perhaps most fundamentally, of mentality. 'A footballer here earns ten times more than a policeman or a miner, but still, when they lose, people say, "It's only sport" ', he said. 'They don't treat them professionally, as they should be treated. There is still the old-style, old-fashioned thinking.' Even Martin Stefański, the PZPN's league director, acknowledged that the old guard had been allowed to dominate for too long. 'Communism died in Poland in 1989,' he said, 'but it only died in the PZPN ten years later.'

It was in 1999 that Marian Dziurowicz was forced to stand down as president of the PZPN after Jacek Dębski, the then Polish sports minister, who was advised by Tomaszewski, accused him of having failed to follow his orders on the reinstatement of a player's registration. Dębski spent the next few months trying, in vain, to find evidence of electoral and financial irregularities but was forced to stop when FIFA threatened to suspend Poland on the grounds of political interference within the federation. The upshot was numerous documents were released, and the culture of the organisation became far more open, but the credibility of the investigation was undermined when newspapers began to report rumours that Dębski had links to organised crime in Austria. Although nothing has ever been proven, it was widely suspected that his murder in 2001 – a single gunshot to the head from close range after he had been lured out of a restaurant by a call to his mobile telephone – was a mafia hit.

Tomaszewski's position as the self-appointed conscience of Polish football does not make him popular. 'He was a very good goalkeeper, but now he's a very stupid man,' said Basałaj. 'He lives alone, he doesn't have good money, he is Mr Nobody, so he has to write bullshit. He has a big mouth. When Clough called him a clown, he got it right.'

Basałaj's loathing for Tomaszewski is perhaps best explained by their clashes over the deal by which Canal+ bought the rights to screen Polish football in 2000. Basałaj at the time was the head of Canal+ in Poland, and he negotiated a $100m deal over five years to buy the rights from a company called Go&Goal. The company had been headed by the former Poland forward Zbigniew Boniek, but he had stood down after becoming vice-president of the PZPN. Tomaszewski, though, claimed repeatedly that Boniek had somehow interfered in the deal. In that instance, he seems to have been significantly out of step, with most pundits suggesting that $100m was extremely generous, and probably saved several clubs from bankruptcy.

At other times, though, Tomaszewski has gone out on a limb, and got it right. Perhaps he does exaggerate, perhaps the relentlessness of his assault is wearing, perhaps his approach is unnecessarily confrontational, but beneath the hyperbole there usually lies a nub of truth. He seems at times a Cassandra, doomed always to be mocked while forcing Polish football to confront its dark heart.

The scandal that followed Poland's victory in the 2001 European Under-19 Championship is a case in point. The morning after the final, a player was arrested having been accused of raping a sixteen-year-old girl. The story, though, was hushed up. 'The worst thing was not that the incident happened and the authorities tried to hide it, but the way they did it,' Tomaszewski said. 'Boniek decided to cover it up, and the players were told to say that the player who was in jail was having a trial with a Finnish club. How can they expect players to behave when they are putting them inside this wicked cover-up?' For almost three years, Tomaszewski worried away at the issue, largely being ignored, until, in February 2005, as Zagłębie Łubin returned from a midwinter training camp in Turkey, their forward, Łukasz Mierzejewski, was arrested by Interpol in Leipzig, at which the PZPN was forced to make the affair public.

He was later fully exonerated, but this, anyway, was not quite such a squalid attempt at a whitewash as it may at first have appeared: Mierzejewski was not the player initially arrested in Helsinki. 'The problem was that the guy they arrested was completely innocent,' explained Stefański. 'The girl went to the hotel, pointed at the first player she saw, and the police arrested him. That's why the PZPN decided not to say anything: they were absolutely certain the boy was innocent. If you are sure the guy was in the hotel all the time, you have to protect him.' That perhaps is understandable, but so too is Tomaszewski's desire for openness. The result, unfortunately, is a series of unseemly squabbles between people who are essentially on the same side. Some kind of reconciliation came in May 2005 when, after two referees were arrested on charges of match-fixing, Tomaszewski was appointed president of the Ethics Commission the PZPN established to investigate the scandal.

ŁKS Łódź were playing KSZO Ostrowiec that afternoon, so we delayed our return to Warsaw to go and watch them. We arrived at the stadium at about ten to three, forty minutes before the scheduled kick-off, but it was immediately apparent that something was amiss. The car park was deserted but for a slightly bewildered-looking steward, and it took only the vaguest muttering of 'English journalist' to get me through the front door. We wandered across an old wooden-floored handball pitch, and headed, unchallenged, past the dressing rooms, down the tunnel and out into the arena, which was empty. True, it was snowing, and it was the second division, but surely there should have been some activity? Then we noticed there weren't even any nets on the goals. Was it so cold the game had been postponed?

Maciej got out the paper and checked again. Sure enough: 3.30. We wandered back inside, and found the club secretary, a middle-aged woman who seemed extraordinarily harassed. The kick-off, she snapped, was at 6.30. There are those who suggest a correlation between people knowing at what time a game starts and them turning up to watch it.

With three hours to kill, we headed up to the stadium café. As we walked in, Maciej was greeted by Piotr Tyszkiewicz, the coach of Kujawiak Włocławek, who was there on a scouting misson and had also been misled by the newspaper. He had formerly coached KSZO, but had been sacked after refusing to pick the club owner Mirosław Stasiak, who, despite being in his late thirties, on the heavy side and having had no formal football coaching, felt it was his right to blunder off the bench for the last few minutes, particularly if there was a penalty to be taken. 'He was the owner, the coach, the president, the sponsor and a player all in one,' said Tyszkiewicz. 'A real Wash and Go man.' Little wonder Tomaszewski spoke of problems of mentality, of the caprice of club owners. That afternoon Stasiak was listed on the bench, as was Janusz Jojko, one of the coaching staff, who sat smoking at the table next to ours until about half an hour before kick-off.

It was a name in the ŁKS starting eleven, though, that drew most of the local press attention: Igor Sypniewski; a forward whose decline has become almost emblematic of Polish football. He began his career with ŁKS, but it was in Greece with Panathinaikos that he made his name, scoring against Arsenal in the Champions League. By January 2001, though, Sypniewski had fallen out with the Panathinaikos manager Angelos Anastasiadis, and was transferred to OFI of Crete.

There were rumours of heavy drinking, but nobody in Poland took them particularly seriously until he signed a hugely lucrative contract with Wisła. His time in Kraków was hugely disappointing, and he managed just five games for them before being offloaded to Kalithea in Greece.

Sypniewski's contract there was terminated after just two appearances, and, without a club, he took five months off football before being taken on by the Swedish side Halmstad. He was so unfit when he arrived that he threw up four times in his first training session, but by June he was the league's leading scorer, his tally including a memorable forty-five-yard drive against Landskrona. That winter he signed for Malmö FF. 'I have left everything problematic behind,' he said. 'I am only looking forward.'

That seemed to suggest there might be some truth in the rumours of alcoholism, but then his coach at Halmstad, the former Sweden midfielder Jonas Thern, hinted that Sypniewski had been threatened by shadowy figures in Poland. The player, unsurprisingly, was highly reluctant to discuss what might have been meant by that. 'It is a difficult question to answer,' he said. 'My real friends are here in Sweden now and my friends in Poland are my family.'

His new life soon began to disintegrate. That March, during pre-season training in the Spanish resort of La Manga, Sypniewski, without giving any warning or offering any explanation, walked off the pitch, lay down on the touchline and refused to rejoin the session. 'He has personal problems,' the Malmö coach Tom Prahl said. 'He is receiving professional help at the moment. It is a difficult problem that the club can't help him with.' The Swedish tabloid *Aftonbladet* then reported that the Polish mafia were hounding him for a cut of his previous transfer fees, to which, for reasons unknown, they seemed to believe themselves entitled.

Sypniewski scored twice on the opening day of the 2004 season, but those were his only goals for the club. In May, he disappeared after raising a middle finger at Prahl, and, having been given a final warning on his return, was fired the following month when the squad came back from a training camp in Dalarna. 'I understand Malmö and I am sorry for everything that has happened,' he said. 'They haven't done anything wrong. It's all my fault.'

An unnamed player then revealed to *Aftonbladet* why Sypniewski had been sacked: 'He was completely uninterested. He didn't engage in the training sessions and when we had a game he didn't bring his boots. The last days he didn't even eat with the rest of the squad. He just lay in his room, watching television.' As three different Swedish newspapers reported that substantial sums had been taken from Sypniewski's bank account, he resurfaced with Trelleborg, but made only two appearances for them before his return to Poland with ŁKS.

Against KSZO, although clearly overweight, Sypniewski had a fine game as a lone striker, his intelligence and touch outweighing his lack of mobility as ŁKS won 2–0. The main worry, though, was less the magnitude of his waistline than of his pay packet. 'Signing him was a completely idiot move,' said Tomaszewski. 'They still owe players their salaries from last year. With some of them earning 3,000 złotys monthly (about £520), they sign Sypniewski for ten times more than any of the others are getting. Sypniewski's own agent said the player needed to be handled by a psychiatrist. He's treated like God compared to all the other players. This is why they will not create professional football.' Threats of strike action by the players soon fizzled out, but they hardly spoke of a united dressing room.

Unfortunately for Tyszkiewicz, his trip to Łódź proved a wasted effort, as he was sacked a couple of weeks later, and replaced by Bogusław Baniak, a coach with a reputation as a promotion specialist. Only the most cynical would suggest his success had anything to do with his friendship with Ryszard Forbrich, the only person ever to be suspended for life by the PZPN. Nicknamed 'the Barber' after his former profession, it was widely alleged that he had an influence over certain referees. (He denies it and the PZPN used the excuse that he had insulted an official to ban him, rather than confront the issue head on.)

Inevitably, given Forbrich's reputation, questions were asked when Kujuwiak came to play ŁKS that April. ŁKS had two men sent off in the quarter of an hour before half time, and another dismissed just after. Facing eight men, Kujuwiak finally took the lead, at which Sypniewski was also shown a red card. The referee, Zbigniew Rutkowski, in the mistaken belief that a game could not continue if one side was reduced to seven (actually, the figure is six), then abandoned the match. Farcically, the twenty-six minutes that remained were played out two weeks later, ŁKS's seven men eventually going down 3–0.

It is not so long ago that ŁKS were one of Poland's better sides and looked like taking advantage of the new financial situation. They finished second in 1993, only for Lech Poznań, who had finished third, to be awarded the title after ŁKS and Legia Warsaw were accused of match-fixing. Nothing was ever concretely proven, but suspicions are always going to be raised when the two sides vying for the title win 6–0 and 7–1 on the final day of the season.

ŁKS were taken over by Antoni Ptak, a millionaire who owns a string of flea markets across Poland and Russia. With Tomaszewski acting as his adviser, they won the championship in 1998, their first for forty years, but then had the misfortune to be drawn against Manchester United in the qualifying round of the Champions League. A 2–0 aggregate defeat was hardly shameful, but Ptak immediately began selling off their best players, and in 1999–2000 they were relegated.

Ptak then bought the third division side Piotrcovia Piotrków Trybunalski, and set up a school for young Brazilian players in the town. Piotrcovia were promoted in 2002, but the following year Pogoń Szczecin, historically a much bigger side, were relegated to the second flight with financial problems so severe that the club were eventually dissolved. Ptak promptly moved Piotrcovia to Szczecin, renamed them Pogoń and began playing games at the council-run ground at which Pogoń had played. Tomaszewski, slightly surprisingly, sees nothing to blame Ptak for. 'He got no help from anybody in Łódź,' he said. 'Instead of being praised for what he had done, he was insulted, so he decided to leave. Now he's got big crowds, he's respected and he's got the support he didn't get here.'

From a pragmatic point of view he may be right. It will be little consolation to Piotrcovia fans, but Pogoń is an older, more established club, and Szczecin a far larger city, and thus Ptak has transformed his team into one of far greater potential. It is difficult, though, not to feel a sense of unease at the arbitrary power wielded by the club owners. At least an argument can be advanced that Ptak's machinations have in some sense been for the good of Polish football; with others that is emphatically not the case.

Polonia Warsaw are one of eastern Europe's most romantic clubs. Founded by the Warsaw intelligentsia, their players fought in the Warsaw Uprising in 1944, and so the Communist government, regarding the club as dangerously independent, ensured their budget was never sufficient for them to rise higher than the second division. 'Polonia was not only football,' Engel said. 'You could meet scientists or artists or painters there. There was a very good atmosphere within the club, because when you don't have a lot of money what you have to have is spirit.'

That spirit lives on among their fans, who continue to arrange choreography, even if it is rare for more than a couple of thousand to turn up at their games. The day after the ŁKS game, I went to see Polonia play Wisła, the league leaders. It was a day of vicious cold and frequent snow showers, and, despite taking an early lead, defeat always seemed inevitable. Their fans, though, continued in displays of flag-waving and card-raising and let off flares at pre-arranged points in the game. Presumably, waiting for the football to excite them was considered futile.

When capitalism came to Poland, Polonia were ripe for expansion. They took their place in the Second Division East in 1991, were promoted in 1993, relegated a year later, and promoted again in 1996; at which they were taken over by Janusz Romanowski. He had been a sponsor at Legia Warsaw, and it was largely his money that took them to the quarter-final of the Champions League in 1996, but he became frustrated with the army's continuing involvement at the club, and, shortly after that quarter-final defeat to Panathinaikos, he walked out and joined Polonia, taking with him a number of players whose contracts he owned. He appointed Engel, who had been coaching in Cyprus, and in 1997–98 Polonia finished second in the table. The following year they were fifth, but in 1999–2000 Polonia did the league and cup double, although Engel left midway through that season to take charge of the national side. 'I completely changed the team,' Engel said. 'I sent away the old players and brought into the team a lot of young ones. I was lucky because some of them were very, very talented boys. When you don't have big money to bring the absolute top players to the team, you have to bring in players who are hungry for results. Fortunately I was always lucky in finding good talents.'

Five of his signings were Under-21 internationals, but, most significantly, two were Nigerian – eighteen-year-old centre-forward Emmanuel Olisadebe, and nineteen-year-old playmaker Emmanuel Ekwueme. With his soup-strainer moustache and fondness for *grzaniec* – a sweet beer drunk warm and dusted with cinnamon – Engel appears quintessentially Polish (for no nation does moustaches quite so well as Poland), but in football terms he is radically modern. Olisadebe had already been rejected by two clubs and was considering leaving Poland after being racially abused and spat upon by Ruch Chorzów fans when Engel took him on. Four years later, having been granted presidential dispensation to naturalise a year before he met the residency requirement, Olisadebe was leading Poland's charge to the World Cup.

The addition of a Nigerian forward captured most of the attention, but it was far from Engel's only innovation as national coach. Polish football, he realised, had become stuck in the ways of the seventies, and unthinkingly persisted with a libero. That, he decided, had to go, but the introduction of a flat back-four took time. 'They were used to a completely different system, some defenders marking one player and doing nothing else,' he explained. 'The foundation was built from defence, and that is why we did not concede too many goals.' They didn't score many either, though, drawing, inevitably, sharp media criticism. 'They started demanding that I should go because we were not scoring in friendlies,' Engel said with incredulity. 'Slowly, slowly, slowly I taught the players the new system. I knew it was getting better and better, but of course the people around the team did not know about it, and most of the press were against us.'

Defeatism is a common Polish trait. Perhaps he had had a particularly bad morning, but when I met Stefański, who gave the impression of spending most of his life banging his head against brick walls, he seemed almost to have given up. 'The mentality of people living in Poland must change,' he said. 'The Poles are always against . . . against everything. We have a long tradition of fighting the Russians, the Germans and also each other. That's the problem; that's why we struggle to create anything.'

He gave as an example Poland's efforts to raise a bid to host Euro 2012. 'We are saying "OK, here is a chance for Poland to grow up," but other people are saying, "No, no, why, why? It's impossible; let's forget about it." Then the same people ask why our country is always treated badly. In Poland everybody would like to have everything, but for free. Even the TV rights: supporters ask why we're selling the TV rights. Everything should be for free. The clubs should have €1m per year, but supporters think people should go free to the games. Some of them probably believe the clubs should pay them to watch it.' When the Nobel Prize-winning poet Czesław Miłosz, returning to Poland, was asked what he thought Poland might have learnt from Communism, he replied 'resistance to stupidity'. Perhaps, though, what has been learnt is resistance, full stop.

With his attacks on negativity, Stefański could perhaps pass as an idealist, but the truth is probably rather that he has become cynical about cynicism. 'We have a long tradition of this,' he went on. 'It's a problem beyond sport. We are all the children of the Communist regime, even if we were against it or born after the collapse of the system; it still is very, very much inside of us. It's in the mentality: the long tradition of fighting against occupiers, and fighting against Communists . . .'

The naturalisation of Olisadebe solved the goalscoring problem, and, the night that England won 5–1 in Munich, Poland beat Norway 3–0 to become the first European side to qualify for the 2002 World Cup. Even before they had arrived in South Korea, though, there were problems, when it emerged that the PZPN had sold the players' image rights without their consent. Engel was diplomatic, suggesting that qualification was the realistic extent of their expectations and that his side had suffered from the climate and their lack of experience; Tomaszewski was predictably scathing. 'The World Cup campaign was devastated because Boniek wanted to gain,' he said. 'The players wanted to sue the PZPN and so every day in Korea there were meetings about the court case.'

Disconcertingly, Tomaszewski told Engel before the tournament that it would see him sacked and replaced by Boniek, and that came to pass even though over 2,000 fans turned up at Warsaw airport to congratulate the national side on their return. Given they had spent much of the summer threatening to sue him, the players understandably failed to respond to Boniek's management and he resigned after just three games in charge, one of which was a home defeat to Latvia. It has even been suggested that Boniek was only appointed because his reforms within the PZPN were unpopular with the old guard, and that making him national manager effectively rendered him sackable.

Engel, meanwhile, after taking a six-month break, returned to football with Legia, before their owner Mariusz Walter decided the club wasn't big enough for the both of them. So, at the beginning of the 2004–05 season, Engel returned once again to Polonia, appointing as his assistant his twenty-five-year-old son, Jerzy Engel Jnr, who had achieved notable success coaching in the third division. The previous season Polonia had finished eleventh, just two points off a relegation play-off, and massively in debt, but, with Engel instigating his policy of youth, they were seventh going into the winter break.

He was making advances off the field as well, and it was reported that Global Soccer Agency Ltd, a company based in Gibraltar, were prepared to invest €150m in the club. Mysteriously, though, in January 2005, the club's owner Jan Raniecki blocked the deal, and Engel was forced out. 'They had the money for sure,' Raniecki said. 'The problem was the guarantees. GSA wanted the land around the stadium, which is owned by the city. They wanted Polonia to pay €1.2m a year to the city until they handed over the rights, and I didn't want to promise that.'

Engel promptly quit. 'I hoped to bring foreign capital and build a completely new team,' he explained. 'Unfortunately the owner didn't agree with this and at the last moment he decided to pull out. I had sided with the other guys and he was against it, so I had to go.'

As if to underline the mess in which that left them, Polonia lost both their next two games 5–0. Even with investment it is difficult to see where the club can go while their stadium is owned by Warsaw city council, which has shown little desire to improve it beyond the bare minimum required for first division football. There is so little money that the hot water is turned on only on match days.

The problem seems intractable. Although the younger Engel, convinced by the panacea of the EU, spoke optimistically of a bright future driven by realistic business practices, Stefański was downbeat. He was probably only thirty, but he had the air of a much older man, perpetually running his fingers through his hair, sighing and staring resignedly into the middle distance. It can't be easy being a universal scapegoat.

Other federations claim they have long-term plans, that things are slowly moving in the right direction, but Stefański was candid enough to admit the PZPN are whistling in the wind. 'Poland,' he admitted at one point, 'is just not a football country.' And that is probably the top and bottom of it: as Poland struggles to emerge from the Communist legacy, football simply is not a priority. The country is neither desperate enough to need football as validation, nor yet comfortable enough to afford it the inflated importance it enjoys in Britain. 'People say it's the responsibility of the PZPN to build the stadiums, to finance them, but it doesn't work like that in western Europe. There, the club is a part of the community, so for the local authorities it's important to keep the club running because people come to see the game, they pay money there, and the money stays in the community. In Poland football is like a very ugly daughter. The parents say, "OK, we have it, so we have to have it" but they don't really want it.

'If we had more pitches, not only for football, but also for other sports, we would have more healthy people living in Poland. Without that we have no chance for success and the situation will get worse and worse and worse. In Poland we have maybe 500,000 people playing football out of a population of forty million. That's a very small number playing football, but it's still half of the total number of people who are playing sport.

'There wouldn't be a problem if my friends and I could go and play football after work, or at the weekend. In England you have thousands of parks where you can play, but in Poland there are hardly any pitches. It's difficult if you're a kid. You can play on bits of concrete between the blocks of flats, but not on grass. So if you cannot play football for real, you have to stay at home and play football on your PlayStation. This is the problem, and all the people responsible for paying for youth and education should face up to it. It's more important to have a lot of people playing different games than for this association to be successful. If you qualify for the World Cup but have only one hundred thousand people playing football, it's a disaster. We need twenty-five million people playing football, basketball, whatever; and then eventually we will have success.'

That will not happen, though, until there is government funding, but that has fallen consistently since Communist times. In 1994, 0.7 per cent of the government budget was spent on sport; in 2004 that figure had dropped to 0.055 per cent. It doesn't help that that money is distributed in direct proportion to success at certain designated major tournaments, irrespective of the level of competition or the costs involved in competing. That leads both to minority sports being overfunded, and also to a reluctance to promote talented footballers who emerge at youth level; it is more profitable to win an Under-17 tournament than for players from that side to be stretched by playing in the senior side. There could, in other words, be no Polish Wayne Rooney.

On either side of the road, the potato fields stretched bleakly through the snow to the grey horizon. Brown and flat and desolate they may be, but it is here, in rural Wielkopolska, that the green shoots of recovery are poking through. The city of Poznań, whose two clubs, Warta and Lech, have won seven titles between them, was once the heart of football in the Polish west, but it is the outlying villages that have enjoyed recent success. Of Poland's so-called 'big four', two – Amica Wronki and Groclin Grodzisk – did not play in the top division until 1995 and 1997 respectively. Both are small-town teams based around one major company, and both have benefited from an unusually astute commercial approach.

The first you see of Grodzisk as you approach from Poznań is the floodlights. They may dominate the skyline, but the ground itself is modest, quaint even, resembling, oddly, a provincial English cricket ground. That is partly because of its size and partly because of the colour scheme – dark-green seats on light-brown brick – but mainly because of the whitewashed wooden grandstand. It is heritage-listed, but in 2005, the club were planning to move it, piece by laborious piece, to a position overlooking a training pitch. From an aesthetic and sentimental point of view that is a shame, because the stand dates back to the club's foundation in 1922; but Groclin did not get where they are today by being emotional. This is a business club run on robustly business lines, and if they are to expand and modernise, heritage has to take a back seat.

In 1992 Dyskobolia were an ordinary village sports club, notable for having been a rallying point for opposition to the Soviet occupation, but little else. Their football team, quite logically, given the size of the village that supported it, pottered along in the fifth division. Then Inter Groclin Auto got involved. Four successive promotions saw the club reach the first division, and, although they were relegated in 1998, they were promoted again the following season and are now a fixture in the Ekstraklasa. Compared to the crumbling wrecks elsewhere in the country, their ground is conspicuously modern and luxurious, small but perfectly formed. Opposite the wooden grandstand is a modern two-storey hotel (it is rumoured the second storey was added because, in Poland, only those hotels with lifts can be granted four-star status; the addition of a swimming pool would take it to five), while the dressing rooms feature heated floors and three different types of sauna.

Inter Groclin Auto is one of the commercial success stories of modern Poland. Its owner, Zbigniew Drzymała, had worked in his father's leather factory, but it was when he bought a Romanian Fiat Maluch (a process requiring not merely money, but also sheaves of paperwork and several years of patience) that he had the idea that made his fortune. The car had headrests, something Drzymała saw as little more than an oddity, until his friends started asking if they could buy them off him. If so many of his friends wanted them, he reasoned, the chances were that there was a much larger market, and so he began producing them at his factory, which already made covers for car seats. Groclin – the name derives from the first letters of Grodzisk and Clinton, the city in the USA where Drzymała briefly lived – is now one of Europe's leaders in the field, supplying Volvo, Mitsubishi, Toyota, Renault, Volkswagen, and Porsche.

Drzymała, a stern, bearded figure, was once an 800-metre runner at the Dyskobolia club, but, for all his protestations of love for the institution and football, his investment has had clear commercial advantages. In 2003–04, Groclin beat Manchester City and Hertha Berlin in their first season in the UEFA Cup, something that did much to advertise the brand across Europe. 'After that,' Drzymała's assistant Jerzy Pięta said, 'we won new contracts in France and Sweden because they had heard of us.'

There are also benefits closer to home. 'The club helps workers identify themselves with the company,' Pięta explained. 'A lot of companies spend huge amounts of money on loyalty schemes, but Groclin has that because of football.' The Grodzisk factory employs 3,000 local workers, most of whom are women – 'the football is for the husbands,' Pięta said – but there are many more who benefit indirectly from the company, and average crowds are around 4,000, about a quarter of the total population of the village. In that sense

Groclin is unusual for Poland, an organic club that is part of the fabric of the community.

In Wronki, forty-five miles to the north, the story is similar. In Communist times, the village was famous for two things: the maximum security prison, and Amica, a company manufacturing household appliances. It has grasped the capitalist nettle with a vengeance, and has expanded to such an extent that it can proudly proclaim that one in three cookers bought in Poland is an Amica cooker. The football club was founded in 1992 by the merger of Bękitnych Wronki and LZS Czarni Wromet Wróblewo, and took Czarni's place in the third division, but moved to Wronki. Like Groclin, they then enjoyed successive promotions, but, as well as establishing themselves in the top flight, also won a hat-trick of Cups between 1998 and 2000.

Both are admirable clubs, well run and deserving of their success. They are both, though, essentially small clubs punching above their weight because of the flabbiness and confusion that pervades so much of the rest of the Polish game. 'We have a lot of fans who just come here, sit down, watch the game and go back home,' said Pięta. 'They are not faithful fans – "Sunday fans", we call them. If we have success and create a good history we will get more people involved, and we want more people to be real fans. On the Internet 45,000 people claim to be fans of Groclin. We're the third most popular team in Poland. Looking at the future, to create a steady crowd it is necessary to have regular good runs in Europe.'

Histories, though, take time to create, and, even then, a village team has only so much potential. Nonetheless, along with Legia Warsaw and Wisła Kraków, Amica and Groclin make up the so-called 'G4' of Poland's leading clubs. Legia and Wisła are both old, traditional clubs, but they owe their continued pre-eminence to recent sponsorship.

The army pulled out of Legia in 1997 (and established another army club, CWKS, who play in the sixth division), at

which they were taken over by the Korean car manufacturers
Daewoo. When they filed for bankruptcy two years later, the
club might have disappeared had not ITI, one of Poland's
largest media companies, stepped in.

Wisła, meanwhile, were only promoted back to the
Ekstraklasa in 1996, since when they have benefited enor-
mously from a sizeable sponsorship deal with Tele-fonika, one
of Poland's largest two mobile telephone companies. The
other is Idea, who, in the winter break in 2004–05, became
the first sponsors of the league. Typically, the PZPN failed to
consult the clubs, and Wisła, bearing Tele-fonika's name on
their chests, refused to add the logo of another telecommuni-
cations company to their sleeves.

Wisła are significantly the most successful club in recent Polish
history, completing a hat-trick of titles in 2005, but even their
background could hardly be said to be stable. They have had
considerable success in the UEFA Cup, beating Parma and
Schalke 04 on their way to the fourth round in 2002–03, and,
given their domination of the domestic scene, European
competition is seen as the yardstick of their progress. Defeat to
Vålerenga the following season was a blow, and if losing to
Real Madrid in a Champions League qualifier in 2004–05 was
excusable, an away goals defeat to Dinamo Tbilisi in the first
round of the UEFA Cup was not. Wisła's owner, the reclusive
Bogusław Cupiał, demanded the whole board resign, but their
coach, Henryk Kasperczak, another member of the 1974
World Cup squad, refused. He, unfortunately, had a contract
worth €22,000 a month until 2008, and, despite being
suspended, refused to budge, even when the Czech coach
Werner Lička was appointed to replace him. 'This is normal,'
Basałaj slightly bewilderingly said. 'In Italy you see this all the
time.' Well, perhaps, but when most Polish clubs struggle to
afford one coach, to pay two seems extravagant.

The G4, frustrated by what they had seen as the PZPN's
conservatism and a voting structure in which much of the

power still lies with the regional federations, took matters into their own hands, and, in the summer of 2005, the top division clubs, after lengthy legal wrangling, disestablished themselves from the PZPN, founding a separate and self-governing company. 'A landmark for Polish football,' Stefański acknowledged. 'Perhaps the start of a new age.'

The financial divisions initially seem fairly equitable, with half of television revenues to be split equally between the sixteen top-flight sides, quarter to be distributed according to league position, and the remainder to be divided by matches shown. Each of the G4 clubs, though, had a representative on the eight-man supervisory board, so it seems reasonable to assume that in time the bigger clubs will profit from the split. That may allow them to compete more equally with top European sides, but there is a danger. 'The PZPN's job is to look after all clubs,' Stefański said, which, by definition, is not true of the new body.

Pięta compared the split to the formation of the Premiership in England, which he seemed to view as some kind of paradise on earth. When I suggested that, for all the improvements brought about by the Premiership, there was a feeling that it had led to the grass-roots being run down, he just laughed. 'In Poland,' he said, 'there are no grass-roots.'

3 HUNGARY

More Bricks than Kicks

Opposite the metro station at Határ út, the penultimate stop heading south-east on the blue line, stands an Ibis hotel. Formed of grubby prefabricated red and yellow blocks, it is a drab and depressing spectacle, entirely in keeping with the neighbourhood. It's halfway to the airport, but it's hard to imagine many tourists or foreign businessmen stay there. While the centre of Budapest has made a virtue of its faded grandeur – its flower stalls, its cafés and its bistros, a nostalgia for the declining years of the Austro-Hungarian empire – here there's just faded concrete, and the ugly orange kiosks that dot the concourse don't seem to sell much beyond bread and porn. Nobody gets nostalgic for the declining years of Communist Hungary. The only things even vaguely quaint are the rattling old chocolate-and-cream trams.

I took the number 42 from Határ út to the end of the line, a wide street that contrived to be dusty despite days of heavy rain. An old brown-brick factory stood at one end, where the tramlines swept left in an arc back towards the metro station. On the wall, beneath two rows of tiny cracked windows, a peeling yellow sign revealed it used to have something to do with the manufacture of aluminium. This was not a thriving area. To one side of the factory ran a railway line, and, as I'd been instructed, I turned right there, walking between the tracks and a row of squat, single-storey cottages, remnants of the days when Kispest was a village, distinct from the city. In the distance, to the left, beyond the tracks and a clump of untidy trees, rose the angled supports of four ancient floodlights.

The security fences were freshly painted in red and black, but that morning the Bozsik Stadium carried a distinct sense of decay. The concrete was crumbling, the seats dulled by the sun. I walked along the back of the terrace beneath the main stand. Nobody stopped me, but then, why would they? There was nothing to steal, nothing that could be defaced beyond what time had done already. At the far end of the ground was a mud training pitch, pocked with puddles and surrounded by dilapidated sheds. In one corner stood a model five-man wall for practising free-kicks, carved of cheap plywood and hanging loosely from one strut. Beyond that was the overgrown cemetery made famous by Antal Végh's book *Why is Hungarian Football Sick?*, the cover of which carried a photograph showing the headstones with a handful of old men standing on the terrace in the foreground, as though queuing for death.

Végh's book was published in 1974, the year before Ferencváros reached the final of the Cup-Winners' Cup. Twelve years later he brought out a follow-up, *Incurable?*. Nowhere else does past achievement so dwarf the present. Picking through the mud that morning, it was almost impossible to believe that the Bozsik Stadium was once the centre of the footballing world, that it was there that the likes of Ferenc Puskás, Sándor Kocsis and, of course, József Bozsik himself were forged into the *Aranycsapat*, the Golden Squad.

An Englishman cannot be long in Budapest without somebody mentioning the *Aranycsapat* and their 6–3 victory over England in 1953 – which, thanks to the unusualness of the scoreline, is happily referred to simply as 'the 6–3'. My train from Belgrade was still chugging through the suburbs when the guard who brought my breakfast coffee felt compelled to point out that we'd be arriving at the Keleti Station, where that Hungary side had received a rapturous reception from 150,000 fans after their victory at Wembley. A few months later, though, as they returned from the World Cup in Switzerland, the mood in Budapest was hostile enough that the players' train was diverted to the north-western town of Tata. Between November 1953 and July 1954, the Golden Squad fell from their zenith to disgrace. Then it fell some more.

What 1966 is to English football, 1953 is to Hungarian. That Hungary side might not have won the World Cup, but, to Billy Wright, the England captain at Wembley that day, they were 'the finest team ever to sort out successfully the intricacies of this wonderful game'. Friendlies then were far more than the anodyne exhibitions they tend to be today, and that game at Wembley was billed as 'the Match of the Century'. Hyperbole, perhaps, with almost half the hundred still to run, but it is difficult to think of another game the ramifications of which stretched so far.

In 1953, Britain was still great. The war was over, and won, rationing was coming to an end, the Festival of Britain was fresh in the memory and there was a young queen newly crowned – her place in the divine order of things seemingly confirmed, as news broke on the day of the Coronation that the Empire had conquered Everest. And, of course, in popular opinion, England were still the best in the world at football, unbeaten at home against foreign opposition – as the joke of the time had it – since 1066. (Provided, of course, you ignored, as most did, the defeat to the Republic of Ireland at Goodison Park in 1949.)

On that foggy November afternoon, though, England were outplayed. Six months later, Hungary beat them again, 7–1 in Budapest. England had believed herself innately supreme, but in two matches Hungary proved just how far the world had moved on, just how far England – Britain – had been left behind. Critically, as Jenő Buzánszky, the right-back in the *Aranycsapat* told me, it wasn't so much that Hungary had better players, great though the likes of Puskás, Bozsik and Nándor Hidegkuti assuredly were. 'It was because of tactics that Hungary won,' he said. 'The match showed the clash of two formations, and, as often happens, the newer, more developed formation prevailed.' Hungary was Communist, radical, perhaps the future; Britain was imperial, moribund, undoubtedly the past.

In the Empire Stadium – the Twin Towers themselves designed to reflect the work of Lutyens in New Delhi, the jewel of the Empire – Hungary struck a shuddering blow for socialism, and not just socialism, but a new, post-Stalinist variant of it. The great dictator had died in March 1953 and, in the July, after being summoned to Moscow to meet Khrushchev, Mátyás Rákosi, Hungary's loathed Stalinist leader, was deposed and replaced by the liberal Imre Nagy. He implemented the 'New Course', abolishing internment camps and granting amnesties to hundreds of political prisoners, stimulating an optimism that was intensified by the continuing success of Puskás and his side.

To understand why England were so perplexed by Hungary's tactical innovations, it is necessary to go back to 1925, when, alarmed at falling crowds caused by increasingly defensive play, the British football associations persuaded the International Board to change the offside law so that only two defenders were required between attacker and goal line to play him onside, rather than three, as had previously been the case.

Until then pretty much everybody had used the 2–3–5 system – that is, two full-backs (what would become numbers

2 and 3), three half-backs (4,5,6), an outside-right (7), inside-right (8), centre-forward (9), inside-left (10) and outside-left (11). After the change in the offside law, though, 2–3–5 became impractical as a defensive formation. Herbert Chapman, the great Huddersfield and Arsenal manager, realised that he could enhance his defensive cover by dropping the centre-half (that is, the player who had been the central of the three half-backs) back between the full-backs. That, though, left him short in midfield, and so the two inside-forwards were also withdrawn, effectively giving a 3–2–2–3 formation: the so-called W-M. His ideas were controversial, but were gradually accepted and adopted by other English sides, even if newspapers until the 1960s continued to print team line-ups as though everybody still played a 2–3–5.

So strong was the sense that such tinkering somehow meddled with what was natural, that, when the FA made shirt numbering compulsory in 1939, they specified the numbers be distributed as outlined above – that is, as though each team lined up in a 2–3–5 system. This, of course, is why 'centre-half' is still used as a synonym for 'centre-back' in Britain, and also why, in the days before squad numbers, teams playing 4–4–2 would commonly line up, reading from right to left, back to front, 1; 2, 5, 6, 3; 7, 4, 8, 11; 9, 10.

In England, tactical experimentation had effectively died with Chapman in 1934. It became accepted that W-M was simply the way football was played, with players shackled to certain areas of the pitch by their numbers. That was probably largely down to an instinctive cultural conservatism; but England's sporting heritage, anyway, militated against the kind of fluidity of movement shown by, for instance, the Dinamo Moscow team that toured England with their *passovotchka* football in 1945.

Johan Cruyff once commented that Total Football could not have developed in a country that didn't play hockey – movement off the ball being key to that sport – and it is probably significant that in eastern Europe it was not uncommon for footballers to play ice-hockey in the winter. English football, by contrast, had grown up in the public schools in tandem with rugby, in which structure is everything and positions have clearly defined objectives. In Hungary, as Buzánszky put it, 'tactics were very much up for discussion', the debate being led by a triumvirate of radical coaches: Márton Bukovi, Béla Guttmann and Gusztáv Sebes.

It was Sebes who led Hungary to glory at Wembley, but it was Bukovi who came up with the critical tactical development. As coach of the Budapest club MTK, he tinkered with the W-M, restoring the inside-forwards to the forward line, and instead withdrawing the centre-forward. It then became apparent that such a system required extra defensive cover, and so another of the half-backs was dropped back, creating what was, in its early days, effectively a 3–1–2–4 that eventually evolved into 4–2–4.

Even had Walter Winterbottom, the England manager, wished to buck England's conservatism, he was restricted to the W-M because that was the formation with which his players were familiar from their clubs. In Hungary, though, the system was far more focused on the national side, partly because of the Communist government's recognition of the propaganda potential of sport and partly because the clubs had little independence following nationalisation in 1949. Sebes, who was appointed sole national coach that year after a brief time as part of a three-man management committee, had seen that the great Italy and Austria sides of the 1930s were predominantly drawn from one or at most two clubs, and sought a similar system in Hungary. Nationalisation gave him his opportunity, particularly given the advantages enjoyed by police and army sides. It was then just a question of deciding which clubs to allocate to whom.

Ferencváros and MTK had been the biggest pre-war clubs, but while the secret police, the AVH, eventually took over MTK (whose name changed from Textiles to Bástya to Vörös

Lobogó – 'Red Banner' – and back to MTK again between 1950 and 1957), Ferencváros were rendered unsuitable by the right-wing traditions of their support. Sebes turned instead to Kispest, in those days a small village club and far from an obvious choice, but, crucially, the side for which Puskás and Bozsik already played. They became the army team, and were renamed Honvéd – 'Defenders of the Motherland'. It was then a simple matter to persuade young footballers that their national service was best spent playing for the club. Kocsis, for instance, reached conscription age in 1950, and, given the choice of playing for Honvéd or serving at a remote border post, unsurprisingly joined Sebes in Kispest. Although there were a number of internationals at MTK, most notably Hidegkuti, Sebes was effectively able to use Honvéd as a training camp for his Hungary squad, facilitating his tactical experimentation.

It was at the Helsinki Olympics of 1952 that the world first began to take notice of Hungary. The eastern bloc nations had an obvious advantage in that all their top sportsmen were technically amateur and therefore eligible for the Games, but, even allowing for that, there was something remarkable in their 6–0 demolition of Sweden in the semi-final. 'It was one of those days,' Puskás said. 'Once we'd hit our rhythm we were virtually irresistible.' Yugoslavia were seen off 2–0 in the final, a result that was a huge relief to Sebes, who, on the morning of the game, had received a telephone call from Rákosi warning him that the government could not tolerate defeat, Yugoslavia's government having manoeuvred themselves into a position of independence from Moscow, placing great strain on their diplomatic relations with Hungary. Buzánszky's memories are rather less politicised. 'At that time,' he said, 'Miss World was a Finnish woman. In itself receiving the gold medal was a wonderful feeling, but it was a great bonus to have Miss World handing over an olive branch and giving us a kiss. I was so overcome with the moment I had to look in the paper the next day to see if she really was as beautiful as I remembered.'

The president of the Football Association, Sir Stanley Rous, had been at the Sweden game, and, impressed, approached Sebes to propose a friendly. Rákosi was concerned about the possibility of defeat, but arrangements for the game were nonetheless confirmed at a meeting of European FA leaders late in 1952, by which time the development of the Golden Squad had taken another major step forward.

Puskás was the greatest player of the *Aranycsapat* – 'If a good player has the ball, he should have the vision to spot three options,' Buzánszky said. 'Puskás always saw at least five' – but England's executioner in 1953 was Hidegkuti. He was not even a regular in the Olympic side, but in September 1952, with Hungary two down after half an hour of a friendly against Switzerland, he replaced his clubmate Péter Palotás. Hungary were level by half time, went on to win 4–2 and such was Hidegkuti's contribution that his position was unassailable. 'He was a great player and a wonderful reader of the game,' said Puskás. 'He was perfect for the role, sitting at the front of midfield, making telling passes, dragging the opposition defence out of shape and making fantastic runs to score himself.'

The England game came increasingly to dominate Sebes's thoughts, and it was in his preparations for it that Honvéd's role as a training ground came into its own. Attitudes to Sebes today are oddly ambivalent, but Buzánszky was dismissive of the critics. 'His role was absolutely decisive,' he said. 'It was like arranging cogs in a wheel – everything had to fit.' Sebes wasn't just a fine coach, though; he was also a political operator of no little ability, as he had shown in organising workers at the Renault factory in Paris before the war.

Shortly after becoming coach in his own right, Sebes realised his system needed a centre-back who was not merely strong and defensively sound, but also capable of spreading play from the back. The ideal man, he decided, was the Vasas defender Gyula Lóránt, but he, unfortunately, was in a detention camp after plotting to lead a team of Hungarian defectors to play a series of exhibition matches in western Europe. Sebes, undaunted, appealed to the Interior Minister, János Kádár, ahead of a friendly away to Austria, giving a personal guarantee that Lóránt would not abscond while in Vienna. Kádár agreed, and Lóránt responded with a superb performance as Hungary beat their great rivals for the first time in twelve years.

For all his political ability, Sebes remained, first and foremost, a football man, as Tibor Nyilasi, the great Ferencváros and Hungary forward of the 1970s, told me. 'When I was a kid, Sebes lived in the same area of Budapest as me,' he said. 'He would come down to the square where I played football with my friends, and take us up to his flat, give us sandwiches, and show us Super-8 films of the 6–3 and 7–1 games. It was he who recommended me to Ferencváros. He was like a grandfather. He lived only for football. In the hard times of the fifties his voice was heard in important circles.'

He was also utterly meticulous, using his position of authority to force opposing sides to adopt 'English' characteristics when playing Honvéd, and ensuring nothing they would meet in England could surprise his team. 'Sebes got hold of some English footballs, so we could get used to the kind of ball that absorbed moisture and got heavier as the game went on,' Buzánszky said. 'He also knew the Wembley pitch was 74 metres across, and widened the pitch at one of our training grounds so we could get used to Wembley's dimensions.'

It was in the matter of the balls that Sebes's concerns proved most justified. In their first game with the English version, a friendly against Sweden in Budapest ten days before the match at Wembley, Hungary played dismally and could only draw 2–2. Concerned about the effect that performance, and a hugely critical reaction in the Hungarian media, could have on morale, Sebes changed his travel plans, deciding that rather than flying to London it would be better for his team to take the train, stopping off in Paris for a warm-up against the works team of the Renault factory where he had been employed before the war. 'It was a big boost for morale,' said Buzánszky. 'We won 18–0 and that proved to us that we weren't that bad.'

Nonetheless, the Hungarian mood in London was far from confident. 'There was great anxiety on the bus before the game,' said Pál Várhidy, who was on the bench that day. 'Before other matches players would chat with each other, but this time there was silence.' For all Sebes's efforts, the Hungarian players knew little of their English counterparts. 'We didn't even know them from photographs,' said Buzánszky. 'At that time, the eyes of the press stopped at the Austro-Hungarian border, and there was no television. But in those days it was clear from the shirt numbers who would play against whom. I was the number two, so I knew I would be against the number eleven, George Robb. When I was in the tunnel before the match I would always look to see what build my opponent was, and try to figure out what kind of player he would be. If he had strong legs he would be fast; if he had bendy legs he would be a dribbler. I had mixed feelings about Robb – he looked fast *and* a dribbler. Wembley was like a holy place for footballers, so there was a certain nervousness in going out there, but that feeling lasted only until the first touch of the ball.'

It didn't take much longer than that for Hungary to take the lead, Bozsik slipping in Hidegkuti to fire home from the edge of the box after only forty-five seconds. It was the beginning of a rout. Jackie Sewell equalised, but Hidegkuti soon added a second from Kocsis's flick, before Puskás scored the game's most famous goal. Zoltán Czibor, notionally a right-footed left-winger but emerging on the right, crossed for his captain, and as he controlled it on the edge of the six-yard box, Billy Wright slid to make a challenge, hurtling 'like a fire-engine heading to the wrong fire', as Geoffrey Green put it in

The Times. Puskás dragged the ball back with his studs, and, in one movement, lashed the ball into the net, leaving Wright sprawling. György Szepesi, who was commentating on the game for Hungarian radio, suggested a plaque should be erected to mark the moment. Bozsik got a fourth with a deflected free-kick, before Stan Mortenson pulled one back to make it 4–2 at half time.

'To me,' Harry Johnston, the England centre-back that day, wrote in his autobiography, 'the tragedy was the utter helplessness . . . being unable to do anything to alter the grim outlook.' Presented with a deep-lying centre-forward in Hidegkuti, England had no idea how to react. The rigidity of the W-M meant that if Johnston followed him, it would leave a hole in the middle of the back-line, but by allowing Hidegkuti time and space, he was able to dictate the play. Bozsik added a fifth shortly after half time, drilling in the rebound after a Czibor header was pushed on to the post by Gil Merrick, the England keeper, and Hidegkuti soon volleyed a sixth from a lobbed Puskás cross. Alf Ramsey converted a late penalty, but there was no doubting the Hungarians' superiority. 'To be honest,' Buzánszky said, 'Kocsis was nowhere near his best. If he had shown his real form, the result would have been even more cruel.'

English observers emphasised the teamwork of the Hungarians, their fluidity and their ability to interchange positions, all of which gave weight to Sebes's insistence that his side played 'socialist' football. Whether Sebes actually believed his claim, or whether he was simply saying what his government wanted to hear is unclear, but it is certainly true that Hungary's strength was in the interaction of members of the team as opposed to the individual talents of England. Nonetheless Gyula Grosics, the goalkeeper of the *Aranycsapat*, and a perpetual opponent of the Communist regime, has always rejected the idea that the victory could be attributed to ideology. 'Football cannot be named after political systems,' he said. 'It is true that the political leadership in Hungary fully exploited our success for their own good, but it would be going too far to say that Communism or the socialist system had anything to do with the Hungarian success.'

England, true to type, remained blinkeredly conservative, and, to the bewilderment of the Hungarians, made no attempt to counter the deep-lying centre-forward when they faced Hungary in the Népstadion in Budapest six months later, losing 7–1. Over a million Hungarians applied for tickets for that game, and, although official figures have the attendance at a little under 105,000, the actual attendance may have been far higher. Many, it is said, having gained entry, used carrier pigeons to send their tickets to friends and relatives waiting at home. These days the Népstadion – now the Ferenc Puskás Stadium – is a wreck, another living monument to Hungary's decline, its top tier permanently closed for safety reasons, and capacity limited to 26,000. Even so, it almost never sells out. 'In a way, 1954 was more important because it proved what had happened at Wembley was not just chance,' Grosics said. 'Never before nor since has there been such interest in Hungary for one match. In those days of dictatorship, it was football that united people in Hungary with the five million Hungarians living outside the borders. There was a feeling of togetherness in the Hungarian nation, something to grab hold of and tie ourselves to.' It was a feeling that would soon evaporate. After four years unbeaten, the 1954 World Cup in Switzerland should have been the Aranycsapat's coronation, the confirmation of their supremacy. It became a nightmare, and the disintegration began.

South Korea were hammered 9–0 in Hungary's opening game in Zurich, and then West Germany were thumped 8–3 in Basle, meaning that, including a 10–0 win over Luxembourg in a warm-up match, Hungary had scored thirty-four goals in their previous four games. In the West Germany game, though, there fell a shadow, and it still clouds Hungarian football today. With the score at 5–1, Puskás was caught from behind by Werner Liebrich and had to go off. He missed the next two matches, with what X-rays would later reveal was a hairline fracture of the ankle, and, although he played in the final – also against West Germany – he was clearly not at his best. Which, of course, begs the question of whether Liebrich's assault was deliberate. Sebes certainly felt so, and, in *Captain of Hungary*, published the following year, Puskás wrote of 'a vicious kick on the back of my ankle . . . when I was no longer playing the ball'.

Time, though, cooled his sense of injustice, and he later said that he didn't believe there had been a calculated plan to injure him. Hidegkuti, in his autobiography, called it 'a correct tackle, and quite accepted in football . . . He was just trying to tackle Puskás, who strained his ankle.' It is true that Liebrich, a player noted for his robust approach, had changed places with the right-half Jupp Posipal only ten minutes before the foul, but there is a big difference between deploying a physical midfielder to mark the opposition's best player and setting out deliberately to cripple him.

Hindsight has lent momentousness to the incident, but at the time that one challenge seemed insignificant alongside what ensued in the quarter-final against Brazil, a match that became known as the Battle of Berne. Goals within seven minutes from Hidegkuti and Kocsis effectively decided the game, which was eventually won 4–2, but the contest was only beginning. Two penalties were awarded and three players sent off, and the final whistle brought both a pitch invasion and a brawl in the tunnel, during which Sebes was cut above the eye with a bottle, and the Hungary dressing room was invaded by furious Brazilians.

The semi-final, against the defending world champions Uruguay, is generally regarded as one of the greatest matches ever played. Hungary again won 4–2, but only after being forced into extra-time having thrown away a two-goal lead with fifteen minutes remaining. Puskás spoke of his pride at the 'fantastic heart' Hungary had shown in seeing off

Uruguay's comeback, but the extra thirty minutes would take their toll. West Germany, by contrast, eased past Austria 6–1.

The Germans call what happened on 4 July 1954 the Miracle of Berne, the day on which a shattered nation re-emerged on to the international stage. Hungarian football, though, has never recovered from the defeat.

The portents weren't good. Hungary's sleep was disturbed by brass bands practising in the street for the Swiss national championship and their team bus was prevented by police from entering the stadium, forcing the players to battle their way through the crowds just to get to the dressing room. And then there was the weather. It rained throughout the day before the final, and then it rained heavily during the game, transforming an already soft pitch into a quagmire that hampered Hungary's passing game. On the positive side – or at least, so it seemed at the time – Puskás was declared fit and played.

The West Germany line-up featured only five of the players who had played in the 8–3 defeat in the group stages. It is possible that was a matter of chance, of Sepp Herberger serendipitously happening upon his most effective eleven, but the theory has developed that the West Germany coach, knowing his team would be too good for Turkey, the other team in the group, deliberately fielded a weakened side for the first game, allowing him to research Hungary while giving nothing away in return. It seems all but incredible that a national manager could take such a risk, but West Germany did beat Turkey comfortably both in the group game (4–1) and the subsequent play-off (7–2), and Herberger's assistant Helmut Schön, who went on to manage West Germany to victory in the 1974 World Cup, always insisted the story was true. As he pointed out, West Germany were under less pressure for that tournament than they ever would be again: if the gamble was the only chance they had of winning the tournament, the minimal repercussions there would have been for a first-round exit made it worthwhile.

As they had in every game in the tournament, Hungary raced into a two-goal lead. (The early surge, in fact, was a constant feature of the golden years, and it has been suggested that a contributory factor in their success was the fact they took warming up far more seriously than anybody else.) Puskás got the first after six minutes, tucking in the rebound after Liebrich had blocked Kocsis's shot, and Czibor added a second two minutes later. Two minutes after that, though, West Germany pulled one back, Max Morlock sliding in after József Zakariás had half-blocked a cross, and then Grosics flapped at a Fritz Walter corner, allowing Helmut Rahn to volley an equaliser. Less than quarter of the game gone and it was 2–2. As they had against Uruguay, though, Hungary rallied. Hidegkuti was less effective than usual thanks to the man-marking of Horst Eckel (a ploy beyond the English imagination), but he still struck a post. Kocsis hit the bar and Toni Turek in the German goal made a string of fine saves, but a third goal would not come. Perhaps fatigue was a factor – the debilitating games against Brazil and Uruguay, the injury to Puskás, the heavy pitch – and perhaps they weren't so fluent as usual, but fundamentally it was bad luck that denied Hungary.

And then, with six minutes left, Bozsik, hesitating uncharacteristically, was muscled off the ball by Hans Schäfer. His cross was headed clear by Mihály Lantos, but Rahn gathered the loose ball, created space for the shot, and drove low past Grosics. In Germany it is known as the goal that made the nation. It would not have been, though, had not the Welsh linesman Mervyn Griffiths – a controversial, authoritarian figure – deemed that Puskás was offside as he ran on to Mihály Tóth's pass and slid the ball under Turek with two minutes remaining. 'I couldn't believe it,' Puskás said. 'It was almost a minute afterwards when he raised his flag. I could have murdered him. To lose the World Cup on such a decision just isn't right.'

No game has been subjected to such agonised analysis.

Kocsis and Hidegkuti both mused afterwards on what would have happened had Puskás not played, but as Puskás pointed out, he did score one and have one controversially disallowed. Besides, a half-fit Puskás – and he was not a player exactly noted for his work-rate even when fit – was still probably better than a fully fit anybody else. His inclusion, though, meant a shake-up of the front line, as Sebes brought in Tóth to play on the left-wing with a brief to cover for Puskás, which meant Czibor switching to an unfamiliar position on the right-wing with László Budai – excellent in the semi, but generally out of form – stepping down. So ineffective were the wingers perceived to be, though, that at half time, apparently under instruction from Gyula Hegyi – the president of the National Physical Education and Sports Authority, and thus his immediate superior – Sebes swapped them over.

Was Sebes, as many have bitterly suggested, determined to shuffle so that he could claim the laurels as the master strategist? Did the pressure and the speculation over Puskás cause him to overcomplicate things? Or, given he had masterminded a run of thirty-two wins and four draws in thirty-six games, including an Olympic title and two annihilations of the mother of football, can we cut Sebes some slack, and accept that, but for outrageous circumstance, his plan would have worked? Budai, after all, the Uruguay game aside, had not played well for weeks, and in the first half Czibor's pace did (as Sebes always said it would) torment the West German full-back Werner Kohlmeyer. Given that fact, it is hard to understand why Sebes accepted Hegyi's demand to switch the wingers; he was not, after all, a man who readily accepted political interference. 'It was our own fault,' Puskás said. 'We thought we had the match won, then we gave away two stupid goals and let them back into it.'

Back in Budapest, disappointment swiftly became anger. 'The reaction in Hungary was terrible,' said Grosics. 'Hundreds of thousands of people poured into the streets in the hours after the match. On the pretext of football, they openly demonstrated against the regime. The atmosphere was so bitter it could be felt months later. In those demonstrations, I believe, lay the seeds of the 1956 Uprising.'

The apartments of certain players and even some journalists were attacked, as rumours circulated that the game had been thrown for a fleet of Mercedes. It was suggested (ludicrously, given Sebes's only daughter was ten at the time) that Tóth had been selected because he was the coach's son-in-law. Rather more credible were the complaints about complacency in the build-up to the final. Sebes had arranged for wives and girlfriends to travel to Berne to watch, but had forbidden players to see them until after the game. At least two players, and possibly as many as six, broke that curfew. Czibor later revealed that 'his room-mate' had stumbled back in at six in the morning after spending the night with a hotel maid, and complained of having to work twice as hard to cover for him that afternoon. He never named the player concerned, and, confusingly, neither of his room-mates, Palotás and Ferenc Machos, played in the final. Czibor also let slip, though, that the guilty party never represented Hungary again, a description that, of the eleven who played, applies only to Zakariás.

Even now the defeat and the reasons behind it provoke furious debate. As Nyilasi said, 'It is as though Hungarian football is frozen at that moment, as though we have never quite moved on from then.'

After spending a few days in Tata until the worst of the disturbances were over, the Aranycsapat returned to Budapest. They went unbeaten in their next eighteen games, but the mood had changed. Puskás was barracked at Honvéd away games, Sebes's son was beaten up at school, and Grosics was arrested having been accused of 'conduct incompatible with the laws and morals of the Hungarian People's Republic'. An erratic goalkeeper and an eccentric character, he had always been a controversial figure, prone to intense bouts of nerves, and such a hypochondriac he would wear a red beret during training sessions because he believed it brought him relief from a brain disease. He had been arrested in 1949 for attempting illegally to leave the country, and felt he was always under suspicion. 'I was born into a religious family, and that wasn't a good sign at all at that time,' he explained. 'I never made any secret of what I thought about the government. My family – especially my mother – had intended that I should be a Catholic priest. I was raised in that spirit, and that was one of the reasons I was not trusted.'

Grosics has a reputation as a loner, an intellectual who preferred to play chess than to drink and watch Westerns with the rest of the squad, but he was engaging enough when I spoke to him – admittedly through an interpreter via telephone – in Budapest. For a man who had seen so much, his outlook seemed remarkably benign. Late in 1954, he was exiled to house arrest in the mining town of Tatabánya and, even fifty years later, he was able vividly to recall the mixture of fear and pride he felt each week as the large black car pulled up at his door to take him off for interrogation.

Through 1955 the structure with which Sebes had surrounded himself was systematically dismantled. He was prevented from taking his place on the bench at a match in Switzerland in the autumn; his secretary was sacked; and his think-tank of coaches was dispersed: Pál Titkos was sent to Egypt, Gyula Mándi to Brazil and Gusztav Hidas to Nigeria. Sebes himself was finally sacked after a defeat to Belgium in March 1956, his place being taken by a five-man committee headed by Bukovi, which recalled Grosics to the team. As the *Aranycsapat* disintegrated, so too did Hungarian optimism.

The Central Committee of the Communist Party denounced Nagy's 'New Course' in March 1955, and Nagy himself was deposed a few weeks later. By the end of the year he had been expelled from the party altogether. He was replaced as Prime Minister by András Hedegűs, but he was little more than a puppet for Rákosi and the other hardliners. Their position, though, was undermined by a continuing process of de-Stalinisation, something that found its symbolic manifestation in Moscow, in September 1956. The players have always denied any political pressure was put on them to underperform against the USSR, but when a goal from Czibor in the Lenin Stadium (now the Luzhniki) gave Hungary their first ever victory over the Soviets, it was widely seen as evidence of Budapest's increasing independence.

Khrushchev denounced Stalin in the 'secret speech' in February 1956, and, that same month, the Hungarian Communist Béla Kun, who had led a brief Bolshevist revolution in 1918 and been executed in Moscow twenty-one years later, was exonerated. By June, the widow of László Rajk, killed in 1949 for supposedly plotting with Tito, publicly demanded that her husband should also be rehabilitated and his body returned to her for proper burial. The authorities acceded, and, on 6 October, as a gesture of goodwill ahead of an official visit to Yugoslavia, Rajk was reburied in the Kerepesi cemetery. The ceremony rapidly became a political event, with numerous speakers condemning the regime. Even more surprisingly, almost 200,000 marched through Budapest to show their solidarity with the liberal values Rajk was seen to represent (although he had actually been just as committed a Stalinist as Rákosi). Within a week, Nagy was readmitted to the party, and a mass demonstration demanding the withdrawal of Soviet troops, a free press, and free elections was called for 23 October.

By 6 p.m. that day a quarter of a million people had gathered in Parliament Square, demanding the reinstatement of Nagy. A statue of Stalin was broken off at the knees by workers using acetylene torches, who then filled its head with petrol and set it alight. The AVH began shooting at the protesters, and, that night, as the violence escalated, the Hungarian government called on the Soviet army to step in. At the time, the Hungary squad were training in Tata preparing for a match against Sweden, desperately trying to follow events in the capital on the radio, and when that game was called off, most returned to Budapest. Grosics, inevitably, was

The goalkeeper Yuriy Degeren, in 1974, shows exactly why Shakhtar Donetsk need their five-star training base.

Miners look on from the top of a convenient slag heap as Shakhtar beat Torpedo 2–0 in August 1966; Oleh Blokhin, the greatest player of a great Dynamo Kyiv side.

Valeriy Lobanovskyi, as a dilettantish left-winger for Dynamo Kyiv taking on Neftchi's Jashar Babyev in a league game in Baku; and as 'the Colonel', Dynamo's greatest manager, Ukraine's Brian Clough.

Mykhalo Koman, who got the winner in the 1954 Soviet Cup Final, goes close again for Dynamo Kyiv; Oleh Bazilevich, a team-mate of Lobanovskyi, and later his first assistant coach, attempts a bicycle kick.

Jan Tomaszewski, October 1973: Wembley's greatest goalkeeping performance.

'The finest team ever to sort out successfully the intricacies of this wonderful game.' Billy Wright exchanges penants with Puskás, prior to England being torn apart by the Hungarians at Wembley, 1953.

Sándor Kocsis leaps for a header in what should have been the *Aranycsapat*'s coronation, the World Cup Final of 1954. They lost 3–2 to West Germany.

The mighty Ferenc Puskás.

the most active. He was there by the statue of St Imre on Gellért Hill when troops again opened fire on demonstrators, and subsequently allowed his house to be used as an arsenal by rebels. 'I had a lot of problems getting rid of the arms afterwards,' he said. 'Fortunately I had a good friend in the army, a captain, who came in a small truck and took the weapons and grenades away. That was my small contribution.'

It did not last long. Honvéd, initially using the excuse of a European Cup-tie against Athletic Bilbao, took their players on a European tour, and MTK soon did likewise. Soviet tanks entered Budapest in early November, crushing the rebellion, and, as reprisals began, Honvéd accepted a long-standing invitation to play a series of exhibition games in Brazil and Venezuela, taking with them a number of guest players including Grosics. The Hungarian FA and FIFA both declared the tour illegal, and, facing suspension and possibly worse, Puskás, Kocsis and Czibor decided not to return, all three eventually continuing their careers in Spain. Guttmann, the brilliant but irascible dandy who led the tour, was something of a wanderer anyway, but he never worked in Hungary again, denying the country of his birth the coaching talent that won two European Cups for Benfica. The national Under-21 team, who had been playing at a UEFA tournament in Belgium when the Uprising began, defected en masse. Hungary were never so good again.

So weakened were Honvéd that they would have been relegated in 1957, had not the Hungarian FA decided to spare them the embarrassment by enlarging the first division. In 2003, though, nothing could save them, and Kispest-Honvéd, as they were by then known, slipped out of the Hungarian top flight. If that seemed symptomatic of the wider decline, worse was to follow. The club was promoted at the first attempt, but, owing tens of millions of forints in taxes, Kispest-Honvéd Sports Circle Ltd, the company that had owned the club, went into liquidation in October 2004.

The problem, Zsolt Kiss, who had owned 10 per cent of the

old company, explained, was that the players had been on entrepreneurial contracts: that is, they were technically not employees, but contractors hired by the club, something that significantly reduced the club's tax burden. The tax authorities protested, and were supported by the courts, leaving the club with arrears they had no means of paying. What followed was a familiar story of infighting and intrigue. Kiss accused another co-owner, Attila Kovács – a former head of the Hungarian FA who had been forced out of office when his personal tax affairs were investigated – of reneging on a deal to pay his share of the debt, and so, in 2003, they and the majority owner Massimiliano Bottinelli, a representative of the Italian meat tycoon Piero Pini, turned to the league for arbitration.

The league came upon the idea of simply setting up a new club, Honvéd FC, which they would allow to take Kispest-Honvéd's place in the first division, provided all 'football-related debts' – that is, player contracts and the outstanding repayments on a loan from the league – were paid off. By the time Kispest-Honvéd Sports Circle went into liquidation, it was little more than a shell. As if that situation weren't tawdry enough, Honvéd began the 2004–05 season with their new coach, György Bognár, being sued by his former club Sopron over allegations he 'borrowed' money from club funds, and gambled it at a casino. He left the club that winter.

To blame Hungary's fall purely on the post-1956 drain, though, is oversimplistic. By the time of the Uprising, the *Aranycsapat* was probably past its peak anyway. Defeat to Turkey in February 1956 was only their third since the war, but it heralded a run of five games without a win, something that reflected and perhaps exacerbated the general mood of discontent. That said, the defections had an undeniable impact, and Hungary, distracted by events back in Budapest, were eliminated at the group stage of the 1958 World Cup in Sweden. Nagy was executed on 16 June, the day after a 4–0 victory over Mexico and three days before a 2–1 play-off defeat to Wales. The referee that day, by a grimly appropriate quirk, was Nikolay Latyshev, a Russian.

Latyshev was the referee again, four years later, when Hungary, led by Flórián Albert, lost in the quarter-finals to Czechoslovakia, and then it was the Soviet team that eliminated them in the quarter-final in England in 1966, only a dramatic goal-line clearance from József Szabo denying them extra time at Roker Park. That at least is how Szabo remembers it; my dad, who was at the game, has no recollection of the incident, although he does remember that the ball burst (this concern with material loss, perhaps, why he became an accountant rather than a sports journalist). Few allege conspiracy – John Charles, in his autobiography, even suggested Latyshev's performance in Stockholm was an apology to Hungary – but the coincidence symbolically delivers a clear message: the Soviets ended Hungarian football. Nonetheless, Albert stands among the greatest centre-forwards the world has known, and Hungary in the sixties were good enough, twice, to reach the last eight of the World Cup.

Hungary's club sides, similarly, flickered towards success. MTK, Újpest Dózsa and Videoton all lost in European finals, but it was the USSR that remained Hungary's *bêtes noires*. Valeriy Lobanovskyi's Dynamo Kyiv beat Ferencváros in the Cup-Winners' Cup final in 1975, and then a young and highly promising Hungary were thrashed 6–0 by Lobanovskyi's USSR in the group stages of the 1986 World Cup. They have not qualified for a major tournament since. Each generation, it seems, has been burdened with the knowledge that they were not so good as the last, and have suffered public resentment as a result. Eduardo Galeano has traced the mentality in Uruguayan football, and David Winner in English, both suggesting that progress is stymied by the constant harking back to a mythical golden age. 'We were always criticised because people compared us to Puskás's team,' Nyilasi said. 'But people would love to go back to that time now.'

There are those who believe that nationalisation itself was

to blame, that it brought the short-term gains that Sebes exploited, but in restricting competition hindered the development of young talents from outside his system. Certainly the habit Sebes's successors had of drawing up long-term plans and focusing their efforts on one competition has rarely brought sustained success wherever in the world it has been tried.

Others blame in-fighting between various factions within the regime, and perhaps for a time it did mean more to Mihály Farkas, the head of the army, for Honvéd to beat MTK (the team of his son Vladimir, the head of the secret police) than for Hungary to prosper in international competition, but in other countries – most notably Romania – such rivalries provided a stimulus for improvement. As Várhidy, who went on to win nine league titles as coach of Újpest, put it, though, football in Hungary in the final thirty years of Communism was not so much different to anywhere else, it just felt worse because of what had gone before.

That at least was true until the nineties, when financial deprivation brought genuine problems. It was only in 2002 that Hungary's GDP returned to the levels of 1989, and private capital does not finance football as the state once did. When something in Hungary is really bad, it is said to be *a béka segge alatt* – under the belly of a frog. Its football is lower now even than that. I went to the Budapest derby between Újpest and Ferencváros in October 2004, having been told repeatedly that the fixture was the biggest of the Hungarian season. Újpest and Ferencváros are the two most successful teams in Hungarian history, they are the only clubs to boast a nationwide support and both, at the time, had realistic championship ambitions, yet the crowd was only 4,520. Yes, the weather was appalling and, yes, the game was played at 11.30 on a Sunday morning (although not, as I initially thought, on police advice, but because Hungarian TV demands its live Sunday football broadcast be over by the time the Formula One starts), but that turnout truly was pathetic.

What would Antal Végh call a book were he to write one now? *Last Rites*, perhaps, or *Requiem*?

Watching that game – a dire 1–1 draw – was an odd experience. It was rather like stepping back into an English ground of the late eighties, albeit one that had gone prematurely all-seater. Both ends were near enough full, and the fans filling them impressively vociferous – a reminder of just how tame so many modern English stadiums can be, even when packed – while the long stands were virtually empty. There were even four Union flags, on each of which was written either 'hooligans' or 'hools'. (This is a matter that is taken weirdly seriously; on one of the many websites devoted to Ferencváros fans it is noted that they dropped the word 'hooligan' in 1997 and replaced it with 'hool', although nobody quite seemed able to tell me why.) The prevailing feel, though, was more Italian, not just in the banks of empty seats, but also in the use of coloured smoke bombs, the style of the chanting and the spinning of scarves above heads. Újpest's fans, indeed, have a conscious link with Fiorentina – the mutual bond of those who wear purple – describing themselves as the Viola and visiting the Artemio Franchi twice a season. Around the ground, the graffiti scrawled on garages and walls was written in a strange mix of Italian and English: 'Viola Fidelity', 'Gruppo anti Ferencváros'.

Few in numbers they may be, but there was no lack of passion among the fans, and there was a real edge, that increasingly rare sense that, with the right trigger, it could all go off. When Ferencváros took the lead just before half time, Újpest fans hurled drinks cans, sandwiches and stones at their celebrating players, and the game was briefly held up in the second half when they took to pelting the Ferencváros goalkeeper Lajos Szűcs. He was always a likely target, having left Ferencváros for Újpest several years earlier, only to return to Ferencváros after two seasons in Germany with Kaiserslautern. Clearly nobody deserves to be bombarded with half-bricks when taking goal kicks, but it must be said that Szűcs is hardly the most sympathetic figure, having himself been at the heart of the disgraceful denouement to the 2002–03 season.

Ferencváros went into their final game a point clear of MTK, and were widely expected to beat their opponents Debrecen, who were severely debilitated by injury. Given MTK faced a tough away game at Újpest, Ferencváros had reason to be confident, and prepared lavish title celebrations, even arranging for hot-air balloons to float overhead bearing banners reading WELCOME TO THE CHAMPIONS. With ten minutes remaining, though, Ferencváros hadn't scored, while MTK led at Újpest through a thirty-fifth-minute Roland Juhász header. As frustration mounted, Ferencváros's managing director József Szeiler ordered that the gates in the perimeter fence should be opened, allowing the crowd to swarm on to the edge of the pitch. The referee, reasoning that an abandonment was only likely to lead to further trouble, played on, but when he blew the final whistle with the game still goalless, fans attacked players from both teams. The Debrecen coach Lázár Szentes was knocked to the ground and suffered such a kicking that he ruptured a kidney. As police tried to restore order, Szűcs could clearly be seen standing on a balcony throwing an aluminium dustbin at officers in riot gear.

After the derby, I spoke to the former Újpest player András Tóth, who, like so many ex-players, was only too delighted to explain why things were better in his day. 'In the seventies, I played a lot of games against Ferencváros in the Népstadion, because at that time all the important games were played there,' he said. 'In those days we didn't have any conflicts with each other. People would come about an hour before the game to see us warm up outside the stadium, crowds supporting both clubs, and they would do it side by side. You would have Újpest and Ferencváros supporters next to each other and there would be no problem.'

So why the change? 'Violence is characteristic of other parts of Europe,' he explained, 'and now we have joined the EU, we have got the kind of trouble you see at Ajax v Feyenoord, or at Austria Vienna v Rapid Vienna, or in Germany.' Only my Englishness, I presume, stopped him naming England.

His argument seemed at first nonsensical – and in the form in which he expressed it, of course it is: violence had been a regular feature of Hungarian football for at least a decade before Hungary joined the EU in May 2004. There is, though, a kernel of truth in there; the increase in hooliganism does correlate with a westward shift in Hungary's perspective. A metaphor I heard regularly in Budapest sees Hungary as a statue that was for years covered in a dustsheet. People believed the statue to be beautiful, but when the cloth was finally removed, it was revealed to be ugly, cracked and dirty. More than most, Hungarians seem to have struggled with their changing national identity since the collapse of the USSR. For many, it is a feeling of dislocation among young working-class Hungarians that has led to the rise in hooliganism, a need both to forge an identity through association with a club and then aggressively to assert it.

For centuries Hungary stood as the frontline of the Christian West, seeing off attempted invasions by the Tartars and the Ottomans, and then, under Communist rule, Hungarians took pride in being the most 'western' of the Soviet bloc – geographically and mentally. Allied to that was a nationalistic pride, a sense of being chosen border people whose specialness was demonstrated by the country's disproportionate numbers of Nobel laureates and Olympic gold-medallists – and, of course, by the *Aranycsapat*. According to János Bali, a lecturer in ethnological studies at Budapest University, by joining the EU, Hungary has lost its unique role. It is now merely an eastern satellite of Brussels or Strasbourg, a cheap destination for stag weekends with a happy chocolate-box capital to draw the tourists, something that has led, in Bali's words, to an 'inferiority complex and a sense of peripheral status nationally'. There is, of course, an inherent paradox in that the form of expression by which these dislocated

Hungarians assert their identity as something distinct from western Europe – the ultra groups that consciously ape their Italian and English forerunners – is itself drawn from western Europe, but such, I suppose, is the nature of globalisation.

Ferencváros remain the most popular side, something that seems not merely the result of their recent history of success, but also because they have always been the most 'Hungarian' of clubs, the nationalism of their fans having first become evident in the 1920s. Hungary held its first secret ballot elections in 1920, voting, perplexingly, for a monarchy. There being no king was a problem, but Admiral Miklós Horthy was appointed (his experience leading the navy of a land-locked country apparently fitting him for the equally paradoxical role of elected king). The early years of his reign saw Hungarian society become increasingly bourgeois, something that led to tension between the new wealth and those who felt they were being left behind. The district of Ferencváros, to the south of the centre of Pest, has always been a working-class area, and it was there that the dissatisfaction was at its strongest.

As the historian Tamás Krausz put it, 'foreign money, i.e. "Jewish capital" and "foreigners" in general, was considered the main obstacle in the way of Hungarian prosperity.' The early years of Horthy's reign also saw the White Terror, by which he persecuted those who had been involved in Kun's Bolshevist regime. As many of those targeted were Jewish, his reprisals both fed off and propagated the more general anti-Semitism.

The Treaty of Trianon, drawn up by the Allies in 1920, was also a source of resentment. Hungary, having fought the First World War on the side of Germany, was reduced to a third of its previous size as land was ceded to Romania, Yugoslavia and Czechoslovakia. It was in the belief that that ground could be recovered that Horthy threw in his lot with Hitler during the thirties, becoming increasingly hard-line and eventually banning Jewish sporting clubs. When Ferencváros protested at the dissolution in 1940 of MTK, a club with long Jewish associations, the twelve Jews among their leadership were dismissed, and Andor Jaross, the Minister of the Interior, made club president. Jaross was later responsible for the deportation of 400,000 Hungarian Jews to Auschwitz, and was executed as a war criminal in 1946. That, though, only completed an ongoing process, Ferencváros having been one of the major sources of support for the pro-Nazi Arrow Cross party, which took power in 1944 after Horthy's failed attempt to negotiate a separate peace with the Allies.

Little wonder that when Rákosi and his Stalinists took power in rigged elections in 1947, they sought to run Ferencváros down, and it is equally unsurprising that Ferencváros fans were at the forefront of the 1956 Uprising, perhaps not in quite the obvious and organised manner of Red Star fans in Belgrade forty-four years later, but a significant factor nonetheless. Many of those who fought in the Uprising came from the slums of Angyalföld and Ferencváros, motivated, it is now widely accepted, less by political conviction than by what the historian Bill Lomax called 'the sport of the fight'. Half a century later, the sport of the fight is to be had with opposing fans.

After the derby I spoke to the gregarious István Sálloi, who at the time was Újpest's sports director. He was relatively relieved at the way the derby had gone, but our conversation was generally depressing. I'd first met Sálloi the previous year when he was sports director at Balaton FC, a team based in Siófok. They finished second in the 2003–04 season, a remarkable achievement given they were so poor that they had no training facility, and practice sessions took place either in the stadium car park or on the verges of the pitch. Twelve months later, they no longer existed, a victim of the chaos that hits Hungarian football each summer, leaving some clubs with new owners, some with new homes, some with new names, and some with nothing at all.

In the summer of 2004 – shortly, cynics would note, before FA elections – the first division was increased from twelve to sixteen teams, with the top four of the second division being promoted and the bottom two of the first division playing off against the fifth- and sixth-placed teams from the second. Both first division sides won, but one of them, DVTK, ran out of money, were unable to present a balanced budget and so were denied a licence. The FA then turned to the team who had finished seventh in the second division, Nyíregyháza, and, with only two weeks remaining before the start of the season, asked them to step in. The club requested a fortnight's grace to prepare their squad, but were turned down; not surprisingly, it was not until their twelfth game of the season that they recorded a victory.

Balaton's owner István Kuti, meanwhile, announced that as money was tight he wanted to move to a town where either the council or local businesses would help out with costs. At first it seemed they would move to Pápa and merge with the local second division team, Pápai ELC, but at the last minute they instead agreed a deal with Lombard-Haladás from Szombathely. It later transpired that Lombard, a firm of pawn-brokers that sponsored the team, had fallen out with the Szombathely city council. That left Balaton without a home, but on the eve of the season, bankrupt and with only four registered players, they agreed a merger with Diósgyőri VTK, a club based in Miskolc, around 300 miles from Siófok. It is perhaps not surprising that few fans bother investing much emotional energy in their teams.

The poverty is perhaps best summed up by an incident in 1999, when a hoax call was made to Dunakeszi warning of a bomb at their ground. The hoaxers could not call the club direct, though, having to leave a message with the factory next door as Dunakeszi's phone had been disconnected.

Given such a background, I asked, what hope was there for Hungarian football? Sálloi rolled his eyes and spoke of the need 'for an Abramovich'. That, I suggested, was a forlorn thought, that there could be no plan for the future other than to hold out desperately, praying that from somewhere a billionaire benefactor would ride to the rescue. 'The problem is money,' he said. 'We can't afford players and we lose any good young players immediately. A lot of young players are going to the fifth or the sixth division in Austria and getting better money than they would here. Sponsors are difficult to find, because they don't want to spend money here, because they think it's not a good level. If the level rises the money will come, but without money we cannot raise the level.'

Less than a month later, defeated by the catch-22, Sálloi resigned.

4 THE FORMER YUGOSLAVIA

Ever Decreasing Circles

THE FORMER YUGOSLAVIA

i Serbia-Montenegro

There was a time when Yugoslavia was the Brazil of Europe. So obsessed were Yugoslavs by the belief that they were the representatives of free-flowing samba football in the old world that Red Star Belgrade's ground is known as the Marakana, after the great stadium in Rio de Janeiro. Ludicrous as it may at first seem, Brazil having won five World Cups and Yugoslavia none, there is some truth to the claim, and Brazil had enough respect for their European counterparts that it was Yugoslavia they chose as their opponents in a testimonial match for Pelé in 1971. Yugoslavia were what Brazil would have been had they been European, self-doubt suppressing imagination and bringing to the surface the cynicism that has always underlain the technical excellence. Self-doubt, in fact, is the defining characteristic of Serbian football: they are Europe's most consistent chokers.

Three times in succession Yugoslavia reached the Olympic final, and three times they walked away with silver. They lost also in the final of the European championships of 1960 and 1968, while Partizan Belgrade were beaten by Real Madrid in the 1966 European Cup final and Red Star lost to Borussia Mönchengladbach in the 1979 UEFA Cup final. Then there are the five European semi-finals lost by Serbian clubs and Yugoslavia's defeats in the World Cup semi-finals of 1930 and 1962. On all but two occasions, when it came down to it, when it really mattered, when the greatest prizes came within their sight, Yugoslav teams collapsed. Yes, the national side won gold at the 1960 Olympics, but it is all too appropriate that Yugoslav football's greatest glory, Red Star Belgrade's penalty shoot-out victory over Marseille in the European Cup final in Bari in 1991, came after a game rendered sterile by mutual paranoia. A characteristic performance brought an uncharacteristic result, but, by then, Yugoslavia barely existed. In this case, the brightest hour came before the night.

It was on April Fool's Day 1992 that Yugoslav football finally expired. It was not even afforded the dignity of dying at home: EU sanctions forcing Red Star out of the Marakana, out of Yugoslavia, for games against foreign opposition. Going into their penultimate match in the European Cup's inaugural group stage, at 'home' to Sampdoria in Sofia, Red Star topped the table, and when they took a nineteenth-minute lead through Siniša Mihajlović, they looked on course for a second successive final. But then the Slovenian Srečko Katanec, once of Red Star's eternal rivals Partizan, equalised, and before half time Goran Vasilijević had put through his own goal – in Yugoslavia, the danger always came from within. Roberto Mancini added a late third, and, a fortnight later, Red Star lost to Anderlecht in Brussels to exit the competition. 'Red Star had a great team at the time and it would have been very different at the Marakana in front of

100,000 people,' Katanec acknowledged. No eastern European team has reached the final since, and it was not until twelve seasons later that Partizan were the next Serbian representatives in the group stages.

The goalkeeper and captain of Red Star's European Cup-winning team was Stevan Stojanović. I met him in Novi Sad at a game between Vojvodina and Sartid Smederevo that he was watching in his role as a scout for an agency based in Belgium. He is one of those huge men who projects an aura of great calm, a welcome attribute given that we'd barely ordered our half-time espresso when some local schoolchildren lobbed a tear-gas canister into the home end, prompting a panicked evacuation. Serbia retains that kind of feel – a place slightly on edge, not quite at ease with itself. The scars of the NATO bombing are still obvious in Belgrade, and, when I was there, Novi Sad was still accessible only by a temporary bridge, the original lying in ruins, a casualty of war.

In that context, there was something disconcerting when Stojanović leant forward and said, 'The tragedy is that we will never know how good we could have been.' In a land that played its part in the bloodiest European conflict since the Second World War, the term tragedy seemed dreadfully exaggerated. In a strictly dramatic sense, though, there probably has been no club so tragic as Red Star, a great side brought down by the fatal flaw in its make-up: the nationalism of its fans. For me, that Red Star team of 1991 remains the apogee of football: not the best side I have ever seen (although I maintain they are generally underrated), but the one that best combined the elements I would most want to see in a team I supported: technical brilliance, fluidity, a capacity for moments of staggering flair, supreme organisation, cynicism, and a pervading sense of mental fragility.

Take the semi-final victory over Bayern Munich. Their equaliser in the first leg in Germany is as close to perfection as any goal can be. In first-half injury time, Brian Laudrup was beaten to an Olaf Thon through-ball by Slobodan Marović, a butcher of a defender who had been hacking lumps out of the Dane all game. Although tight by his own corner flag, Marović played a delicate pass to the right-back Duško Radinović, who flicked it inside to Miodrag Belodedici. The Romanian, still in his own box, helped the ball on to Robert Prosinečki, who glanced up and curved a sixty-yard pass down the line for Dragiša Binić to chase. He outpaced Hans Pflügler, and whipped a low cross between Jürgen Köhler and the goalkeeper Raimond Aumann for Darko Pančev, arriving at the far post, to slide home. Everything was controlled, precise, and yet, because of the pace of the move, it was virtually undefendable.

When I spoke to Binić about it, though, he was frustratingly dismissive. 'We scored a lot like that,' he said. 'We were a quick team, so we played on the counter.' The speed was the key, Binić was keen to stress, because that, you see, was the bit that involved him. I have interviewed few more voluble players, and I have interviewed none so voluble on the subject of themselves. The only thing that saved him from being an insufferable egotist was the occasional suggestion that his self-aggrandisement might have been ironic in intent. 'I was the fastest player in Yugoslavia,' he said, with a flourish of his cigarette. 'I was the fastest player in Europe. I'm still the fastest man in Yugoslavia, and I'm faster than any English player in a one-off sprint, even though I began smoking three years ago. It was well known that I was fast. I could run a hundred metres in ten point five seconds. There was a stunt for the newspapers and I ran against a Yugoslav sprinter. I was wearing my boots, and he had spikes, but I was faster from the start and led until seventy metres, and then he eased past me, but in football you don't have to run a hundred metres. When Carl Lewis came to athletics meetings in Belgrade, I wanted to run against him.' Hans Pflügler didn't have a prayer.

Red Star's second also came on the break, Dejan Savićević racing on to Pančev's flick before smacking a superb low finish past Aumann. I once arranged to interview Savićević in his brief time as national manager of Serbia-Montenegro. I'd fixed a date with his secretary, but she asked me to phone the day before to confirm a time. When I suggested meeting in the morning, she tutted loudly. 'He is a Montenegrin,' she said. I thought at first this was just a slightly disrespectful joke, the stereotype of a Montenegrin being of a layabout who spends his life dozing under trees, but then she agreed to pencil me in for his first appointment of the day – at noon. He was over an hour late even for that. Sublime he may have been as a footballer, but as an interviewee he was hopeless: tick the box marked 'unreliable genius' and move on.

The general rule seems to be that the better the footballer, the worse they will remember their greatest moments – an indication, perhaps, of how the best football stems from unconscious instinct – but Savićević, after mumbling about how 'I just hit it and it went in', did vaguely recall that there was a degree of complacency about the crowd in the Marakana for the second leg. When Mihajlović scored with a deflected free-kick midway through the first half, the tie seemed won, and that was when the doubt kicked in. The composure that had marked their performance for the first three-quarters of the tie disappeared, and Red Star conceded twice in the space of four minutes. 'Klaus Augenthaler scored a goal that went under Stojanović – a mistake,' Binić said. 'The Germans started running for everything, and suddenly it was 2–1 from Manfred Bender. We were very tense because the momentum had turned against us. The Germans hit the post and if it had gone to extra-time we probably would have lost, but in the last minute we had a counter-attack. Mihajlović crossed from the left. He had me in the middle and Pančev just behind, but he hit a bad pass. It was low, and Augenthaler . . .'

Even Binić was unable to find the words for it, perhaps dreaming of the volley he would have creamed into the top corner if only Mihajlović hadn't miskicked. With his hands, cigarette still clamped between his fingers, he traced the loop of the ball as Augenthaler, in attempting to clear, scooped the ball backwards, so it hung, and, spinning cruelly, dipped with languid perfection over Aumann and into the far corner. 'Luck is very important in football,' Stojanović said with a grin, 'and at that moment it shone on us.' It was just as well it did, because mentally they were shot. That brittleness, though, was part of their beauty.

Yet it was Red Star who held their nerve better in the final, beating Marseille in a penalty shoot-out after a dire 120 minutes of anxious goallessness. That said, with Manuel Amoros, Chris Waddle and the former Red Star hero Dragan Stojković in their line-up, Marseille had gathered a squad of players with a history of suffering penalty trauma. Stojković declined to take one, less because of his failure in the 1990 World Cup against Argentina than because he could not bear to down the club where he was so revered. So too did Waddle, the memories of West Germany and Turin too fresh. Amoros, the French full-back, having had nine years to get over the World Cup semi-final defeat against West Germany, volunteered to go first, only for Stojanović to save. It was Pančev who converted the final kick, winning Red Star a trophy they fully deserved – even if the final was the worst in the competition's history. That anticlimax will always cloud the perception, but it is a measure of how good they were that when the Rangers manager Graeme Souness sent his assistant Walter Smith to scout Red Star before the sides met in the second round that year, he is said to have returned with a two-word report: 'We're fucked.'

Yet admire them as I do, it is impossible to discuss that Red Star side without reference to atrocity. Nowhere was football so entwined with the disintegration of the Communist regime, and nowhere was the disintegration so prolonged and so bloody. Their fans – the Delije as they are now called – are widely condemned, pariahs of the European game, and, to an extent, their reputation is deserved. Some of them are racist, some of them do fight, and some of them did commit war crimes, but the organisation itself has a warmer side, and the draw it holds is readily understandable.

Before a Partizan–Red Star game in 2002, I had lunch with Milena and Ljiljana, two journalist sisters, in a small restaurant opposite the Marakana. The place was packed with Red Star fans, preparing for the short walk to the Partizan Stadium, but the atmosphere was far from raucous. Showing people to their tables, instead of a *maître d'*, was a tall, slightly balding man in his thirties, dressed in jeans and a leather jacket. Occasionally, with great politeness, he would ask diners to move tables or to shuffle up to make room for another guest. He was, Milena later told me, one of the leaders of the Delije. Older fans, some barely able to walk unassisted, were invariably treated with great deference. It took me a while to work out why everything felt familiar, but then I realised that the scene was a staple of gangster films, the extended mafia family coming together over dinner.

The day before, after a press conference at the Marakana, I chatted briefly to the doorman, whom everybody knew by the nickname Mile Šnuta. He was probably only in his sixties, but he looked older, his face yellow and wizened. 'I was one of the chant-leaders,' he told me, his voice scarcely more than a croak. 'Everywhere Red Star went, I went too. But now my heart is too weak, so my doctors have told me I cannot go to games, because I get very excited.' I asked if he would watch the derby on television. 'No,' he said, smiling toothlessly. 'I will be in the stand if it kills me. To die for Red Star would be an honour.'

I later learned it was the Delije that got him his job. That afternoon I met a younger fan, his legs twisted horribly inwards, who propelled himself on a pair of sticks. The Delije, he told me, helped him out, even took him to the odd away game. They may be violent and anarchic, but the Delije are also a community. Milena and Ljiljana both have tales to tell of how the Delije have spirited them away from trouble. They look after their own, and their own are often those members of society least able to look after themselves: from that point of view, their appeal is obvious.

Red Star were founded at Belgrade University in 1945. So impoverished were they that they might never have got off the ground had Obilić and FK Slavija not donated footballs they'd protected through the war. In their first game Red Star beat a Yugoslav army team 3–2 in front of a crowd of over 3,000, and, as they embarked on a twenty-match unbeaten run, they gathered a devoted following. 'These guys,' the Delije's website says, 'had something special, because they represented the very soul of our capital. Mostly they were rough guys or bohemians, young Belgradians who did not like the army or the Communist system, which had already begun to rot.' The claim bears a degree of self-serving revisionism – it is scarcely credible that a team founded by Communists and whose very name is a Communist symbol should have harboured a significant anti-Communist support – but, even allowing for that, Red Star have always been a club for the poor and the disaffected, and thus for anti-Titoist and anti-federalist feeling.

By the seventies, thousands of fans would gather on match days in central Belgrade, before marching to their home on the North Stand – the 'Epicentre of Craziness', as a famous graffito dubbed it. 'If, by chance,' the website says, 'they met opposing fans, clashes were inevitable.' Seizing the banners of rival groups became such a common practice that legislation was passed outlawing flags above a certain size. Mocking the humble origins of most of Red Star's support, opposing fans taunted them with chants of 'Gypsies', a term that was swiftly appropriated. 'We are Gypsies,' they would return. 'We are the strongest'. In the eighties, as attendances and ethnic tension boomed, Red Star's support split into two major groups – the Ultras, who were concerned mainly with choreographing displays of flags, and the Red Devils, who 'adopted Serbian habits mixed with English habits', as the website puts it: 'drinking to death, beating rivals and consuming marijuana'. As with their English counterparts, the general violent nihilism coexisted with an extreme right-wing philosophy. Red Star's fans, though, always insisted on their independence from any political body, stressing that the people they really hated were fans of Partizan. Similar groups in Croatia, by contrast, allied themselves to Franjo Tudjman's ultra-nationalist Croatian Democratic Union (HDZ) party.

The rivalry with Partizan extends even into international fixtures. I went to see Yugoslavia play Finland at the Marakana in one of their final games before they ditched the pretence and became Serbia-Montenegro in February 2003. Four days earlier Yugoslavia had earned a surprising draw against Italy in Naples, but there was little of the optimism I had expected. Red Star fans, wearing their club shirts and occupying the North Stand as they would for a league game, jeered the Yugoslav anthem, chanted 'Serbia, not Yugoslavia' and sang Serbian folk songs. When the former Partizan forward Mateja Kežman – a particular hate figure for Red Star, having scored against them in each of the five Belgrade derbies in which he played – misplaced an attempted backheel, he was mercilessly jeered, and faded from the game. It was as though the match itself – which, after an iffy first half, Yugoslavia won 2–0 – was an irrelevance, merely a stage on which Red Star fans could express their continuing commitment to Serbian nationalism, while at the same time deriding the wishy-washy federalism of Partizan.

Such has been the victory of nationalism that Partizan, these days, is a club in search of a role. Named after the guerrillas with whom Tito battled Nazi occupation, in Communist times they were the team of the army, and so represented everything hard-line Serb nationalists opposed. To start with, Tito was half Croat, half Slovene, born in Kumrovec, Croatia, and his Partizans, as well as battling German forces in the Second World War, also clashed with the Chetniks – right-wing Serb guerrillas. After the war, with Tito in power, the army, quite aside from symbolically representing the federal ideal of Yugoslavia, suppressed the Serb Orthodox Church, pictures of whose saints Red Star fans took to brandishing at matches in the eighties. Partizan's black-and-white colours are even the result of a decision taken by Tudjman during his unlikely stint as club president in the late fifties. It is too simplistic, though, merely to define Red Star as a Serb team. The side of 1991 contained several non-Serbs: Robert Prosinečki was a Croat, Refik Šabanadžević a Bosnian Muslim, Marović and Savićević Montenegrins, Ilija Najdoski and Darko Pančev from Macedonia FYR. That said, in the famous photograph of the Red Star players celebrating their victory on the running track in Bari, it is noticeable that while eight players are clearly extending the two-fingers-and-a-thumb Serb salute – signifying the Trinity and affiliation to the Serb Orthodox Church and, by extension, Serbia itself – Prosinečki, pointedly, is not.

At another time their victory might have galvanised federalist feeling, but in May 1991 the cracks in Yugoslavia were so wide as to be irreparable. It is debatable at what point war became unavoidable, but it was arguably from the moment of Tito's death in May 1980. The Albanian Communist Mahmet Bekalli, for instance, wrote of his funeral, 'Little did we know we were also burying Yugoslavia.' Certainly by 1988 preparations were at an advanced stage. In August that year I went on holiday with my parents to Žabljak, a dusty village high in the mountains on the Montenegro–Bosnìa border. We were supposed to make our return to the airport at Budva Tivat, seven hours away on the Adriatic coast, by bus, but the fan belt broke, leaving us frantically to arrange a taxi. Behind schedule, the driver raced along a series of side roads, and we seemed to be back on track when we turned a corner and came upon a military roadblock. I was only twelve at the time and so my memories are perhaps not to be relied upon, but my parents confirm a long conversation took place between the driver and a tall figure in a greatcoat (given it was

August this detail seems unlikely, but I suppose we were high up). He eventually let us pass and for several miles we drove through what was clearly a military training area. Most striking – and again I've checked this with my parents – was the sight of a group of soldiers with bazookas propped on their shoulders. When we at last reached a checkpoint at the far end of the valley, the driver turned to us and explained, 'They are getting ready for the war.' It seems bizarre – an indication, I would suggest, of how underplayed the situation was in the Western media – but the next year we happily went back to Bohinj in Slovenia, and, two years after that, were booked to go to Rogla near Maribor.

By 1991, Slovenia and Croatia had both declared themselves to be sovereign states and announced their intention of declaring independence, while Serbs in Krajina, an area of Croatia with a Serb majority, had begun their rebellion. Tensions were such that on 16 March Slobodan Milošević admitted, 'Yugoslavia is finished.' The first casualties of the war fell on 31 March as Croat troops clashed with Serb militia, to the horror of a large group of Italian tourists, in Plitviće National Park. In April, between the two legs of Red Star's semi-final victory over Bayern, a group of extreme Croat nationalists fired three Ambrust missiles into Borovo Selo, a village near Vukovar, and, at the beginning of May, twelve Croatian policemen were killed and twenty wounded in a failed attempt to free two colleagues captured in a senseless earlier raid on the town. The European Cup was won on 29 May; within a month, Slovenia had declared independence and the federal Yugoslavia was dead.

Prosinečki, asked about the wider context of Red Star's victory, was uncomfortable and defensive, insisting that the players were focused simply on the football. 'We had a great generation,' he said. 'Politics has nothing to do with it. I can't talk about things I haven't felt. Perhaps there were some at the club who thought that way, but I really don't know about it. Sportsmen are people who aren't preoccupied with politics.'

Maybe so, but he was the only member of the side who did not return to Belgrade in 2001 for celebrations of the tenth anniversary of the victory in Bari, citing prior commitments.

Politics, anyway, cannot be so easily separated from sport. Seven months after the victory, the nationalism hinted at by the salutes in Bari was shown undisguised in the Marakana as Red Star celebrated victory in the Intercontinental Cup. By then Slovenia was officially independent, Vukovar had fallen to the Serbs after weeks of bombardment and the siege of Dubrovnik had begun. That August, when the Krajina Serbs had taken the Croatian town of Kijevo and instigated the first act of ethnic cleansing of the war, General Milan Martić, the head of their police force, had symbolically ripped down a signpost in Latin script; at the Marakana, after the victory over Colo Colo of Chile, the crowd were brought to a frenzy by Arkan, the head of their fan club, similarly brandishing a street sign he had stolen in Croatia. In that act, redolent both of a general displaying the standard of a vanquished enemy and of a hooligan showing off the colours of a rival fan he has beaten, football's part in the Balkan horrors is laid bare.

In the eyes of the Delije, it was they who fought the war's first battle, during a league game against Dinamo Zagreb. Dinamo's ultras, the Bad Blue Boys (BBB), seem to agree. Outside the Maksimir Stadium in Zagreb there is a statue of a group of soldiers, and on its plinth is written: 'To the fans of this club, who started the war with Serbia at this ground on 13 May 1990.' Tudjman, as leader of the HDZ, had been elected president of Croatia on a nationalist ticket a fortnight earlier. His use of the *šahovnica*, the red-and-white chequerboard emblem that had been a symbol of the Ustaše, the Croatian fascists who collaborated with the Nazis and slaughtered hundreds of thousands of Serbs during the Second World War, seemed deliberately provocative. Unsettled Serbs could hardly have been encouraged when he commented, 'Thank God my wife is not a Jew or a Serb.' As Croatia simmered with nationalist fervour, Tudjman invited back several emigré Croats, many of whom Serbs considered war criminals, and vowed to lead the republic to independence. When a Serbian team whose fans were themselves avowedly nationalist went to play against a team whose fans had pledged allegiance to the HDZ, violence was unavoidable.

There are as many different accounts of the subsequent battle at the Maksimir as there were people there, but what seems clear is that the conflict was to a large degree premeditated. Rocks had been stockpiled, while fans used acid to burn away security fences. The Delije, it is said, even brought huge numbers of Belgrade licence plates with them and fixed them over the Zagreb plates on local cars, tricking the BBB into attacking Croatian vehicles. Zvonimir Boban, the Dinamo captain who went on to play for AC Milan, became a national hero in Croatia by launching a flying kick at a policeman who was beating a Dinamo fan, while Red Star players had to be rescued from the rioting by police helicopters. In all, seventy-nine police officers and fifty-nine fans were injured that day, and hundreds were arrested. Among them, one name stood out: Arkan.

Arkan – or Željko Ražnatović, to give him his original name – was the son of a colonel in Tito's air force, but he soon rebelled, dividing his time between studying at catering college and purse-snatching in Kalemegdan Park. When he was seventeen he was arrested for the first time and sentenced to three years in a juvenile detention centre. It seems that when he was released, his father, in an attempt to straighten him out, put him in touch with contacts in the Yugoslav State Security Service (UDBA). Arkan, though, moved to western Europe and took up a career as a bank robber. He was jailed in Belgium in 1974, but escaped; he was jailed in Holland in 1979, but escaped; and he was held in a prison hospital in West Germany after being wounded in a raid, but escaped. Insouciant and seemingly unimprisonable, he became an almost mythic figure, on one celebrated occasion strolling into a courtroom in Sweden where an associate of his was on trial and securing his release by pointing a gun at the judge. It now seems likely that he was at least in part aided by the UDBA, by whom he was probably employed as a hit man. It wasn't just his slipperiness that made his name, though. Where other gangsters revelled in excess, Arkan was noted for his abstemiousness. One story has him standing by an open window going through his exercise regime while behind him his associates celebrated a successful raid with whisky, cigars and prostitutes. Then, in 1986, he returned to Belgrade, opened a patisserie just over the road from the Marakana, bought a pink Cadillac and began working more overtly for the UDBA.

That was also the year in which members of the Serbian Academy of Sciences and Arts published their memorandum expressing discontent at the Serbs' position within the Yugoslav constitution, and the year in which Slobodan Milošević became leader of the Serbian Communist Party. The following year, after a riot among Serbs in Kosovo had alerted him to the political capital to be made from nationalism, Milošević replaced Ivan Stambolić as president of Serbia. Red Star fans, who had taken to holding aloft pictures of the dissident novelist Vuk Drašković, leader of the Serb Renewal party, were largely supportive of his right-wing agenda, but Milošević knew their anarchic passions could soon turn against him – as, eventually, they did. Accordingly, he asked Arkan to take them in hand. 'We trained fans without weapons,' Arkan said. 'I insisted on discipline from the very beginning. You know our fans – they're noisy, they like to drink, to joke about. I stopped all that in one go. I made them cut their hair, shave regularly, not drink. And so it began, the way it should be.' Under his tutelage, the Gypsies became the 'Delije' – the 'Strong Ones' or 'Heroes'.

They had been one of the most feared hooligan firms in Europe, but under Arkan the Delije became something more sinister, as he drew from their ranks to form his Tigers. Weeks after the victory in Bari – when there was 'choreography

Europe will never forget', as one fan told me – the Tigers, chanting the songs they had sung from the North Stand, marched to the front. They were there in Vukovar in 1991, when hundreds of Croat patients were herded from a hospital, packed into trucks and shot in a field, and they were there too the following year in Bijeljina, killing Muslims or chasing them from their homes at the onset of the conflict in Bosnia.

When the Croat counter-offensive began in 1995, Arkan was back in Belgrade with his new wife, the pop star Ceca, whom he had met in October 1993 at a celebration to mark the third anniversary of the formation of the Tigers. (Their wedding was an orgy of kitsch on the theme of the 1389 Battle of Kosovo, Arkan dressing as a warrior and Ceca as one of the women who had tended the injured. He rode up to her parents' house on a white charger and, as was customary in the fourteenth century, was asked by her father to prove his worthiness by shooting an apple off the top of the door with a crossbow. His first effort missed, as did his second, and his third, so, before it got too embarrassing, he nodded to his henchmen, who blew it to pulp with Kalashnikovs.) Arkan watched on television as the Croats retook land he had helped conquer, and, if legend is to be believed, was so enraged that he donned his uniform again and made a phone call to the Delije. Within half an hour, his Tigers had gathered outside the Marakana, ready to return to war. In Bosnia, there were more atrocities. It became not simply about land, but also about financial gain. It was said that you could always recognise the Tigers because they had soil under their nails from digging in the gardens of houses they had looted, looking for hidden jewellery. The war made Arkan notorious, but it also made him rich.

Arkan built a house near the Marakana, and tried to take over Red Star, but the club's then president, Dragan Dzajic, rebuffed him. So, in 1996, Arkan took charge of Obilić, one of Belgrade's oldest clubs, but not one of its most successful. The attraction to him, though, is obvious. Obilić are named after Miloš Obilić, the knight who supposedly killed the Turkish sultan Murad at Kosovo. The defeat suffered at the hands of the Ottoman Empire then remains central to the Serbian psyche: they are the wrongly oppressed but glorious losers. What better for Arkan than to cast himself as a latter-day Obilić, scourge of the infidel.

Obilić's rise was astonishing. Promoted in 1996–97, they lost just one game the following season to win the first championship in their history. They might have won a second the following year, having gone twenty-four games unbeaten from the start of the season, but the league was suspended on 14 May when the NATO bombing began. This was not, though, anything like the rags-to-riches fairy tale the club likes to present.

Referees arriving at the Obilić stadium would be greeted by heavies in fatigues, opposing players would mysteriously withdraw hours before matches, and the Tigers, many carrying guns, packed the terraces, a visible warning to any team tempted to try too hard. And then there were the rumours that sedative gases were pumped into the away changing room before kick-off; implausible perhaps, but taken seriously enough that when Red Star played there, they changed in the car park. And even if there were no gas, there was always the possibility that Arkan might pay a visit to the away dressing room at half time. On one occasion, according to a common tale, he threatened to shoot an opposing centre-forward in the knee if he scored in the second half.

Thanks to such shenanigans, and an admittedly impressive defence, Obilić approached their final game of the season two points clear of Red Star at the top of the table. Both faced away games against sides threatened with relegation, Red Star at Železnik and Obilić at Proleter. A few days before the games, Železnik's president Juša Bulić was shot in a Belgrade bar in what appeared to be an underworld hit. Suitably encouraged, Železnik won 2–1. Obilić's game, curiously, started slightly late. They led 1–0 when the news came through that Red Star had been beaten, meaning they only needed a draw for the title. Proleter promptly equalised, and so got the point they needed to avoid a relegation play-off.

UEFA, though, weren't keen on the idea of an indicted war criminal leading a team in the Champions League, so Arkan stood down as president, allowing his wife to take over. He remained in an advisory capacity until January 2000, when he was shot thirty-eight times in the chest as he sat drinking a coffee outside the Intercontinental Hotel in Belgrade. His killers have never been caught, and theories abound as to why he was assassinated. Some say his murder was ordered by Milošević's son, Marko, jealous of Arkan's stranglehold over the black market; some say it was the secret police, afraid of what he might reveal if he ever reached the Hague for questioning; some say it was a simple gangland turf war; there are others, though, romantics perhaps, who suggest that his partners at Obilić were resentful of how much money he siphoned from the club, and that, in the end, it was football that destroyed him.

Arkan's legacy lives on in the cosmetically enhanced figure of Ceca. I went to Belgrade in the summer of 2003 having made preliminary arrangements to interview her. Unfortunately, she was unavailable, having been arrested in connection with the assassination of the Serbian prime minister Zoran Djindjić a few weeks earlier. As excuses for skipping interviews go, being in solitary confinement is pretty much beyond reproach. From the VIP lounge in the main stand at the Obilić stadium, looking out over the trees that line the street behind the other stand, I could see the red roof of the prison where she was being held, but that was as close as I got. Instead I ended up interviewing Binić, her acting president, but, forthcoming as he was on himself, he was reluctant to discuss either Ceca or anything to do with the club's recent past.

We met in her office, on the wall of which were three framed photographs: one of the 1997–98 championship-winning team, one of Ceca in concert in front of a 100,000 crowd at the Marakana, and one of Arkan, in full combat gear, emerging from billowing smoke and firing a machine-pistol into the air. Down in the lobby, there was still a bronze bust of Arkan, standing alongside a plastic model of the proposed redevelopment of their stadium. The two long stands, all stainless steel and blue plastic, have already been built, and are hugely impressive, but as Obilić's average home gate is under 2,000, they are also largely pointless. Given finances at the club are such that they took a decision in 2003 only to field Under-21 players, it is highly unlikely that the project will ever be completed, and so the half-finished stadium will remain as a monument to the madness of the 1998 league title.

Whether or not it was football that did for Arkan, it was not long after his death that it turned against Milošević. Otpor, the student opposition group, and the NATO bombing certainly played their parts, but, as far as the Delije are concerned, it was they who led the internal opposition, they who enacted Serbia's anti-Communist revolution. Defeat in Bosnia and the hardships brought about by sanctions and the NATO bombing had hardened feeling against Milošević, but, beyond a few student demonstrations, fear kept outright public dissent in check, until 26 July 2000 when Red Star played Torpedo Kutaisi of Georgia in the second qualifying round of the Champions League.

'I was there,' Ljiljana told me. 'What happened was unbelievable. You have to understand that before that day, even if we didn't like Milošević, we wouldn't dare say that.' As Red Star romped to a 4–0 win, the Delije shouted, 'Do Serbia a favour, Slobodan, and kill yourself' – a taunt with a particular barb given the history of suicide in Milosevic's family. The police weighed in, but the Delije fought back. A Red Star banner was seized, and two policemen trampled on it. As they did so, though, they were approached by the Red Star coach, Slavoljub Muslin, who persuaded them to give him the flag, and threw it back over the restraining hedge and into the crowd. Symbolically, Muslin, and thus Red Star, were seen to have joined the protest.

Dissent spread to other stadia. Virtually every game became an anti-Milošević rally. On 24 September, Milošević suffered a humiliating election defeat to Vojislav Koštunica. Still he tried to cling to power, first demanding a second round of voting, and then securing through the courts an annulment of the election. This time, though, the movement against him was too strong. There was a general strike. Pockets of protest began to spring up across Serbia. In Čačak, sixty miles south of Belgrade, Mayor Velja Iljić, a hard-line Milošević critic, gathered opponents of the regime and marched on the capital. By the time his column, a bulldozer at its head, reached Belgrade, it was 10,000 strong. Once there, Iljić's forces were joined by Otpor and the Delije. Chanting 'Do Serbia a favour, Slobodan, and kill yourself', they smashed down the doors of the state television station, and set the building on fire. 'We were sick of watching state television,' said Iljić. 'We got fed up with living in Milošević's Serbia. I planned it all with my mates. It was Čačak's humble contribution. We got sick of the way the opposition was going. It was useless. We'd march, criticise Milošević and then everybody went home and he was still there. We decided, "We are men, let's do it."'

And so the crowd moved on to the parliament, which by then had been ringed by police. The chanting continued, and tear gas was fired. The Delije, though, were used to clashing with police, and, despite Iljić's appeals for calm, refused to be dispersed. The police line broken, the protesters surged into the building, ransacking it as they looked for evidence that Milošević had attempted to rig the elections. It didn't take long to find, and soon the air outside was filled with ballot papers, each marked with a cross next to Milošević's name. Studio B, once an independent channel that had been turned into a propaganda outlet for the government, went off air, only to return a little later as its old self, referring to Koštunica as the elected president. Shortly after, Koštunica appeared before the parliament, and began his address to the rebels with the words: 'Good evening, liberated Serbia.'

A week later Red Star faced Partizan at the Marakana. It could have been a day of glorious celebration in which rivals put aside their differences and recognised the contribution each had made in dethroning a tyrant – several Partizan fans had played a prominent role in the storming of the parliament – but it became a riot. Partizan's then chairman was Mirko Marjanović, the Serbian president and a close ally of Milošević. In the eyes of Red Star fans, they were facing the same enemy they had overthrown a week earlier. The banners in the North Stand made their feelings clear. 'Mirko to jail; Partizan to the second division', said one; 'The sun of freedom rises on our victory', read another.

Before kick-off, chants went up from the Partizan end calling for the resignation of Marjanović and his cronies. Gradually the protests became more violent, and seats and fireworks were thrown at police, who also in some way represented the old guard, and who had, after all, for several months brutally suppressed dissent. Three minutes into the game, Red Star fans, angered by the destruction of their stadium, charged. As hundreds of fans poured on to the pitch, even the players became involved in scuffles. The journalist Dejan Nikolić was in the North Stand that day. 'The surge was immense and there was no point trying to fight against it,' he wrote. 'You had a choice: either run with the crowd or be trampled on by several hundred fans. All around people were losing their balance and disappearing under the stampeding crowd. One fan said to me, "They were never in the front line during any of the demonstrations. They never fought with the police – at least not while wearing the Partizan colours. Now suddenly here they are, claiming all the credit – we'll not let them do that."'

Two years later, the atmosphere was calmer, but not much. As Red Star fans were herded through the city from the

Marakana to their tribune at the Partizan Stadium, they were
pelted with coins, but nobody seemed too bothered. That was
just what happened at derbies. Just behind the away end is a
small, almost quaint, church, surrounded by the cemetery
from which the Partizan fans took their name, 'Grobari' –
'Gravediggers'. The group was officially shut down several
years ago after an incident in which a rocket fired from the
home end killed an eight-year-old Red Star fan – the Delije
continue to leave his seat empty – but several banners in and
around the ground still bear the Grobari name.

There were checkpoints and searches every few yards on
the approaches to the Partizan Stadium (so thorough that I had
a packet of Lemsip capsules confiscated), but fans still
managed to smuggle hundreds of flares into the ground. Up
in the press box, a rickety wooden structure perched like a
pigeon loft on the top of the main stand, though, it all felt
very safe, mainly because there was nobody anywhere near
me. Away to the left, Red Star fans held up large sheets of red
card, to the right Partizan fans twirled black bin liners above
their heads, for the derby, of course, is not just about fighting,
but also about choreography. Immediately below me, though,
the stand was virtually empty. There was a scattering of red-
and-white shirts and a scattering of black-and-white, but they
paid each other little attention. The hostility, it appeared, was
reserved for those who wanted it. Police ringed each end, but
despite the occasional scuffles and the showers of flares, they
made no effort to intervene. The reasoning seemed to be that
those who go in the ends surrender themselves to the ends.
Serious trouble, indeed, broke out in a UEFA Cup-tie between
Red Star and Chievo in 2002 when police broke the unwritten
rule and entered the North Stand at the Marakana.

Straddling the fence at the front of the Red Star fans, I saw
Petja, a Delije member I had met the day before. His response
to my question about why he supported Red Star led me, not
for the first time, to wonder if the ideology were not all a bit
of an excuse. (Milošević used nationalism to retain political

power; Arkan used it to make money; the Delije use it to give a logic to the violent assertion of their identity as Red Star fans.) 'We are normal people,' Petja said. 'We are students or people who go to work. Partizan fans are cattle or geese.' There is a sense in which you just are red-and-white or black-and-white. Without exception, every player to whom I spoke insisted he had been a lifelong fan of the club for which he played.

This is a common enough claim the world over, of course, but given that only seven players have played for both clubs, it has more credence in Belgrade than most places. It helped that at the time every player was a Yugoslav, but even those who were born far from Belgrade supported one or the other. The then Red Star forwards Mihjalo Pjanović and Branko Bošković both insisted they would rather not play football at all than play for Partizan. 'From the youngest age you choose Red Star or Partizan even if you are not from Belgrade,' said Pjanović, who is from Prijepolje. 'I remember coming to the European Cup semi-final against Bayern Munich in 1991. I had relatives we came and stayed with in Belgrade, so I first came to a game when I was very young.' Bošković is from even further away. 'Red Star is like Manchester United,' he said. 'You choose at a very early age to support them. I lived in Montenegro so it was too far to come to games when I was younger, but I was a Red Star fan.'

There is a TV studio in the Marakana, but the Partizan captain Saša Ilić has vowed never to do any interviews there, insisting the cameras come to him, while Ljubisa Tumbaković, who coached Partizan to six league titles in the nineties, hated Red Star so much that he once hurled a cup of coffee across a restaurant because it was served with a red spoon.

The day before that game, which ended 2–2, I met Red Star's marketing manager, the frighteningly ebullient Zoran Avramović. Serbian football, he admitted, suffered from the same problem as all leagues post-fragmentation, both in the former Yugoslavia and the former USSR: the big clubs were simply too dominant. 'Nobody wants to watch a league where everybody knows who will win,' he explained. 'The smaller sides have to build their schools and try to catch us up. These days people go home from work on a Friday, they sit in a chair and drink a beer, and over the weekend they can watch seven or eight games from across Europe on their televisions, free of charge. But if our league is competitive, people will want to watch that.'

In the financial problems that struck the larger Western leagues in the earliest years of the twenty-first century, though, he saw hope. 'How can we develop if we keep on selling our stars?' he said. 'At Red Star we have worked on creating a stable financial situation so we do not have to sell our players, and because there are not so many transfers in England and Spain and Italy at the moment, we can hold on to them for two or three additional years. But still, a time will come when a player is offered ten, twenty, fifty times what we can offer, and then we cannot expect players to stay, however much they love Belgrade. We have been through a difficult spell. It has taken everybody a long time to adjust, and the gap is still huge, but perhaps now at last there is a little hope.' Avramović is a man who would talk excitedly about the future even as the noose was slipped around his neck, but there is perhaps a suggestion that things are improving.

For much of the nineties, Serbia was a gangster economy, dominated to such a degree by Arkan that Belgrade's major shopping centre was known jokingly as Arkansas. Not surprisingly, football was similarly dominated by organised crime taking advantage of the system of so-called 'private contracts' which were finally outlawed in 2001. The arrangement, by which individuals owned players and paid their wages, leasing them to clubs in the hope of being able to sell them abroad at a profit, initially suited everyone. Players enjoyed more benefits and better conditions than the clubs could have offered them, the clubs were relieved of the financial burden of satisfying top players, and the FSJ saw young Yugoslav talent stay in the country longer before departing for bigger wages abroad. And then organised crime took over.

I have spoken to several players about the issue; all of them asked me not to name them. For some, the injustice was simply financial; one player, for instance, discovered his agent-cum-owner was taking 80 per cent of his salary. The testimonies of others told of an all-pervading corruption. 'I was in a youth squad of Partizan when I signed a private contract,' one player said. 'I needed to play somewhere else because, being realistic, I knew I had no chance next to the great generation of players that emerged at the club at the time. I just wanted a chance to play first-team football, so I signed a contract that guaranteed no money or other payments to me, but only an agreement from my new manager, who was a respectable businessman, that he would find me a club where I would be able to play. He arranged for me to move to a smaller club, but soon he fell out with the club officials and he gave up on me. A powerful local figure picked up my contract from him. Then it became messy. He first arranged for me to be loaned to a minor league team. He just told me over the phone that I had to pack my things and go two hundred kilometres from Belgrade the next morning. I was to play twelve games and then return to my club. The two best players from that little team went the other way.

'I was the great hope for that club in a fight for survival. I played one game, scored twice and then my manager called and told me that I had to get injured. I tried to tell him that I was doing all right but he just said that I had to think of a way to get on the injury list or he would put me on it. What could I have done? I faked stomach troubles and got myself off the team. They lost three consecutive games and became certain to be relegated.'

Another, a young goalkeeper, admitted that he had been lured in by thoughts of the high life. 'My father's friend saw me playing at school and suggested that he would try to get me a trial with a big club from Belgrade,' he said. 'My father and I signed a contract, and in return I got a mobile telephone and a place of my own. My manager was to receive 20 per cent of my salary at the club as well as 15 per cent of the fee from any transfer that occurred in the following five years. Although I wasn't in the first team, I was considered to be talented and had special training with a goalkeeper's coach. After a while I was loaned to a smaller second division club. I was told that it was necessary for me to gain experience.

'But one day, my manager called and said that I had to do something for him that would mean a lot to my career. I had to concede four goals in a game that had no meaning for the other club, but was very important to us. Those three points could have proved decisive in a race for promotion to the first division. I objected, and knowing that he was my father's friend, I was pretty sure that nothing bad would happen. The day before the game, he called and asked me to return to Belgrade to discuss my decision. I agreed, and went to the house where he had told me to meet him. He was not there but there were four men who told me they were his friends and that he would arrive shortly. I was kept there for two days but my manager never showed up. I missed the game, which we lost 4–1. When I returned to the club no one asked me where I had been. They acted as if nothing had happened. My manager called me the day after and told me that the next time I had better do what he asked voluntarily. I really wanted to get back to Belgrade and play in the big league, so I obeyed. During the next season, he asked similar favours from me several times.'

Private contracts may have been outlawed, but the underlying problem they initially addressed remains. 'Red Star and Partizan are not what they used to be,' Katanec explained. 'They can't be what they used to be, because as soon as they produce a decent player, he thinks, "Great, off we go," They have to take the millions that they're being offered. And they aren't the worst off; other clubs have to sell for even less, and when you start selling your boys for extremely small amounts of money, it's a dead end.'

This, of course, is an issue throughout eastern Europe. The problem is not just that the domestic league is weakened when young talents leave, lowering attendances and thus advertising and sponsorship potential, but also that the players themselves, elevated too soon and thrust into an alien environment, find their own development impaired. There are those who have succeeded: Dejan Stanković was nineteen when he left Red Star for Lazio, for instance, and became a regular almost immediately, but for every player like him, there are dozens who fail. 'I played well in my first season at Lazio because I was euphoric,' Stanković explained, 'but I struggled for the next two seasons. It's very different to Serbia, because you have to sort yourself out. Nobody asks how you are, or pushes you to train harder.'

Stanković speaks as a genuinely top-class player, but a significant number of those who are traded are simply not top class, and many deals are done for the benefit of the agent rather than the player, even after the abolition of private contracts. I inadvertently became involved in blocking one such deal in 2003, when an official from the Ukrainian club Karpaty Lviv asked me what I knew of three players his club were considering signing from OFK Belgrade. Karpaty were under the impression that all three were first-team players, but when I asked Milena to check, she replied that only one had ever featured in a senior game.

In Communist times, players were forbidden to move abroad until they were twenty-eight, a system pretty much everybody I've spoken to in eastern Europe − players excepted, of course − would like to see reintroduced in some form. 'The small countries have to find a mechanism to stop all this talent from flying away and instead concentrate the quality of the area in their own league,' said Katanec. 'How do we do that? Either by having rules that are strong enough to stop the kids from going away, or by having sponsors who are rich enough to keep them. But I'm speaking hypothetically. The EU, FIFA and UEFA would immediately come in and say we couldn't have such a rule, and sponsors here simply can't compete with sponsors from the big countries.'

The market has such countries as Serbia trapped in a vicious circle. Players leave to make more money, making their league less attractive, making it harder to raise funds to keep other players. Yet Avramović's optimism is perhaps not entirely misplaced. In 2004 Serbia-Montenegro finished as runners-up in the European Under-21 Championship, and that generation of players is generally recognised as the best from the region since the majestic Yugoslavia team that won the World Youth Cup in Chile in 1987. Players such as Simon Vukcević, Boško Janković, Marko Perović and Dušan Basta augur well for the future of Serbian football, and, while Vukcević has certainly been distracted by the money he has been offered, there at least seemed a general willingness on the part of their clubs to resist the temptation to make a quick profit. Red Star, it was reported, turned down a £4m offer for Janković from Porto. 'Red Star need Boško Janković,' his coach Ratko Dostanić explained. 'We want to make a strong team capable of competing in Europe. Every club depends on money received from selling players, but we will not sell players we need. Every player, Janković included, should think about winning trophies rather than about transfers.' Janković himself spoke of having plenty of time, of having more to achieve in the red-and-white shirt.

Noble sentiments, for sure, and Red Star is a club with an exceptional emotional pull, but Serbia has been holding a fire sale since 1990. Even if the exodus is slowing down, clubs and players, no matter how great their mutual affection, never resist the market for long. It says much, anyway, for the decline that fourteen years after winning the European Cup Red Star were celebrating simply because a young player had decided to stay with them for another season.

ii Slovenia

In one chair Srečko Katanec slumped, his tie still neatly positioned over his top button, but his face betraying his exhaustion. In the other sat Rok Tamše, a bright-eyed TV interviewer in a rumpled brown shirt. Slovenia had just lost their first game of the 2002 World Cup 3–1 to Spain in Jeju, and Tamše was clearly anticipating difficulty drawing post-match comments from a man notorious for his disregard for the media. Katanec, though, was not his usual prickly self. The interview began ordinarily enough: how did he feel it had gone? What if the referee had given that penalty for the trip on Sebastjan Cimerotič? Was the penalty that Spain won justified? With hindsight, though, in Katanec's tired answers, there were clues to what had really gone on. 'We have two more games,' he said, 'and then the cycle finishes . . .' A careless phrase? An admission that Slovenia would not get through the first round? Or an indication that he already knew he was going to resign?

'Certain players haven't done anything in attack,' he muttered a few minutes later; an assault, surely, on Zlatko Zahovič, the great star of the team, but Tamše let it pass unchallenged. And then, apparently accidentally, Tamše asked a question that struck at the heart of the issue: 'What is going on behind the dressing-room door?' Given the tenor of the rest of the interview, it was probably meant as a simple what's-the-mood-like inquiry, but there was just a moment when Katanec clearly wondered if Tamše knew, as he glanced sharply to his right, his features snapping from their habitual droop into the hard profile of an Easter Island statue. 'I will not be talking about that,' he said, 'but in the next few days I will tell you what happened behind the dressing-room doors after the game.' An oddly intriguing answer to a straight question, but Tamše failed to pursue it, and went on to discuss the fact that the next game, against South Africa, would be played during the heat of the afternoon.

Given the furore that followed, it is hard now to assess just how much people did know at the time, but it seems probable that nobody had any inkling that there was anything badly amiss. Slovenia had played reasonably well, had been a little unlucky to lose 3–1, and, for all Katanec's pessimism, still had a realistic chance of reaching the second round.

Two days later, though, the news broke. I am fortunate that Aleš Selan, once onefootball's correspondent in Slovenia, chose to video every mention of the incident on television in the hours that followed, creating through the agonisingly fragmented detail of rolling news a comprehensive record of Katanec's final battle.

24ur, the main evening news programme of POPTV, Slovenia's largest commercial channel, began with footage of Zahovič being substituted against Spain. 'Shocking news from South Korea,' came the headline, 'where it is reported that there has been a row between Katanec and Zahovič.' The picture changed to show France Arhar, a former governor of the Banka Slovenije: 'France Arhar will run for office . . . ' The rupture was deemed a bigger story than a senior politician announcing he would stand for the presidency: a revealing set of priorities anywhere, but extraordinary in Slovenia. For much of their history, they hadn't been particularly good at football, and hadn't really seemed to care. They were a nation of skiers, and football was something with which the southern republics ('Bosnians' as they dismissively lumped them together) concerned themselves. By the time of the World Cup, football was important enough for the president Milan Kučan to write a letter urging the warring parties to find a peaceful solution, having arranged to meet the players in their first official engagement on their return.

Football has been hugely important in Slovenia's self-definition as an independent nation. Many probably still do confuse it with Slovakia, but far fewer than did before Euro 2000. 'The results were achieved at an important time for our country,' Katanec said. 'We were adapting to Europe and trying to get into the European Union. The football team was a way of promoting the country. With the European Championship and the World Cup, we qualified in the November, so there were six or seven months of presentations about Slovenia on television all over the world. You can't buy that kind of advertising. When we arrived in South Korea, for instance, they ran an hour-long film about our country, showing Lake Bled and all the other gorgeous features. Imagine how much it would have cost if we'd had to pay for it . . .'

Katanec is right to emphasise his achievement. This book has largely been a tale of disappointment and decline, but Slovenia's qualification for Euro 2000 and the World Cup two years later represented an intoxicating, unimaginable success. In 1998, Katanec took over a side that had taken just one point from eight games in failing to qualify for the France World Cup, a dire record about which nobody was particularly bothered or surprised. Aleš, the unacknowledged archivist of his world, has every match Slovenia have ever played taped and neatly catalogued – where possible with both Slovenian and English commentary – as well as the scenes of manic jubilation at Ljubljana airport when Slovenia returned from Kyiv having beaten Ukraine in the qualifying play-off for Euro 2000.

It is probably the first leg of that game that provided the greatest moment in Slovenian football history. It is a goal I know well, because every time I've been in the Loški, the bar over the road from Aleš's house in Škofja Loka, they've insisted on putting it on the big screen for me. The Ukraine goalkeeper Oleksandr Shovkovskyi rushed from his goal towards the corner flag to clear, but scuffed his kick, which was gathered by Milenko Ačimovič just inside the Ukraine half. As Shovkovskyi, realising all too late what was going on, hurtled back across his box, Ačimovič lofted the ball goalwards. It pitched on the six-yard line and, a fraction ahead of Shovkovskyi, slithered into the netting just inside the post.

'David Beckham,' roared Dave Farrar on Eurosport, 'where are you now?' It has become the catchphrase of a generation.

Only seven Slovenians ever played international football for Yugoslavia, and it wasn't until 1974 that Brane Oblak became the first Slovenian to play at a World Cup. Even his call-up, he admitted, was probably politically motivated: 'There was a key, and it said there had to be one or two Slovenians in the squad, two Montenegrins, five Croatians, ten Serbians, a few Bosnians, but because I was good, I stayed in the team. If I'd been rubbish, they'd have dropped me and called up another Slovenian. They had to include one because that way everybody kept quiet and there'd be no problems. That was just the way things were done in the old times.'

Such a system of quotas sounds in keeping with Tito's general policy of suppressing nationalism and promoting federalism wherever possible, but Katanec, who came into the side a decade later, after Tito's death, insisted there was no such system in his day, and seemed doubtful there ever had been one. 'If you were crap, the coach wouldn't just "use the key" and pick another Slovenian,' he said. 'I don't believe that. Nobody would keep you in the team of you weren't of a high enough quality. Oblak played at the same time as Danilo Popivoda, so that was two Slovenians in the national team, and that's because they were both top class. If there'd been more top-class Slovenians I'm sure there'd have been three or four in the side.'

Whether there for quota reasons or not, Oblak made the most of his World Cup opportunity, hitting the bar in Yugoslavia's opener against Brazil with a header so powerful it rebounded out of the box, and having a good enough tournament to come fifth in the vote for player of the World Cup, behind the illustrious quartet of Johan Cruyff, Franz Beckenbauer, Kazimierz Deyna and Johan Neeskens. After drawing that opening game 0–0, Yugoslavia hammered Zaire 9–0 – still the record margin of victory in the finals – before a draw with Scotland saw them top their group on goal difference. 'We'd prepared very hard for the game against Brazil,' Oblak said, 'which cost us eventually because we hardly knew about anybody else, and also we hadn't sorted anything out regarding bonuses. When we qualified for the second round, we wanted money. There was a dispute, and everything was really in the balance ... '

A Balkan side in dispute? So far, so familiar, but then Tito came to visit, and solved the problem with typical verve. First he lightened the mood at the official photoshoot by suggesting his wife Jovanka should join the players kneeling in the front row (no translation can quite capture the crude pithiness of the original: '*Ajde Jovanka, čučni i ti*'), then he suggested that as the players were doing well, it might be an idea for them to be paid a little extra. With Tito watching in Düsseldorf, though, Yugoslavia lost their first game of the second group phase 2–0 to West Germany, which effectively ended their hopes of a place in the final even before defeats to Poland and Sweden. 'You know how things are,' Oblak explained. 'You get the money, somebody goes shopping ... '

For all Tito's efforts, ethnicity was always an issue. 'Back then we had some problems with the nationalities,' Oblak said. 'It was tough for me because I didn't know very well the differences between certain words in the Serbian and Croatian languages, which are usually very similar. They have slightly different words for "coffee" and for "soup", for example, and I didn't know that. But they put up with me because I was a Janez [the stereotypical Slovenian name is often used to denote a Slovenian], so they'd just say "fuck it, he hasn't a clue anyway". Sometimes in the old national team, though, watching Serbs and Croats deal with each other wasn't pretty. When we played well, these things wouldn't happen, but if we didn't play well, it quickly showed.'

Slovenians may have been virtual bystanders in that dispute, but since secession the relationship between the capital Ljubljana and the eastern region of Styria has rapidly deteriorated. As so often, the ill-feeling manifests itself most clearly in football, and clashes between fans of Maribor, the main club of the Styria region, and Olimpija Ljubljana have become commonplace. 'You have to have rivalry,' Oblak said. 'And if there isn't any other way, you have to create it artificially. Now, though, perhaps between Olimpija and Maribor it has gone too far.' When I first went to the Loški, it was frowned upon to drink Laško, the Styrian beer (nicknamed 'Goat' after their logo), rather than Union (from Ljubljana, nicknamed 'Piss'). Now Laško, sponsors of Maribor, own both breweries.

For four years, though, Katanec held that rivalry at bay, and the Ljubljančan with his Styrian playmaker performed minor miracles. And then Jeju. In that first news bulletin, nothing was entirely clear. There were rumours that the two had had to be pulled apart as they squared up to each other. It all came to a head, it seemed, when, after sixty-three minutes, Katanec replaced Zahovič with Ačimovič. The same clip was replayed over and over again: Zahovič walking from the pitch, slapping hands with Ačimovič, and then, out of focus in the background, kicking out at a bottle of water.

Katanec and Zahovič may have been the two architects of Slovenia's unexpected success, but they had never got on. Irrespective of the Ljubljana–Styria issue, they were never likely to. Katanec was disciplined, ascetic, a believer in the primacy of the team; as a player he had represented the characteristic Slovenian virtues of solidity and industry (although both his parents were Croatian). Zahovič, by contrast, was a free spirit, technically gifted, individualistic. Both carried unhelpfully large egos.

POPTV turned to the usually forthright Oblak for his views. Recognising that he was probably among the leading candidates to replace Katanec, though, he trod what for him was a fine diplomatic line, concerned to alienate neither Zahovič nor the Slovenian Football Federation (NZS). 'We know the first guy, and we know the second guy,' he said. 'I have worked with both of them, and I have had problems with both of them.' He acknowledged, though, that the substitution was probably a mistake, recalling a World Cup qualifier against Yugoslavia in which Zahovič had done nothing all game and then scored the equaliser four minutes into injury time.

At midnight Korean time, the NZS held a meeting to decide whether to send Zahovič home, but, back in Slovenia, the exact nature of the dispute remained unexplained. Katanec and Zahovič, the news went on, happy to have some bona fide facts backed up with archive footage, had clashed before, most notably in August 2000, when Katanec said in an interview with the Slovenian sports paper Ekipa that Slovenia lacked a true leader, an obvious dig at Zahovič, the leading goal-scorer, leading assist-maker and, blatantly, best player, presumably designed to provoke him into working harder at training. Zahovič, though, spoke of being 'very hurt', went into a sulk and was dropped for a friendly against the Czech Republic. As insults were traded through the media, the president of the NZS, Rudi Zavrl, forced the two to get together and talk through their differences. That seemed to be that as Slovenia went unbeaten through their qualifying campaign for the 2002 World Cup, but, when Zahovič was substituted against Ghana in Slovenia's final preparatory friendly, rather than making his way to the bench, he stomped straight off to the dressing rooms.

At lunchtime on the third day after the game, the NZS finally announced that Zahovič would not be sent home. 'The incident was a big one, and went over certain limits,' Zavrl said, speaking on a crackling phone line from Jeju. 'Our decision is not meant to lessen the weight of the incident . . . The rest of the players have accepted our decision with relief. That doesn't mean condoning what Zahovič did, but they want peace, to get prepared and to train normally.'

It was only when Katanec then gave his press conference that it became clear what the 'incident' was. 'There were things going on during the game,' he said. 'I was a "ljubljanska P . . . "' – the Slovenian P-word is the English C-word – I was

subbing only Styrians and I should take another one off so that
another Ljubljančan could play. After the game I heard that I
was a prick of a coach and had been a prick of a player, and
that he could buy me, my house and my family . . . ' At that,
he began to weep. ' . . . and Šmarna Gora [the mountain near
Ljubljana where Katanec owned a house and where he had
taken the players for pre-tournament training] . . . ' A long
silence followed. ' . . . So now you know what happened, but
I am an employee of the NZS and I will put everything I've got
into this. I will coach this team for I hope three or four more
games and after that my story is over. I'm sorry it had to end
this way, but I guess that's part of football. Football gives you
something, and it takes a little away. That's it, but I'd like to
say something else. I'm terrified of Slovenia being so small
and still dividing itself into I don't know what. I'm proud to
be Slovenian, and I'm proud my parents were Croatian, my
father and my mother . . . ' At that, the tears came more
freely, and he stood up and left.

The players had been told not to discuss the incident with
the media, but Zahovič, wearing his Slovenia baseball cap
backwards in a curiously banal assertion of his rebellious
nature, responded with an impromptu press conference
outside the training camp. 'People who dig a hole for others
often end up falling in that hole themselves,' he said – a
Slovenian proverb implying that Katanec had plotted to
damage him, only to end up having to resign himself. 'Yes,
there were hard words exchanged, but I never mentioned his
parents or their nationality. Šmarna Gora was mentioned and
he [Katanec] was mentioned. I'm sorry about that . . . it was
wrong. This has been going on a long time . . . he wanted to
provoke my reaction from day one of the preparations. Things
were happening and I didn't want to react, even though I was
having to listen to somebody putting me down every day. It
wasn't only about me, but also about other players.'

Katanec, he alleged, had told Ačimovič that Glenn Hoddle
had only signed him for Tottenham for his own personal gain.

There is, it must be stressed, absolutely no suggestion that there was anything inappropriate about that transfer, or even that Katanec believed there to be; the remark was presumably intended to goad Ačimovič into greater effort.

'He should stop competing with me and the thirty-two goals I've scored,' Zahovič went on. 'He should stop competing with my fame and he should stop competing with the other players because we've been hugely important in getting him where he is today. Nobody wants to take this away from him. Yesterday there was a meeting, and I wanted to hear what the rest of the players thought. They were very honest. They said that my reaction was not appropriate and they didn't agree with it, but they think I deserve more respect from my coach . . . They wanted me to stay. That's what he was crying about . . . He wasn't crying because he felt insulted . . . '

Eventually Zahovič came round to the game against Ghana, and one of the least contrite apologies imaginable. 'If he thinks I'm not in form,' he said, 'he should tell me and I'd be happy to sit on the bench, but when I'm on the field, he shouldn't underestimate me. The first time I miss one or two passes he shouldn't – I won't mince words – say he will fuck my mother, because he didn't fuck my mother and he won't fuck my mother. If he wants to he can start talking to me . . . I'm apologising in public to return the ball to his court.'

The 'apology', though, was in breach of the NZS's stipulation that players should not discuss the incident with the media, and so, finally, the decision was taken to send Zahovič home. With him went all hope.

Slovenian TV news, unwilling to leave the story alone, but with time to fill before Zahovič made his way to the airport, occupied themselves by interviewing various fans. Most of those in South Korea spoke of a feeling of having wasted their money in going to watch a team that was tearing itself apart, while those at home tended to focus on the Ljubljana–Styria divide. The Viole, the hard core of Maribor's support, accused

Zavrl of simply backing the Ljubljančan horse. This was a familiar moan. That Slovenia wear green and white – the colours of Olimpija Ljubljana – is taken by the Viole as a deliberate slight, while there was anger that the NZS had subsidised the Green Dragons, Olimpija's Ultras, to go to South Korea. 'We are always prepared to help organised fans,' Zavrl replied. 'The Green Dragons asked us about a subsidy, and nobody else did.'

As Zahovič pushed his luggage through the airport, head bowed, eyes radiating hurt, a microphone was shoved in his face. If the players really were on his side, the reporter asked, why hadn't they stuck with him until the end. 'They don't have the guts,' he said.

Slovenia proceeded to lose tamely to South Africa and Paraguay, and returned to Ljubljana dispirited and disillusioned. The Zahovič incident, Katanec claimed at his final press conference, had nothing to do with his resignation, but 'a new man' was needed to 'repair the squad'.

Katanec was so upset that the interview he gave for this book was only his second in two and a half years that followed. 'I look at it this way,' he explained. 'Even in a family, where there are only two people, it often happens that interests grow apart. When you are at the beginning of the story, you have the same interests, but that doesn't mean it will always be like that. Two people get to know each other, they like each other and have common interests. But as years go by, many realise that perhaps it wasn't meant to be. And just as these things happen between two people, they also happen between twenty people and they can happen between two million people.

'So, it happened to us. It happened in basketball as well, but in terms of media coverage, football is simply so much bigger that everything appears bigger. Football is magical for people. It creates these emotions, this huge national pride . . . From the European championship qualifications on, this thing happened in Slovenia and it grew at and after each and every match. You could feel it in Slovenia when you went on the street. You felt something in the air.'

As the national team prospered, though, the domestic league slid into chaos, as exemplified by the trials of Olimpija. Backed by the local UDBA, in Yugoslav times they were Slovenia's only regular representatives in the top flight, often attracting crowds of over 20,000, although less because the standard of football was better than today – although it certainly was – than because there was nothing else to do. 'Back then, the lights were on for two hours per day, the rest of the time you had to use candles,' Oblak said with characteristic overstatement. 'There was no television. If you had electricity, you could listen to the radio, but that was it. Kids today can't imagine what it was like. Nobody went to the seaside, nobody went on trips. People went hiking and climbing the mountains, that was it, so obviously everybody went to watch football.'

The links to the UDBA meant a place on Olimpija's board for Janez Zemljarič (or Johnny de la Terra, as his name was mockingly translated), a former president of the Slovenian government and vice-president of the federal Yugoslav government, but financing was largely provided by SCT, a construction firm whose president, Ivan Zidar, was also president of the club. Zidar, a rough, forceful personality, had begun his working life doing menial jobs in Germany before being educated as an engineer, hauling himself inch by inch towards power. A keen boxer, he was fiercely proud of his imposing physique, and once mocked his son-in-law in the Slovenian broadsheet Delo for not being able to lift a 60kg weight with one arm. 'Zidar was autocratic,' said Oblak, who coached under him in 1994–95, winning the Slovenian championship. 'He didn't know much about football though, that's for sure. But he was the director of a company that employed over 3,000 people from southern republics and that's why he was made president of Olimpija. Politics put him there so the Bosnians who were building houses would have something to do – watch football.'

Zidar is a man around whom anecdotes flock. On one occasion, faced with a strike among SCT workers, he approached the pickets and asked who was in charge. When the leader came forward, he laid him out with a single punch. 'And who's his deputy?' he then asked. Nobody volunteered, and the strikers returned to work. Oblak may have spoken of being 'friends for ever' with Zidar, but he also admitted to having pursued him through the courts for more than a decade over an apartment he was given as payment when Zidar was short of ready cash.

Zidar's presidency was a hangover from totalitarian days. Players would accept contracts in the knowledge they would be paid only eight or nine months out of twelve, and, if anybody complained, a harangue from Zidar would usually silence them. Olimpija had finished fourteenth of nineteen sides in the final pan-Yugoslav league, but were a big enough fish in a small enough pond that they won the first four independent Slovenian championships. It was in those days, though, as average attendances fell from 7,400 in 1989–90 to 1,100 in 1991–92, that the seeds of their downfall were sown. As market economics began to take hold, players began suing Olimpija for unpaid wages. Worse, Gorica and Maribor began to challenge Olimpija's pre-eminence, and so the financial rewards of being champions – advertising, sponsorship, European football – could no longer be taken for granted.

Zidar's response was to keep spending, trying desperately to re-establish Olimpija's superiority. Nastja Čeh, the inspiration behind Maribor's championship success in 1998, was brought in at huge expense, but Maribor, better organised and better structured, continued to dominate and even reached the group stages of the Champions League. At Olimpija, the debts continued to mount, thanks in part to the government's decision to impose a mandatory penalty interest rate of 25 per cent on unpaid debts. One creditor who sued for two million Slovenian Tolars in 1992 was finally paid twenty-six million (about £80,000) in 2004, and that was still under half of what he was owed. By early 2005, the club admitted to a debt of around €3m, although it was suggested the true figure could be double that. Either way, with an annual budget optimistically stated at €1.2m, the sum was unpayable.

So out of control were the debts that in 1998 the club's assets were frozen. They began trying to trade through ZŠD Olimpija – the largely ceremonial umbrella body to which all Olimpija clubs in various sports belonged – but their accounts were also frozen. Frustrated, Zidar, who had been distracted anyway as he extended his influence at SCT, declared he would quit. As players stopped receiving even two-thirds of their salaries, performances dipped. For the Green Dragons, the final straw came when the board vetoed on health and safety grounds their plan to mark their tenth anniversary by hanging a giant number 10 shirt between the floodlights at the Bežigrad Stadium.

At the time the Dragons were led by Kefo, a short, plump and undeniably intelligent web designer with a flair for organisation. In November 1998, he called a strike, and so the Dragons, rather than going to games and cheering on Olimpija, spent match days handing out fifteen-page pamphlets written by Kefo outlining their grievances. In under a decade, he noted, Olimpija had gone from a season in which they beat each of Yugoslavia's big four – Red Star, Partizan, Dinamo Zagreb and Hajduk Split – to losing to teams from Slovenian villages. Changes were needed, he said, not necessarily at presidential level, but certainly at the level of the director, Jože Prostor, with whom, as Zidar increasingly became only a figurehead, most of the power lay.

When Zidar finally dealt with the protest in April 2000 it was in characteristic fashion, calling Kefo, telling him to meet him in quarter of an hour and slamming the phone down. Kefo and two other Dragons hurried to obey. At the SCT offices, the receptionist took some persuading that three ultras in Olimpija colours had a meeting with her boss, but when she finally let them through, Zidar was bullishly welcoming. He offered them drinks, and when one of Kefo's lieutenants, a teetotaller, asked for orange juice, he gave him a double vodka. Then he asked Kefo how much money he wanted, and agreed to replace the director. At that, his secretary came in to tell him that some Italian trading partners had arrived to see him. 'Tell the fucking Italians to wait,' he said. 'My boys are here.' Prostor was sacked shortly afterwards and replaced with Miro Gavez, who had been on the board of a firm that imported BMWs. Zidar himself then resigned, although he remained as president for a year as no assembly was called to vote for his successor.

The changes, though, could not alter the fact that the club was facing an unmanageable debt. They weren't the only ones: Gorica, Mura, Koper, and Publikum were all struggling. There was, though, an alternative for clubs faced with the possibility of declaring themselves bankrupt and starting again in the second regional leagues (effectively the fifth division), pioneered by Gorica. Previously NK (Football Club) Gorica, they reformed themselves as ND (Football Society) Gorica. They had the same address, the same personnel and the NZS allowed them to carry on playing in the first division, but, magically, they were free of debt. Koper and Mura, seeing that Gorica had effectively got away with it, did the same.

Zidar finally departed in 2000, and was replaced by Anton Colarič, the deputy mayor of Ljubljana. By May the following year, he and Gavez had decided that Olimpija also had to go down the bypass route, and NK Olimpija became NŠD NK (Football Sports Society Football Club) Olimpija. They were granted a first division licence for 2001–02, and it seemed that they, like the others, with a quick finagle, had freed themselves of debt. The precise legal position of the club, though, remained unresolved. In September 2001, Olimpija played Brøndby in the UEFA Cup. When UEFA sent the proceeds from that game to the NZS to pass on to Olimpija, though, the NZS, acting on the basis that the club's accounts were still frozen, confiscated them. NŠD NK sued the NZS, an action that seemed sure to provoke a ruling one way or the other on the legality of the bypass procedure. The courts, though, ducked the central issue, determining that as the entry to UEFA had been made under the name of NK Olimpija, and as all the players were still technically registered to NK Olimpija, that was the club that had played in the UEFA Cup, and therefore the NZS's confiscation was legitimate. Three years later, however, when bailiffs tried to seize gate receipts from a match between Olimpija and Maribor, they were unable to do so as it was determined that that club was NŠD NK Olimpija, and therefore not responsible for the debts of NK Olimpija.

Even with that lifeline, Olimpija's overspending continued, and, as sponsors deserted them, players soon found that their salaries were not being paid. Performances suffered, which was particularly frustrating for fans who had thought they were witnessing the beginning of an Olimpija to match that which had dominated the early years of the Slovenian championship. Coached by Bojan Prašnikar and with Sebastjan Cimerotič and Ermin Rakovič forming an exciting front pairing, Olimpija beat Espanyol 2–1 at the Bežigrad in the UEFA Cup and would have claimed the Slovenian title if they had won against Maribor in their final game of the season. Over 10,000 turned out in Ljubljana – the largest crowd for a league game since Yugoslav times – but Olimpija were undone by Nastja Čeh, who by then had rejoined Maribor. He set up Barnabas Sztipanovics for the opener, and, although Cimerotič equalised, Olimpija were unable to force a winner. Denied Champions League football, Cimerotič, Rakovič and Prašnikar all left the club, and Olimpija finished just fifth in 2001–02.

That was where Jurij Schollmayer came in. A former model and a successful entrepreneur, he was persuaded to get involved with Olimpija by Pero Lovšin, the front man of Pankrti, the band that started the punk movement in Slovenia. Schollmayer established Olimpia Ltd and through that promised to pay the club €1.5m a year, plus €250,000 to the youth system, in return for all revenues gained through television, sponsorship, advertising and gate receipts. Olimpia Ltd's assets, though, were only worth around €10,000 – the minimum required to establish a limited company under Slovenian law – and so Schollmayer himself had virtually no personal liability. Privatisation had left Slovenian football clubs in the hands of their members, so nobody could actually 'own' the club, but, under the terms of the contract, Olimpia Ltd had the right to appoint half Olimpija's board, meaning that Schollmayer effectively had a contract with himself.

Schollmayer arrived promising Champions League football within three seasons, appointed Oblak as coach and brought in Robert Prosinečki and the Slovenian legends Mladen Rudonja and Miran Pavlin. A run of seven games without a win towards the end of the season, though, did for their title chances, and Oblak, who was sacked in the middle of it, was quick to cry foul. 'He didn't want us to be champions, because my contract read that all my bonuses would be doubled if we were champions,' Oblak said. 'He quickly cut me to pieces because he was having to pay me too much each month. He started to undermine the whole thing and he sacked me. If he hadn't done that, we'd have been champions, I can guarantee that. We had points to spare and there'd have been no problem, but then he started to tell me to substitute Prosinečki, Rudonja and Pavlin. I didn't want to do that, so he ended up substituting me.' His allegations are virtually impossible to prove, and it is hard to believe that the potential rewards of Champions League football would not have outweighed whatever bonuses were owed.

Olimpija went on to finish third in the league, but the Slovenian Cup still offered the prospect of European football. Oblak had taken them to the last four, and they advanced a stage further when their semi-final opponents, Korotan Prevalje, went bankrupt. A spectacular Prosinečki free-kick gave Olimpija an away goals victory in the final, but he still left that summer. 'He was the best player ever to play in an Olimpija shirt,' said Oblak. 'He's an extraordinary talent, sheer class. But I don't think a Slovenian club could afford such a player. I think he was conned and that's why he came. Even the Porsche he was driving was taken away from him at customs because Schollmayer had stopped paying for the lease.'

Oblak has a habit of exaggerating, but whether that is true or not, Schollmayer quickly realised that, even with UEFA Cup qualification, Slovenian football was no cash cow and cut his investment to €700,000 for his second season. He managed to persuade the investment group KD to sponsor Olimpija, but the club's financial position continued to deteriorate, and with Slovenia being used as a test case for UEFA's new licensing rules, the situation became increasingly serious. Under the system, clubs had to meet various financial stipulations before being granted a licence to compete in European competition from the 2004–05 season, with the programme being extended to cover the Slovenian top flight from 2005–06. Providing the necessary guarantees proved beyond Olimpija, and so, despite finishing second in the league in 2004, they were denied entry to the UEFA Cup in 2004–05. (Maribor, who had finished third, qualified as Cup winners, and, as Koper and Mura were also refused UEFA licences, Primorje, who had finished sixth in – that is, bottom of – the championship play-off, took Slovenia's second place in the UEFA Cup.)

Realising that the licensing rules threatened Olimpija's existence in the top flight, Aleš and various other members of the forum on the club's website decided to take action. Who, he asked, were these members who theoretically owned the club? Mystifyingly, he was told, such information was confidential, although all playing staff at the club had a vote at the general assembly. How, then, did a fan become a member? That was simple: turn up at the club offices, fill in a form and pay a nominal fee. So he did, as did various other fans. The old guard, many of whom had been involved in the club since Communist times, realising their power was being eroded, made some (amateurish) efforts to prevent the new influx. Boris, the head of the website, for instance, repeatedly found the club secretary unavailable when he turned up to register.

Schollmayer, finally accepting there was no money to be made, pulled out in summer 2004, but agreed to sell Olimpia Ltd for one Tolar to anybody prepared to take on the debts. In the autumn, with an assembly due, Aleš, representing the forum fans, went to Zemljarič and Colarič, the senior board member and the president, and suggested the best thing to do would be for the club to fold, and start again in the second regional league, thereby preserving some kind of integrity. He found Zemljarič stubborn and irascible, still apparently stuck in the seventies, demanding to know who had authorised journalists to write that Olimpija were struggling to survive, and parroting the old saw that Slovenia was 'still paying for the Bosnians'. These 'Bosnians', though, had legally binding contracts.

For the fans, the next step was to convene an assembly at which Gavez could be challenged and replaced as director. The club statutes provided for an annual general meeting, but at that stage the board had managed to avoid one for over two years. An extraordinary general meeting, though, could be called if a third of the members demanded it. Since Gazev would not reveal how many members there were, it was impossible to know exactly how many people that constituted, but, in October 2004, a demand for an EGM signed by twenty members was presented to the board. 'Our first ambition was just to watch and choose the best option that presented itself,' Aleš explained. 'As we realised they might fuck us again and have no assembly, we made a request for an extraordinary assembly.'

The Green Dragons, meanwhile, were pursuing a more militant course. Kefo had been replaced by Koma, a nickname that means what it sounds like it means, and was entirely appropriate. Kefo's stunts had at least been alleviated by a degree of wit. In April 2000, for instance, at a game in Maribor, which at the time suffered over 20 per cent unemployment, the Dragons unveiled a banner, reading: 'We would congratulate you on Labour Day, but none of you have jobs.' Koma, though, was a far wilder figure, and under his leadership the Dragons attacked players' cars and sprayed insulting graffiti around the ground. In mid-September they issued an ultimatum to Colarič and Gavez, warning them they had until 1 October to resign. Or what? Aleš asked. Or else, Koma replied.

In a 4–1 defeat to Publikum on 26 September, they put their threat into action, around twenty Dragons charging on to the pitch with three minutes remaining and forcing the abandonment of the game. The Olimpija goalkeeper Ermin Hasič, terrified, sprinted for the dressing rooms, and following his lead, most of the players followed, although the Dragons' anger was not really directed at them. The Bosnian defender Enes Handanagić, by contrast, gained great kudos by sauntering off, as indifferent to the chaos around him as if he were walking his dog through a deserted meadow. Milivoj Bračun, Olimpija's Croatian coach, was also slow to leave because of an injured leg, and he was seen on national television being struck over the head with a flagpole. 'It was nothing personal, just something that had to be done,' the Dragons said, admitting Koma had had coffee with Bračun two days earlier.

As the Slovenian media lamented the morals of the nation's youth, Olimpija's board took the opportunity to blame the Dragons for the absence of any new sponsors. They'd had verbal agreements with several companies, they implausibly claimed, but all of them had been scared off by the violence.

The petition calling for an EGM still had to be dealt with, and, on the thirtieth day of the thirty-one they were permitted under Slovenian law, the board responded by calling the AGM for the end of November, although that date was eventually postponed by a week. By then, the former Olimpija and Slovenia forward Primož Gliha had declared himself a candidate for the club presidency. He, though, was acting as a figurehead for Janez Sodržnik, once a major figure in Ljubljana local government. Candid to a fault, Sodržnik was greeted with suspicion by Olimpija fans, partly for his political past, but more particularly because he had been born in Styria. Sodržnik and Gliha broadly agreed that the club had to be refounded, and, after the assembly had finally been convened, approached the forum fans for support.

Aleš was doubtful, but recognised in Gliha a realistic candidate for the presidency and in an alliance with him the best way of reclaiming the club from the likes of Zemljarič, Colarič and Gavez. 'When the regular assembly was finally called, they started contacting us from all sides,' he said. 'On one side were the old boys who for the first time in their lives had an opponent; on the other side were the new boys – Sodržnik and Gliha.' With the fans roughly equal in numbers to the old guard, the balance of power lay with the players. That represented a significant problem for the Gliha group, because their proposals necessarily entailed the renegotiation or termination of all player contracts. Nonetheless, Aleš spoke to them, explaining that since they weren't being paid what they were owed under their existing contracts, it didn't make much difference anyway.

The forum fans put forward a series of proposals: that the next assembly should be called for the end of the season, that the term of the new president should be limited until then, that the debt should be calculated and made public. The players backed them on every point, until it came to electing the president, when they ignored Gliha and instead voted for Borut Gaberšek, a former director of SCT who had been on the board for twenty years. Gliha, bizarrely, wasn't even entitled to vote at the AGM, his membership having been denied on the grounds he had applied too late, although no deadlines are laid out in the club's statutes.

Predictably, there turned out to be no money to pay the players' wages and, within a matter of weeks, seventeen players had left. Olimpija, remarkably, still qualified for the championship play-offs, but did not even bother to apply for a licence in March 2005. In the 2005–06 season, they were effectively replaced by NK Bežigrad, a new club named after the national stadium in Ljubljana which started out in the fifth division. Coached by Gliha, their side featured several ageing legends of Slovenian football, most of whom, apparently, played for free. Their first game, a friendly against the fourth division side Arne Tabor 69, was won 4–0, all the goals being scored by the 43-year-old Milko Djurovski, the so-called magician of Macedonia and one of the very few men to have played for both Partizan and Red Star. Having an all-star veterans XI in the regional leagues, though, is hardly a consolation. Olimpija were the biggest, most presitigious club in the richest of the former Communist nations. If they cannot survive when Slovenian football is going through an unprecedented period of success at national level, you begin to wonder who can.

iii Croatia

On a wet night in Kyiv in November 1997, Croatia played Ukraine in the second leg of a World Cup qualifying play-off. Already 2–0 up from the first leg, their passage to the finals in France was secured twenty-seven minutes in, as Alen Boksić equalised Andriy Shevchenko's early goal. Needing to score three, and disillusioned after Vitaliy Kosovksyi had had a goal wrongly ruled out for offside, Ukraine meekly accepted their fate, and, in the hour and a bit of anaemic football that followed, there was plenty of opportunity to ponder the surroundings. Most striking were the advertising hoardings, control of which seemed to have been divided between the two countries. While the Ukrainian ones were mainly for beer and vodka, on the Croatian side, one stood out. It read: U boy, u boy, za narod svoy: To battle, to battle, for your nation.

Buoyed by that nationalistic spirit, Croatia had reached the quarter-finals of Euro 96, playing some sparkling football. Peter Schmeichel, in particular, will remember the rapid break that led to Davor Šuker nonchalantly chipping him from twenty-five yards in Croatia's 3–0 win over Denmark at Hillsborough.

In France in the World Cup they did even better. Their group, featuring Japan and Jamaica, was admittedly not as testing as it might have been, but there was no doubting the quality of their performance in the quarter-final as an ageing Germany were picked apart, Robert Jarni scoring for the only time in his seventy-four-match international career before late goals from Goran Vlaović and Šuker (with his right foot, extraordinarily) completed a 3–0 win. Although France beat them in the semi-final, Croatia beat Holland in the play-off for third. 'I had wonderful players, full of a sense of patriotism,' their coach Miroslav Blazević said, 'players who were ready to do big things for their country. One of the biggest advantages Croatia has in sport is that patriotic feeling.'

That team, emerging from the war, was a powerful symbol of the new Croatia and was exploited as such by the national president, Franjo Tudjman. Their success may have been less unexpected than that of Slovenia would be, but it served a similar function, advertising the bright new nation to the world. 'We knew we were the first generation to play for the new Croatia,' the defender Slaven Bilić said. 'We knew we had a bloody war behind us. Tudjman said to us that we were like ambassadors for Croatia. But there was no extreme national-ism. In 1996, OK, there was extra motivation when you heard the national anthem, and especially when you saw the reaction at home. By 1998 we were just thanking God for our country and I was proud to play for them, but it was different to 1996.'

However much he tries to underplay it, though, the pride was sufficient to carry Bilić through that tournament despite a stress fracture of his hip, a determination to play that effectively ended his career. He still walks with a limp, and has to drive a jeep because he finds sitting in lower cars too uncomfortable, something which rebuts the accusations of malingering still cast by Everton fans upset that a player for whom they paid West Ham £4.5million managed just twenty-six league starts for them.

I met Bilić in Split in early 2005. As he drove me from my hotel to a restaurant overlooking the Adriatic, he apologised for the cold. After several days in Slovenia, where the snow still stood frozen by the sides of the roads, though, Split felt gloriously springlike. It's a wonderful city anyway, especially early in the year before the tourists have moved in, the Roman remains all the more impressive for being incorporated into the modern fabric of the town rather than being preserved and exhibited in a metaphorical glass case. Even the old stadium, now used only for rugby, with its white bricks and red tiles, feels as though it's been around for a couple of millennia. 'Split didn't really suffer in the war,' said Bilić. 'My mother is from a village ninety minutes drive from here, and they went there with tanks and destroyed everything, but here we lived a normal life. There was shelling from ships for a couple of days and they were in the town for a couple of weeks, but it wasn't real war.'

I have dealt with few more instantly likeable footballers than Bilić, and I certainly can't remember any others who have insisted on paying for the coffee. A qualified lawyer, Bilić learnt his English from music – he still plays in a rock band – and speaks with an engaging mid-Atlantic fluency that occasionally lurches into Cockney or Scouse. An Anglophile, he maintains a flat in London – primarily so he can watch major tournaments without constant distractions from the Croatian media – but Bilić does not have the best of reputations in England.

That is partly the result of his lengthy absences for treatment in his final season at Goodison, but more because of the way he collapsed at the slightest touch from Laurent Blanc in that 1998 World Cup semi-final. Blanc was sent off and, as a result, did not play in the final. 'I'd got a yellow card against Romania earlier in the tournament,' Bilić explained. 'I loved Billy Costacurta [the AC Milan and Italy defender] as a player, and I'll always remember that in 1994 he missed the Champions League final and the World Cup final because of being booked in the semi. So, I thought to myself before the game, "Don't do anything stupid: if you commit a foul, then OK, but don't argue or anything like that. Don't do a Billy."

'They had a free-kick, and I was marking Blanc. I really liked him as a player, and at Barcelona he'd played with Prosinečki, who'd been my room-mate for five years. And he smoked. So I thought, what a great guy. I had my hand across his chest, and with one hand he pushed my hand down, and with the other he went to my face. He didn't hit me like Mike Tyson, but he gave me a push.

'At that moment I was panicking, because in nine out of ten situations like that the referee goes yellow, yellow to both players. And I heard Igor Stimać tell me to go down. So I thought, no final, no third place whatever, so I went down. I didn't think "Is he going to miss the final?" I just wanted to protect myself.

'I didn't do anything wrong. He hit me, and the referee came and gave him a red. I swear if I could change it so he could play in the final, I would. But I was just acting to protect myself. A lot of French journalists went mad saying I dived – and the English were obsessed by diving because of what had happened with Beckham being sent off for hardly touching Simeone – but the bottom line is that he made a mistake. Nobody can say he didn't and that was a red card, but because it was the final, and because it was in France, blahblahblah it's a big story.'

Whatever the rights and wrongs of that – and, to be honest,

I doubt many in Croatia saw anything in the incident beyond the advantage it had gained them: 'In the past,' Blazević said, 'we had to find a way to survive as a small nation, so genetically we have the ability to trick people' – it should not be allowed to distract from how good that Croatia side was. Thanks to Bilić's less than happy time at Everton and the ageing Davor Šuker's disappointing spell at Arsenal, it has become a commonplace almost to dismiss their achievements in the mid-nineties as the result of riding the crest of a nationalist wave. True, given organisation, team spirit and a fair wind, essentially average sides (Greece in 2004, for example) can prosper over the month's span of an international tournament, but Croatia were more than that. In Robert Prosinečki and Zvonimir Boban, they had two of the greatest midfielders of the nineties.

They first played together in Chile in 1987, when Yugoslavia won the World Youth Cup with what was probably the best Under-20 side in history. Including not only Prosinečki and Boban, but also such players as Stimać, Šuker and Jarni, all of whom became regulars in the full Croatia side, they averaged a record 2.83 goals per game over the tournament.

Some great teams are designed, planned from the very first in painstaking detail; most have some element of luck in their constitution; that Yugoslavia side seems almost to have been randomly flung together, triumphing despite internal tensions and a football federation that openly admitted they were sending a team only to fulfil their obligation to FIFA. Their captain, Aleksandar Djordjević, was sent off in the final qualifying match in Hungary and banned for four games, and with Igor Berečko, Dejan Vukicević, Igor Pejović and Seho Sabotić injured and Boban Babunski left out because he was in dispute with his club, the FSJ withdrew Siniša Mihajlović, Vladimir Jugović and Alen Boksić on the logic that they would gain more by playing league football. They refused even to finance any journalists to cover the tournament, and the only

Yugoslav reporter to travel to Chile was Toma Mihajlović, who worked for *Arena*, a Zagreb-based Sunday magazine that was interested in a piece on the large Yugoslav emigrant population in Santiago. 'Nobody had any expectations from the team,' he said. 'We thought they'd play the three group games and go home. But when they got to Chile those players found another face. They found a nice country and good accommodation in excellent hotels, and so many girls around . . . '

Heavy rain forced the postponement of the opening ceremony for three days – much to the frustration of the organisers, who had thought having Yugoslavia play Chile in the first match would ensure it was witnessed by a full stadium – but the game went ahead regardless, Yugoslavia winning 4–2. 'After that,' Mihajlović said, 'everything was upside down. Everybody in Chile started supporting Yugoslavia because they had played so well. The boys realised that if they won the second and third games they would be able to stay in Santiago.'

And Santiago was worth staying in. Mirko Jozić, the Yugoslavia coach, had a reputation as a disciplinarian, and tried to rein in his players, but Stimác had met the winner of Miss Chile 1987, herself of Yugoslav descent, and nothing was going to get in the way of his socialising. 'There were no out and out fights,' said Mihajlović, 'but there was constant friction between them. I was with the players most nights, and there was nothing wild. They stuck together and didn't drink, but they did stay in the clubs until three or four every morning.'

Australia were despatched 4–0 and Togo 4–1, at which Red Star decided they could do with Prosinečki for a UEFA Cup-tie against Club Bruges, and attempted to recall him. The players protested to FIFA, and João Havalange, then the organisation's chairman, intervened to keep Prosinečki in Chile. He responded by bending a last-minute free-kick winner against

Brazil in the quarter-final. It was later voted the goal of the tournament.

Yugoslavia then beat East Germany 2–1 in the semi-final, but at some cost. Predrag Mijatović was sent off, and Prosinečki was booked in the last minute, meaning both would miss the final through suspension. A plot, clearly, for no Balkan victory could be complete without a triumph over perfidious forces. The Australian referee, Richard Lorenc, it turned out, had had a major confrontation with the Red Star legend Dragan Sekularać, then coaching in Melbourne, only a year earlier. And hadn't the Australian coach, Les Scheinflug, who had been born in Yugoslavia of German parents, warned Jozić about him?

Well, perhaps, but if there really were a conspiracy, why let Yugoslavia win? Why wait until the final minute, when there could be no guarantee he would make a tackle, to book Prosinečki? None of it sounds very convincing. Boban gave Yugoslavia an eighty-fifth-minute lead against West Germany in the final, and, although Marcel Witeczek equalised with a penalty two minutes later, he went on to miss his kick in the shoot-out, giving Yugoslavia victory. 'The team stayed in Chile for two days afterwards to celebrate,' Mihajlović recalled. 'It was Robert Jarni's birthday so there was a party for him. In the semi-final Dubravko Pavličić had had two teeth knocked out by Matthias Sammer, so they invited the dentist who'd repaired them to the party and presented him with the match ball. There was a real family atmosphere with the Yugoslav community there, and when they went home after three weeks everybody was crying.'

Bilić was not in Chile, having fractured an ankle, although it is debatable whether he would have been in the final squad anyway. He is too modest and too satisfied with what he did achieve to make an issue of it, but it remains an oddity that he never represented Yugoslavia at any level. 'It was definitely harder for Croatians to play in that team,' he said. 'Of course, if you were Boban or Prosinečki and much, much better than anybody else you would play, but I wasn't that good. I don't know why I was never picked for Yugoslavia, but people say it was because of my father.'

Bilić's father, a doctor of economics at Split University, was one of the organisers of student demonstrations in 1971 that demanded greater autonomy for Croatia within the Yugoslav Federation. 'Tito cracked down on it, and a lot of them went to jail,' Bilić said. 'My father was one of the top five men in Croatia, and after that the situation was very difficult for my family. He didn't go to jail, and he kept his job, but it wasn't great.'

In the rest of the former Yugoslavia, people wonder what would have happened in the nineties had the 1987 World Youth Cup-winners been allowed to grow together with the likes of Stojković, Savićević, Jugović, Mihajlović, Pančev and Katanec. A glimpse of what might have been was offered in the 1990 World Cup when Yugoslavia, inspired by Stojković, beat Spain in a superb second-round match in Verona, only to lose on penalties to Argentina in the quarter-final, a game in which they had survived with ten men for eighty-nine minutes. Two years later, though, having been imperious in qualifying, Yugoslavia were expelled from the European Championship. Denmark took their place, and won the tournament. 'If the country hadn't fallen apart,' Katanec said, 'I guarantee we would have crushed the world.'

Bilić, though, was rather less convinced that a Yugoslavia team could have been better than his Croatia side. 'Where would you put Savićević?' he asked. 'We had a midfield that was the most creative ever – Boban, Prosinečki, Asanović. To put Savićević there, who would you leave out? There were some great players from the other republics but I wouldn't have added a single one of them to our squad. We didn't need a creative midfield player. We didn't need anybody on the flanks – we had Jarni and Stanić. We didn't need a defence. We didn't need a goalkeeper. Up front, OK, there is Pančev, but we had Šuker and Boksić. They had a great team, and I don't know what would have happened if it had still been Yugoslavia, but I really don't think we could have done any better.'

The advantage of being a purely Croatian team, of course, was that the internal rivalries, particularly in the years immediately following the war, were less pronounced. 'The most important thing for us was that we were a team,' Bilić said. 'We were friends. We had quality on the pitch, but our biggest quality was team spirit. When you talk to other internationals they tell you that in the camp they don't mix that much – they go to their rooms, play on the PlayStation or read. We were together 24/7.'

At its head, that squad had the incomparable Miroslav Blazević, an eccentric whose braggadocio bordered at times on genius. How would Yugoslavia have done in the nineties if it had stayed together? 'Oh, they'd have won the World Cup,' he said. 'So long as they'd appointed me as their coach.' An emotional, temperamental man, he consulted astrological charts before making team selections, and attributed Croatia's success in the World Cup to good fortune brought by wearing the cap of a gendarme beaten almost to death by German hooligans earlier in the tournament.

'He would always say he was the best in the world,' said Bilić. 'I'm not saying he was a bad coach or a great coach, but he was the ideal coach for us. If you'd given us Capello, Ferguson or Wenger, it wouldn't have worked. He was everybody's father, a great motivator.

'You would play against, let's say, Estonia, and you know it's only Estonia, but he would gradually motivate you. Every day he knew in his head when he was going to create an incident to wake everybody up a bit, then he'd tell us all to go to a nightclub or something. At team meetings he'd be talking about Estonia as though they were fucking Brazil. You'd know he was lying, you'd know it wasn't true, but you say, fuck, yeah, it's going to be hard. And he would always say, OK, Estonia's left-back is whoever, and he'd be talking about their players, and he'd be writing their names on a board, and you'd know it was wrong; he'd be saying, like, this guy, he's so quick, he's so good, and you'd know when he was talking to you that he'd never seen him in his fucking life.

'Anyway, it would motivate you, but whoever we played against, he always told us we were better than them. So when we played Argentina in the World Cup, he came to me and said "Son," because we were always his sons, "Son, you have to come with me and talk to the press." So, OK, it's me and him in the press conference. And I know even the twenty-second player in their squad plays for Inter, and everybody else is at AC Milan, Real Madrid, Barcelona . . . all at the best teams, and we have Boban at Milan, but he doesn't play, and Šuker at Real Madrid, and he doesn't play. The rest of us were playing in great leagues but not for great teams. So he says to the press, "Argentina, not a bad team, not a bad team, but none of their players play for the best teams in Europe." So I look at him, and say, "What the fuck are you talking about?" But that's what he was like. It was all nonsense, but it was great nonsense.'

Or, as Blazević saw it: 'I convinced my players we were the best in the world and they accepted it. We were packed with confidence. We destroyed the German machine 3–0 in the quarter-final and we showed them how Croatians play football.'

Born in Travnik, Bosnia, in 1935, Blazević played for FK Sarajevo and the Croatian sides Rijeka and Dinamo Zagreb before moving to Switzerland with Vevey and Sion. As a coach, he won a Swiss championship with Grasshoppers and a Cup with Sion, and briefly took charge of the Switzerland national team before returning to Croatia. In 1982, wearing a lucky white scarf to every game, he led Dinamo Zagreb to their first Yugoslav championship in twenty-four years. He also rejected Prosinečki, vowing, with typical hyperbole, to eat his degree certificate if the midfielder ever made it as a player. In 2001, when coach of Iran, he said he would hang himself from the crossbar if his side lost to the Republic of Ireland in a play-off for World Cup qualification: despite being wrong on both counts, his degree certificate and his neck remain intact.

Blazević was also a close friend of Tudjman, and the president, wearing the trademark white uniform he thought lent him the gravitas of Tito, was often to be seen both at Croatia games and at the squad's training camps. 'President Tudjman was a big football enthusiast, a crucial man in Croatia's football success,' Blazević said. 'I was very close to him and we had a special relationship. He helped a lot.'

Not, Bilić insisted, that that made the team any more nationalistic. 'Tudjman was a big Croatian, and he was crazy for sport and mad for football, and that was good,' he said. 'Why should we be ashamed when our president comes to watch us play? If I were playing for England, I would be proud if Tony Blair came to watch. There's nothing wrong with it. They said we were a nationalist team, but why? I had lunch with Tudjman once and that was one of the best memories of my life. Why not?' Serbs ethnically cleansed from Krajina would presumably be able to find a reason.

Many of those doing the cleansing were drawn from the Bad Blue Boys, Dinamo Zagreb's Ultras, who took their name – always written in English, of course, for all the best hooligans are English – from the Sean Penn film *Bad Boys*. Founded in 1986, that watershed year for nationalism in Yugoslavia, they soon developed a reputation for violence. 'Not so rare were the big fights,' as their website says. 'Numerous blows were given and taken; to prove one's love for the club, they didn't mind. Dinamo was and still is something sacred.' They affiliated to Tudjman's HDZ, and four years later, the website goes on, they went to 'defend Croatia . . . from Vukovar to Prevlaka. Many of them never returned to "their" north. In honour and everlasting glory of the fallen Dinamo fans, beneath the western stands a monument was built, an altar for the Croatian heroes who forever had the blue colours in their hearts.'

Tudjman, who had been president of Partizan Belgrade in the fifties, was a fan of football in general and Dinamo in particular, and, after returning to Croatia, he used his influence to the club's advantage. The future Leeds and Middlesbrough forward Mark Viduka joined Dinamo after Tudjman had rung him at home in Melbourne; while, in 1994, at a league match against Primorac a few days before a Cup-Winners Cup tie against Auxerre, Tudjman walked into the opposing dressing room and suggested it might be an idea if they didn't try too hard. He thought 6–0 might be a suitable boost for Dinamo. Sure enough, Primorac lost 6–0.

Tudjman's most notable act at Partizan had been to switch their kit from red-and-blue stripes to black-and-white, an early indication of his penchant for cosmetic change. Having convinced himself he was the father of the nation, he then appears to have decided that his role demanded a spree of re-naming. Most cities in Croatia now have at least one street named after him.

Most significantly, in 1993, he changed the name of Dinamo (Communist, hence Titoist, hence federal, hence not nationalist, hence unacceptable) to HAŠK Gradjanski, after the two clubs from which Dinamo was formed when the Communists took power in 1945. Then he changed it again, to Croatia Zagreb. Few of the fans took any notice, most continuing to call the club Dinamo. When one turned up at a political rally with a Dinamo banner, Tudjman berated him, at which the crowd began chanting 'Dinamo, not Croatia'. A month later, the HDZ was defeated in local elections. Not quite as dramatic as the impact the Delije had on Milošević, perhaps, but a demonstration of the power of the fans' bodies nonetheless.

Croatia played Yugoslavia (by then consisting of just Serbia

and Montenegro) for the first time in a European Championship qualifier in Belgrade in August 1999. Bilić missed the
game with his ongoing hip problem, but he and Alen Boksić,
who was also injured, were invited by Blazević to travel with
the squad. 'It was incredibly hostile,' he said. 'They were
calling us Ustaše and everything, and then in the second half
the lights went off. It was completely dark. All you could see
were the infra-red beams on sniper rifles.' The night before I
met Bilić, his Croatia Under-21 side had played a friendly in
Bosnia that had been abandoned at half time because of a
floodlight failure. 'I turned to Aljosa Asanović, who's now my
assistant,' he said. 'And I asked him about that time in
Belgrade. I asked him if he'd shat himself. He looked at me,
and he said: "Of course I fucking did." I was in the VIP
section, so I was safe, but for those on the pitch . . . ' There is
even a theory among Croatians that the power was deliberately cut because Croatia had seemed to be getting on top. In
what might have been seen as a diplomatic gesture, were such
a thing conceivable in Belgrade, the match finished in a 0–0
draw.

The return in Zagreb two months later, a game Croatia had
to win to qualify, was hardly less intense. Before kick-off
Croatian fans unfurled a huge banner reading 'Vukovar 91' – a
reminder of an atrocity to be avenged – while wounded war
veterans were presented to the crowd before kick-off. The
incident for which the game will be remembered, though,
came five minutes before half time. Jarni and Zoran Mirković
tangled in chasing a ball towards the goal line and Mirković,
making the most of it, tumbled to win a free-kick. Jarni,
angered, stood over him and shouted in his face, at which
Mirković – regardless of the fact that Yugoslavia, needing a
win to be sure of qualification, led 2–1 – reached up, grabbed
Jarni's testicles and gave them a sharp tweak. He was sent off –
giving the two-finger-and-a-thumb Serb salute to the Croatian
fans as he went – but, far from being hung in effigy back in
Belgrade for having damaged his side's chances, he was hailed

as a hero. Faced with a slight to his honour, he had taken his revenge. Perhaps it would have been different had Yugoslavia not qualified – although Croatia came back to draw, the Republic of Ireland succumbed to a last-minute equaliser in Macedonia FYR – but the reaction said much of Balkan priorities nonetheless.

Much of the Croatian crowd's bile was directed at Siniša Mihajlović, who has, by dint of some less than diplomatic statements in the media, come to symbolise Serb nationalism. I have, I confess, a soft spot for Mihajlović. For one thing, it amuses me that the most reviled player in European football used to be known as 'Barbika' because of his fluffy Barbie-doll hairstyle. For another, amid the controversy that clouds him, it is often forgotten just what a good footballer he was. Sven-Göran Eriksson rated his left foot alongside David Beckham's right, and took him from Roma to Sampdoria and then to Lazio. Nobody – not Platini, not Maradona, not Zola – has scored more free-kicks in Serie A than him. So good is he that when, at a Yugoslavia training session, the midfielder Albert Nadj offered to buy the whole squad dinner if Mihajlović could hit the crossbar from the halfway line with two shots out of three, he didn't need the third attempt. He clearly has some pretty significant personality flaws, but I can't quite understand how he has come to be so hated. And he is hated – even the *Guardian* ran a piece asking, 'Is this the nastiest man in football?'

That headline followed a Champions League game between Chelsea and Lazio in November 2003 in which Mihajlović spat into Adrian Mutu's ear. That is pretty much indefensible, although it should perhaps be considered that it is a very British attitude that sees spitting as the ultimate taboo – Mutu, significantly, seemed far less bothered by the incident than anybody else at Chelsea. Bad as that was, far worse was the incident in October 2000 that saw him banned for two games by UEFA after Patrick Vieira claimed he had called him 'a fucking black monkey'. Mihajlović could, under Italian law, have been jailed for up to three years, but after he made a public apology and disavowal of racism from the centre-circle at the Stadio Olimpico, ahead of Lazio's next home Champions League game, no charges were pressed.

Mihajlović's defence, though, is worth hearing, not because it excuses what he said, but because of the insight it offers into his mentality. 'Yes, I insulted Vieira,' Mihajlović said, 'but only as an answer to his insults. He called me "a gypsy shit", and so I answered back with "black shit". I'm proud of being a gypsy, so I wasn't offended, and I don't see how he could be offended because I called him black. I certainly didn't call him a monkey. Vieira provoked me from the first minute, and whatever colour his skin is, I'm not going to let somebody treat me like that. I am who I am and I would have reacted the same way even on the street. I've played football since I was fifteen years old and in that time I have been kicked, spat upon and insulted. In football these things happen. What made me really angry is that off the pitch, back home, Vieira gave a press conference to talk about incidents that occurred during the match and must be kept on the field. If I am a racist, so is Vieira.' Vieira was never charged over the 'gypsy' allegation, which may say something about the western European attitudes that dominate at UEFA: racism against the Roma remains one of Europe's forgotten evils.

For Mihajlović, like Mirković, an attack on his honour had to be settled. It was that belief that provoked the incident with Mutu, who, it appears, had deliberately set out to wind up Mihajlović, having been sent off in an international in Bucharest following a clash with the defender. 'I reacted like that because I was provoked in a dishonourable way,' Mihajlović, said. 'As a kid I got into a lot of fights. I got beaten up and I beat people up. I fought with older children. I didn't get frightened. I remember there was a teacher who lived on our street who didn't want me in her class because she thought I would cause trouble. However, I was always an excellent student and later that teacher told me she regretted not having me in her class because I was a very different person in school to how I was on the street.'

Age has not diminished that divide between public and private selves. Eriksson's adviser Athole Still, who has known Mihajlović socially for several years, has spoken of him as 'a Jekyll-and-Hyde character' who 'is transformed on the pitch'. 'As a family man,' Still said, 'he is the most benign, relaxed, pleasant character.' Even Mihajlović, though, accepts that he has issues. 'When I sleep, I dream of snakes,' he said in an interview with the Serbian magazine Tempo. 'I hate snakes. People who understand these things tell me the snakes are my enemies.'

He has certainly made enough of them over his career, but he has suffered too from an element of scapegoating. Just as the loathing felt in England for Diego Maradona was in part shaped by the anti-Argentine attitudes that followed the Falklands War, so the perception of Mihajlović has been conditioned by the wars of the nineties and the NATO bombing of Belgrade. The war is central to the man. Mihajlović was born to a Serbian father and Croatian mother in Vukovar in the far east of Croatia. He grew up just outside the city – then a peaceful place with an ethnically mixed population of 50,000 – in Borovo Selo, the village into which Croat extremists launched three Ambrust missiles to ignite the war in April 1991.

By July the war was in full swing, and Vukovar was surrounded by the Serb-dominated Yugoslav National Army (JNA). For four months they bombarded the town, reducing the 15,000 largely Croat inhabitants who remained to living in cellars without water or electricity. Those who tried to flee were picked off by snipers. Vukovar fell on 19 November and, despite the international community's efforts to organise an evacuation, several hundred Croats were massacred. Four years later, as the Croats swept back through the land they had lost, Vukovar changed hands again. To what extent revenge was taken against the Serbs who remained is unclear, but what is certainly true is that the Vukovar Serbs, mindful (and constantly reminded by propaganda from Belgrade) of the atrocities committed against Serbs by the Ustaše, were terrified. Given their son's status as a hero of the local Serb community, Mihajlović's parents had more to fear than most, but, in the hours before the Croatian army arrived in Borovo Selo, they escaped. It is not known for sure who smuggled them away, and Mihajlović is understandably reticent on the subject, but the strong suspicion in Serbia is that it was Arkan.

Mihajlović returned to Borovo Selo in 2000. 'It was wiped out,' he said. 'Our house was reduced to rubble. I stopped the car near my old school because I wanted to walk along the path I used to take every day, but the school wasn't there any more. When I went through the ruins of our house, I found an old poster of the Yugoslavia national team. There was a bullet hole where my heart should have been.' When German television showed footage of the house shortly after the region was handed back to Croatia, several photographs of Mihajlović could be seen amid the stones. In each of them, the eyes had been cut out – an obvious reference to the Ustaše leader Ante Pavelić's insistence on having the eyes of murdered Serbs brought to him in a bowl each morning to prove the massacres were continuing apace.

Two weeks after Arkan's assassination, Lazio fans displayed banners commemorating his death during a Serie A game against Bari at the Stadio Olimpico. That may just have been coincidence – his right-wing militarism, after all, is just the kind of thing to appeal to the more extreme Ultra groups – but Mihajlović is widely believed to have given at least his tacit consent. For that he has been condemned, but if Arkan really did save his parents' lives, the tribute is perhaps understandable.

Croatia's ill-feeling towards Serbia is only to be expected, but Croatian football has seen a more general rise in violence. In Yugoslav times, the rivalry between Hajduk and Dinamo was a friendly one, akin, Bilić said, to that between Liverpool and Everton. 'It was a big day for Croatia to celebrate,' he said. 'In the stadium they would sing the same songs together.' Now, with the two clubs having won thirteen of the first fourteen independent Croatian championships, it is far more bitter. Away fans have been banned after a series of violent clashes, but Bilić admitted that, even with that restriction, he would not take his son to a Hajduk–Dinamo game were they not guaranteed seats in the VIP section. To paraphrase what Brane Oblak said of the situation in Slovenia, it is as though rivalry, if it does not exist, must be invented. The effect is further to depress attendances that had fallen anyway since fragmentation; where Hajduk Split could once expect average gates of up to 15,000, they now get less than a third of that, which has an obvious financial impact. Only the intervention of Bilić, Asanović, Stimać and Boksić averted bankruptcy for Hajduk in 2001. 'They were in a terrible state and the players hadn't been paid for months,' Bilić said. 'So we invested some money. It was probably the worst investment ever.' That, in turn, has diminished the quality of the Croatian league. I was repeatedly given the blithe assurance that the Croatian league is the most developed of any in the former Yugoslavia, but, even if that is true, Hajduk's defeat to the Irish side Shelbourne in a Champions League qualifier in 2004–05 suggests it is a fairly empty boast.

The decline of the league, though, has not as yet affected the national team, few of whose players play in Croatia anyway. There too, though, recent years have been marked by increasing violence among fans, and a surprising hostility has developed with Slovenia since independence. On the face of it, they would seem to have a lot in common. Both were once part of the Austro-Hungarian empire, both are predominantly Roman Catholic, and both use Roman script. Certainly they had more in common with each other than with Serbia, where the influence was Ottoman, the religion Orthodox and the script Cyrillic. Yet the same week that the two were drawn together in a qualification play-off for Euro 2004, a poll in a Croatian newspaper reported that while only 45 per cent of Croatians hate Serbs, 60 per cent hate Slovenes.

The two nations may have fought wars of independence against essentially the same enemy, but it was in those conflicts that the present day hostility has its roots. Slovenians are bitter that Tudjman, reneging on an earlier agreement, allowed the JNA to march through his country in an effort to force Slovenia back into the federation. Slovenia, nonetheless, unhindered by an indigenous Serb population, achieved secession within ten days. Croatia's subsequent war lasted four years.

During that period, the Slovenian-owned Ljubljanska Bank shut down its offices in Zagreb, and, in so doing, seized all assets held by Croatians in foreign currency accounts. In a similar manoeuvre to that practised by the football clubs, the Nova Ljubljanska Bank was then formed, and the debts of its previous incarnation written off. Croatian investors were understandably outraged, but the Slovenian government argued that their money was circulating in other former Yugoslav republics, and therefore couldn't be reclaimed.

Partly because of the Ljubljanska Bank issue, the Croatian government stopped paying costs for the Krsko nuclear power station, which is in Slovenia, but since its foundation had been jointly owned by Slovenia and Croatia. The Slovenian government reacted by cutting off the power supply to Croatia. Agreement was eventually reached and an international treaty signed – largely because the Slovenians feared the Croatians would refuse to pay their share when the plant came to be decommissioned – but the issue still rankles.

And then there is the sticky issue of borders. Initially Slovenia and Croatia agreed to maintain the borders as they had been in the federal Yugoslavia. That was fine for the land boundary, but it had never been necessary to draw up a sea border. International conventions exist for such matters, but geography, unfortunately, doesn't comply. Slovenia, tucked up in the north-eastern corner of the Adriatic, has just twenty-six miles of coastline, and only has access to the open sea through the Bay of Piran. That would be split by strict application of convention, closing off Slovenian waters where Croatia's sea border meets Italy's. Quite aside from the absurdity of a country with a coastline being technically landlocked, such a resolution would have a devastating economic impact on the Slovenian port of Koper, one of the major southern gateways into central Europe. The Slovenians, anyway, argued on the uti possidetis principle that as they had always been responsible for the gulf, they should continue to be so.

An agreement was reached whereby Croatia allowed Slovenia free access to the open sea in return for concessions over the land borders, but it fell apart when the Croatian parliament refused to ratify it. That the Slovenian government had revealed it was prepared to negotiate over the land border, suggesting that line did not quite have the permanence that had been assumed, only complicated the issue. The situation was hardly helped when the radical Croatian nationalist politician Slaven Letica visited the disputed Slovenian peak of Trdinov Vrh decked out as the legendary early nineteenth-century Croatian hero Ban Josip Jelačić. He had intended to ride up the hill on a white charger, but complications over transportation meant that the horse didn't arrive, and he ended up struggling up on foot, only to be chased straight back down by Slovenian border guards.

That may all sound a touch abstract for the average football fan, but politics in the Balkans is far more central to everyday life than it is in Britain, and a banner at the Maksimir at the first leg of the play-off called on Croatia to win 4–0: one goal for the Ljubljanska Bank, one for the Bay of Piran, one for the land borders dispute, and one for the Krsko power station.

The hostility had boiled over on Slovenia's previous visit to Croatia, for an ill-advised friendly in March 2002. The BBB lay in wait at traffic lights, and when Slovenian cars stopped, set about them with baseball bats and metal bars, leaving several Slovenian fans needing hospital treatment. Slovenians were horrified – in the unwritten rules of Balkan hooliganism, attacking 'ordinary' fans as opposed to other crews simply isn't acceptable. Slovenian flags were burnt in the stadium, and the traditional chant whereby one half of the stadium would shout 'Dinamo' and the other reply 'Zagreb' replaced by one side calling 'Ubi', and the other answering 'Janeza' – 'Kill Janez', the equivalent of an English crowd taunting Scotland fans by chanting 'Kill the Jocks'.

That violence, in itself, was simply the culmination of a series of incidents at other sporting events over the previous six months. Croatian fans travelling to support the slalom skier Ivica Kostelić had clashed with Slovenian fans in Kranjska Gora the previous winter. Then, in January 2002, the BBB turned up in Zlata Lisica near Maribor to support Ivica's sister Janica, and began pelting her rivals with snowballs. This time, the Slovenians were expecting them, and a huge fight broke out between the BBB and the Viole.

The worst incident, though, came at the final of the European Men's Water Polo Championship, held in Kranj, Slovenia, which, to the dismay of the organisers, pitted Croatia against Serbia-Montenegro. Around 3,000 Croatians packed the stands, outnumbering by far the 200 Serbian fans who were segregated into an area next to the enclosure for VIPs – among whom sat the Serbian foreign minister. Serbia won, at which their supporters were attacked by a group of Croatians. Slovenian police, in an effort to protect the VIPs, piled in, and the incident escalated. Chairs and other missiles were thrown, and a Croatian fan was seen on national television being dropped from a height on to his head.

Thanks largely to a massive police presence at both games, the play-off passed peacefully, but the level of hostility was evident in the vehemence of the celebrations in Zagreb after Croatia had secured a 2–1 aggregate victory. Fans gathered in Trg Jelačića, the main square in Zagreb, where they were entertained by the Croatian band Psihomodo Pop. At the end of their act, the lead singer thanked his audience and then bellowed, 'Slovenian pussies!' which captured the mood perfectly. It is as though without Serbs on whom to focus their aggression, enemies have had to be found closer to home. As Katanec said, it seems that the Balkans cannot stop Balkanising.

iv Bosnia-Hercegovina

Walk east along ul Zelenih Beretki through the old part of Sarajevo, and you come to the Orthodox cathedral. Just up to the left is the Catholic cathedral, and next to that is the old synagogue. A few yards further on is the peaceful courtyard that surrounds the Gazi Husrevbey mosque. As my attention was drawn to their remarkable proximity, I was reminded, strangely, of the scene in JFK when Kevin Costner points out to his subordinate that each of the intelligence services in New Orleans has an office on the same square, as though gathering around the headquarters of the pro-Cuba organisation for which Lee Harvey Oswald worked. In Sarajevo, the point of triangulation is the scene of another assassination, the spot outside the City Museum at which ul Zelenih Beretki meets the river, where, on 28 June 1914, the Archduke Franz Ferdinand and his wife Sophia were shot dead by the Serb nationalist Gavrilo Princip, precipitating the First World War. A plaque bearing Princip's footsteps used to be set in the pavement there, but it was ripped out by Muslims during the war.

In *Black Lamb and Grey Falcon*, the novelist Rebecca West chides the river in Sarajevo for running red, accusing it of prostrating itself too obviously before pathetic fallacy. Seven decades later, despite having yet greater and more local carnage to commemorate, the Miljacka runs largely dark green, the red showing only where the current is strong enough to part the thick weed that all but covers the river bed. Nonetheless, there is little danger of anybody forgetting the city's tragic history. Just along from the museum, for instance, is the shell of the national library, hit by an incendiary in August 1992, a hundred years to the day after construction had begun. Everywhere, walls are dotted with bullet holes and pavements marked with 'Sarajevo roses', the small craters left by mortars, many of them now filled with red rubber as a memorial to the siege.

Looking straight across the river from my room in the Saray Hotel I could see a Muslim cemetery, the uniform whiteness of the gravestones itself testimony to how many died how recently. Beyond that are the hills, range upon range surrounding the town. Some are green, covered in pines; some, those closer to the city centre, the ones that were not controlled by the Serbs, are brown, stripped bare, every tree taken for firewood after the electricity supply was cut off.

It was on 2 March 1992 that Serb troops first took up positions in those hills, and laid siege to the police academy at Vraca above Grbavica, a Serb district to the south of the river. Three days later, responding to the decision by the Bosnian president, Alija Izetbegović, leader of the main Bosniak (that is, ethnically Muslim) party, to mobilise the Bosnian civil defence, a small crowd gathered in the west of the city and marched towards the centre. As the demonstrators progressed, they were joined by thousands of others – Bosniaks, Croats and Serbs alike – carrying Yugoslav flags and portraits of Tito – all protesting against a conflict based on ethnic divisions. The march swung right over the Vrbanja bridge, towards the Serb barricades in Grbavica. Shots were fired. One man was hit in the foot, but the march continued. There were more shots, then a hand grenade was thrown, and, in panic, the demonstrators dispersed. In the chaos, Suada Dilberović, a twenty-one-year-old medical student from Dubrovnik, was hit in the chest. She was pronounced dead on arrival at the Koševo Hospital, Sarajevo's first casualty of war. By the end of the month, the airport had been sealed and the blockade was complete. On the last plane to leave was Hasan Salihamidžić, a fifteen-year-old schoolboy who would go on to become the greatest player in Bosnia's independent history.

Salihamidžić lived in Jablanica, about thirty miles east of Mostar on the road to Sarajevo. Most people seem to agree that, although a decent footballer as a child, he was nothing out of the ordinary. What set him apart was his will to succeed, his desire for self-improvement. Every morning, the young Hasan would get up at 6 a.m. and run for ninety minutes before school. After classes, he practised the piano, and then caught a bus into Mostar to train with Velež, which at the time was the only top-flight club in the city, supported by Croats and Bosniaks alike. In 1991, he even took the prize for the best pupil in his elementary school with fives (the top grade) in every subject. He was, in short, one of those sickening people who are good at everything.

Then, in April 1992 – shortly after the EC had recognised Bosnia-Hercegovina's independence – Salihamidžić received a call-up to play for the Yugoslavia Under-16 side against the CIS. The squad was to meet in Belgrade on 1 May, so, on 30 April, Salihamidžić's father, Ahmed, drove Hasan and his team-mate Vedran Pelić to Sarajevo to catch a plane to the Serbian capital. After driving for half an hour, they came to a Serb checkpoint at Bradina, where they were held up for four hours while soldiers checked that the documents from the Yugoslav Football Federation (FSJ) were genuine. By the time they reached Sarajevo, it was dark, but they hurried to the airport anyway, and caught the last flight that night. By the following morning, the city was completely besieged.

After the match, which was played in Cyprus, Salihamidžić, Pelić and another Bosnian, Edis Mulalić, unable to fly back to Sarajevo, stayed in Belgrade and began to train with Red Star, who offered them contracts. All three refused, and, ten weeks after returning from Cyprus, realising that the siege was unlikely to be lifted any time soon, they set out by land, making their way back to Bosnia through Hungary, Slovenia and Croatia. Salihamidžić continued to train with Turbina, a local club in Jablonica, and started to work as a bartender, while his father did all he could to find his son a club in western Europe. It seemed for a while that Salihamidžić might join his father's friend Jerko Tipurić at Club Bruges, but eventually his salvation was Ahmed Halilhodzić, the cousin of the future Lille and Paris St-Germain coach Vahid Halilhodzić. Although born in Jablonica, he had lived in Germany for twenty years and secured Salihamidžić youth terms with the Bundesliga side SV Hamburg.

All that was needed then was exit papers, which took three months to procure, after which Ahmed Salihamidžić put his son in a car to Zadar in Croatia, from where he took a bus to Hamburg. Ahmed Halilhodzić's wife Djula was supposed to meet Salihamidžić at the bus station, but when he arrived, he couldn't see her. Gradually people drifted away, until he was left alone. Tired and frightened, he went to the bus station's small café, where, so intimidated he could barely speak, he whispered the only two words of German he knew, 'Bitte limonade.' The waiter, though, could not understand him, so he tried again.

'Bitte limonade.'

'Pa tako mi reci brate!' ('So, speak to me, my brother!') the waiter replied; he was a Bosnian Croat. The two chatted, calming Salihamidžić until Halilhodzić finally arrived half an hour later.

'As soon as I left Bosnia for Germany,' Salihamidžić said, 'I realised that all life is a fight. People talk about the kings, about Zidane, Cantona, Ronaldo, but there are no kings in football. You can be a king for a day, but tomorrow the king will be somebody else. In every game, every practice, every minute of every day, you have to give everything as though it were a Champions League final.'

Salihamidžić spent six months living at Ahmed Halilhodzić's house in Hamburg, and after that moved into the club's academy. There, his energy levels undiminished, he was the only player to represent three different teams, and impressed sufficiently that when he was eighteen he was offered a professional contract by Felix Magath, who would coach him again at Bayern Munich. That meant that he had to leave the academy, so he moved in with his Spanish team-mate Paco Copado, who lived with his parents and his sister, Esther. For Salihamidžić, though, the war and his family remained a constant concern. 'This coach, Magath, is really good,' he wrote to his parents. 'He's teaching me properly, but he never wants to talk to me. He never asks if I miss my family, how they're getting on in the war . . . I miss my sister a lot, but also I miss my father's criticism. He always knew what the best thing for me was. I think a lot about my mother – I'm a mama's boy. I can't wait to see her, and to sit on her knee.'

In 1995, Copado was transferred to Real Mallorca and returned to Spain with his parents. They wanted Esther to go with them, but she decided instead to stay with Salihamidžić. The following year Salihamidžić played nine times for Hamburg, making his reputation with a stunning performance away to Eintracht Frankfurt on the final day of the season. Needing a victory to qualify for the UEFA Cup, Hamburg won 4–1, Salihamidžić scoring twice and setting up the other two. The following night, he was a guest on a chat show on ARD TV, who unbeknown to him, had sent a camera crew to Jablonica on the day of the game to interview his family. When Salihamidžić saw the piece, he began to cry; when, later, contact was made for a live link-up, he all but broke down.

'My son has three basic characteristics: hard work, ambition and a desire to progress,' Ahmed Salihamidžić said. 'He has two faults: he's too ambitious and he can't stand to be beaten. When he's lost a match, he switches off his phone for two or three days and nobody can talk to him. Maybe that's a good thing, maybe that's the reason he's so successful.'

Successful he has undoubtedly been. A year after his debut for Hamburg, he was in pre-season training with the club in Spain when he received a telephone call to tell him he'd been called up for the Bosnia-Hercegovina Under-21 side. 'He was so happy, he started jumping up and down on the bed,' said his father, who seems to regard embarrassing his son as a parental duty. Esther, you imagine, would not have had to wait long to be shown the album with the baby photos. After just one game for the Under-21s, Salihamidžić was elevated to the full national team, making his debut in Bosnia-Hercegovina's first competitive match, a World Cup qualifier against Croatia. Bosnia lost 4–1, but Salihamidžić got the goal, a fitting beginning for the player who would become his nation's footballing figurehead.

The man who gave him his international chance was Fuad Muzurović, the first coach of an independent Bosnia. The Bosnian Football Federation (NSBiH) was established shortly after the declaration of independence – initially representing only the Muslim clubs – but it was not until November 1995, two weeks before the Dayton Peace Agreement, that Bosnia-Hercegovina played their first international – a friendly away against Albania in Tirana. 'We set up our headquarters in a hotel in Zagreb, but I was really doubtful as to whether we should make the trip because I had only eight players,' he said. 'We decided to call up Husred Musemić who had played in Scotland for Hearts, even though he had already retired. In the end I had only twelve players and no reserve goalkeeper, and when we got to Tirana I was worried because the players who were coming from Slovenia were late. There was a while when it looked like some of my coaching staff might have had to play.'

I met Muzurović in the café at the Koševo Stadium, although, it being Ramadan, he refused anything to eat or drink. A white-haired man with an intense gaze, he seemed principally concerned to discuss heading with me, having specialised in the subject as part of his coaching qualification – 'not just scoring,' he explained, 'but passing and clearing as well'. It took me a while to work out why he thought I could possibly have anything new to say on a subject about which he had already written a sixty-page dissertation, but then I realised it was just a matter of national stereotyping. 'If you see a good nice goal scored with the head, we say it is a goal in the English style,' he told me. 'A goal with the foot is a Euro-goal.'

Muzurović had to deal with rather more consequential regional divides. 'I could only call on players from one part of the country,' he said, 'so there were big problems.' Muzurović wanted to pick Risto Vidaković, who had played for Red Star Belgrade and FK Sarajevo before the war, and went on to play for Real Betis in Spain, but he refused. 'He told me he was scared,' Muzurović said. 'The same with Savo Milošević – he's also Bosnian but he plays for Serbia. Mario Stanić was born in Sarajevo, but he played for Croatia. They were afraid of the reaction of the fans in Croatia and Serbia and in the places in Bosnia where their parents were.'

During his first years as national coach, when he was also in charge of FK Sarajevo, Muzurović's main role was simply to keep football in Bosnia alive, and to that end in 1993 he took his side on a foreign tour of 'humanitarian games' to raise money for orphans and veterans, and to raise awareness of Bosnia's plight.

Mirza Varešanović was a player with FK Sarajevo when the war began. He had served for over a year on the front line when he was invited to rejoin the squad to prepare for the tour. 'We trained in the basketball hall,' he said. 'Every day going to and from training we were under fire from the snipers and the cannons, but our love for the club and for football was bigger than the fear for our lives. It was our way of fighting for Bosnia. People who lived in Sarajevo under the siege think that maybe it's not a good way of behaving during the war, but because we were well known, the people in the Bosnian presidency thought it was more useful for us to go abroad and play as the team of the besieged city than to stay back and practise. We were some kind of Bosnian ambassadors.'

Quite apart from the problems of training, though, there was the issue of getting out of the city, which, where it wasn't surrounded by Serb troops, was sealed by the UN. The squad was split into four groups of seven players, each of which was placed under the control of a member of the special forces. 'The idea was that we would go across the airport on four consecutive days,' Muzurović said. 'I remember the night we went. We knelt out of sight in front of the airport, and then the officer with us said: "Run like hell." We had to run with our bags on our backs. There was no stopping for two hundred yards, because we knew if we did we'd be killed. The middle of the airport was the most dangerous place because that was where you came in range of the Serb concentration camp at Kula. As we ran across, they were shooting at us.

'It is hard for me to talk about this, because my son was with me and I was afraid for him. He was caught by the UN forces, who gave him a bit of a kicking.' Muzurović's son, Mirza, who by that stage had joined us, nodded ruefully. 'I went to the players and told them to go on without me,' Muzurović went on, 'but one of the police officers promised he would bring my son, so we kept going.

'The UN forces didn't allow anybody to move across the airport, whether you were going in or out of Sarajevo. They had a tank with a spotlight, so when we saw the light we just turned round and made it look like we were going into the city from the free territory. That was the game you had to play. We turned round and lay down in the snow, and the UN force picked us up, put us in a transporter and took us to the free territory.'

'Like a taxi,' said his son.

The players, still dodging Serb patrols, crossed the mountains by night, walking through the snow until, two days after they'd set off, they arrived in a small village where they were able to hitch a lift in a refrigerated meat truck to Pazarić. From there they caught a bus across the border to Split. 'Leaving my parents was the hardest part,' Varešanović said. 'I didn't know if they'd still be alive when I came back. For six months after leaving I knew nothing about them. I tried to make contact through the radio station, and I tried to make phone calls. It's really hard when you hear the phone ringing, and you don't know whether there's anybody in the house to pick up and say "I'm alive".'

Once the squad reached Zagreb, Miroslav Blazević, at the time the president of Dinamo Zagreb, provided accommodation and equipment, and they played Hajduk Split in the first leg of a tour that would eventually take in fifty-four matches in seventeen countries as diverse as Austria, Saudi Arabia and Indonesia. They met the Pope in the Vatican, and then, after beating the Iran national side 3–1 in Tehran, the Iranian president Ali Akhbar Rafsanjahni. 'He said to us: "Congratulations on your victory,"' Muzurović told me. '"This is your way of fighting. This is the best way to present your young state to the world. I wish you all the best and I'll see you in a free Bosnia."'

Back in Sarajevo, the intervention of the UN Protection Force (Unprofor) allowed football to begin again in a limited form. In March 1994, despite knowing Serb artillery was trained on the Koševo, a game was played between teams representing Unprofor and the city of Sarajevo (Unprofor lost 4–0), and later that year, the situation was sufficiently improved for the inaugural Bosnian championship to be played, the top four sides after a series of regional play-offs meeting in Zenica, away from the worst of the fighting.

It's easy enough wandering around Sarajevo to see why, despite Unprofor's efforts, playing in the capital was all but impossible. From the inside, the Koševo, the national stadium and the home of FK Sarajevo, which was rebuilt for the 1984 Winter Olympics, seems almost untouched, but outside, where the training pitches used to be, there are graveyards, one field dotted with the plain white stones of the Muslims, the next with the more ornate crosses and sculptures of the Catholic Croats. On the other side of the ground, across a shallow valley itself covered in headstones, stands the hospital which, somehow, kept operating throughout the siege. The Grbavica Stadium, the home of Zeljeznicar, the other Sarajevo team, fared even worse.

It is now one of those quaint little grounds UEFA seem to be doing their best to stamp out. They have one modern stand, all homogenous blue plastic, but the end behind the other goal consists of nothing more than a series of concrete steps cut into the natural banking of the hillside. The main stand is constructed of delicately carved wood, apparently designed to resemble a cuckoo clock, and, facing that, is a shallow terrace that would be unremarkable were it not for the ancient steam engine that sits level with the halfway line, a nod to the club's origins in the railways. The stadium stood on the front line, and when the siege was lifted in 1996, the first thing players and officials had to do was to clear the pitch of mines.

The area around the Grbavica is typical of those parts of Sarajevo that lay near the front. Renovation has begun, but it is far from complete. I met Dželaludin Muharemović, at the time the captain of Zeljeznicar, in a pizzeria a hundred yards from the stadium. It seemed a pleasant enough place, a small fountain bubbling in the courtyard, and it was only when I came out and happened to glance up that I realised that from the second storey up the building was a shell, the walls still perforated by bullet holes and the more ragged tears inflicted by mortar bombardment.

Muharemović is a popular figure in the city, even among fans of FK Sarajevo. He was undeniably friendly and charismatic, but there was a hauntedness about his face, a premature hardness to the lines around his eyes. Muharemović had played for Zeljeznicar for six months when the war began. 'I joined the special police force to defend the city,' he said. 'There were quite a few guys who stayed in Sarajevo during the siege. We played football for fun sometimes, but it was difficult because there was constant danger from snipers and shells and we didn't have space to play real football. We started to play properly again in 1994, in the hall of a school near the centre of town; just a few of us got together and started to do something with the ball. The biggest problem when they decided to start the championship was to put the team back together.'

Zeljeznicar finished bottom of the final group – which was won by Čelik, a team based in Zenica – but the results were largely academic. 'That was the time when we started to think about the other things, not just the war and the fighting and our duties in the police or the army,' Muharemović explained. 'Zenica was a more peaceful place than Sarajevo. We weren't in danger from snipers or mortar shells, and for the players from Sarajevo it was a really good feeling to walk on the streets without thinking that somebody could get hurt or be killed. I started to feel like a football player again and that was a great feeling, one of the most beautiful things I can remember.

'We came out of Sarajevo very hungry. We'd lost lots of weight and we hadn't trained a lot. Čelik were playing in the free territory, in almost European conditions, and that was why they won the championship. We could play against them for forty-five minutes or an hour, but after that we just disappeared from the pitch. The worst thing after the tournament was the thought that we had to go back to Sarajevo.' Muharemović was lucky, though. NK Zagreb had scouts in Zenica, and they were impressed enough to sign him.

As the siege continued, so too, remarkably, did the football, often in absurd conditions. Muzurović, who brought his FK Sarajevo side back to compete in the first championship, told me about travelling for a game in Bihac, taking three days over a journey that would usually take six hours. In May 1995, a mortar landed on a game taking place in Sarajevo, killing several players and spectators. Yet, still the football continued, a flickering of normality and hope in the darkness.

*

Once the war was over, priorities changed, and in 1998, Muzurović resigned as national coach. 'During the war, I wasn't doing it for money,' he explained. 'I had been doing it for love. But after 1998 when we began to play seriously, I decided to talk about a professional way of doing things. The time of love was over, but because they didn't want to discuss my contract, I decided to move away. I didn't have any money, and the only way I could make some was to move abroad.'

Money is a constant problem. Varešanović, a wiry, worried-looking man with extraordinary snakeskin winkle-pickers, was, when I met him, the youngest sports director in Bosnian football. On the wall behind his desk in the FK Sarajevo club offices hung two portraits, one of Safet Sušić, once of Paris St-Germain and probably the best Bosnian player in history, the other of Asim Ferhatović, a star of the FK Sarajevo side of the sixties who broke a contract with Beşiktaş because he missed Sarajevo so much.

They serve now as painful reminders of the good old days, far removed from the troubles of the present. Varešanović seemed all but despairing about the state of his club and Bosnian football in general. 'You can't make progress at the moment,' he explained. 'You can only survive. We are like beggars knocking on the door asking for money. It's hard for us to do that because we are a club with a name, with a tradition in Europe. We have to be honest, and with the hard economic situation in the club we can't promise the title every year, but the fans keep the pressure on us.'

The government, he said, should offer tax breaks for those investing in clubs, provision should be made to set up shops and restaurants at the Koševo, the league should be reduced in size so there are fewer second-rate teams, the infrastructure and youth coaching set-up should be improved. That last point was something Muzurović stressed. 'Conditions for work with young players are far worse than when we won the league in 1967,' he said. 'Behind our best training pitch is a pitch without grass. You see every day around five to six hundred small kids playing in the dust, without water, without anything. Sarajevo youth teams are the best in Bosnia, the champions, but they practise in and have their matches in the mud, in the dust. Could you imagine how good we'd be if we had a decent pitch, warm water and everything? I know all there is to know about teaching young kids to head the ball, and none of this generation can head the ball in the right way. At dusk you can't see anything, so they close their eyes and head the ball in the wrong way.' It is hard not to sympathise with people as genuine and passionate as Muzurović, but there remains a terrible bathos about his complaints: when training pitches have been turned into cemeteries, heading technique just doesn't seem that important.

Since the Dayton Peace Accord, Bosnia has been split into two entities — 51 per cent of the country is administered by the Federation of Bosnia-Hercegovina (the Croat and Bosniak portion), and the remainder by the Republika Srpska — while the presidency cycles between each of the three groups. That speaks more of grudging acceptance than genuine reconciliation, but, slowly, things are improving, and in that process football has had a significant symbolic role.

On Easter Monday 1993, the Serbs began shelling Srebrenica, a small town about two hours' drive from Sarajevo. Before the war its population had been around 8,000, but with the influx of refugees fleeing ethnic cleansing in the surrounding villages that figure had grown to 40,000, most of whom lived rough. In a twenty-minute bombardment, the Serbs worked the length of the high street, killing fifty-six people, several of them children who had been playing on a nearby school football pitch. One boy, a grim icon of the war, had his eyeballs burst by the force of the shock waves. Louis Gentile, the only UNHCR official left in the town, spoke of seeing flesh hanging from the fence that surrounded the schoolyard. Unprofor withdrew and declared Srebrenica a 'safe area'.

Western governments, though, allocated only a fifth of the forces it was estimated were needed to implement such a zone. In July 1995, supposedly reacting to a guerrilla attack from within what was theoretically a demilitarised area, the Serbs bombarded and took Srebrenica. As many as 8,500 Bosniak men were then systematically slaughtered.

Four years later, a number of Bosniak football teams of various ages travelled to Srebrenica and played a series of matches against Bosnian Serbs. It is hard to be entirely sure, but it seems likely that it was on the pitches on which they played that at least some of the victims for the massacres were selected. 'It's difficult,' Sadik Vilić, the coach of one of the Bosniak sides, said. 'I lost ninety per cent of the people I loved in these hills, but the children are making the first step.' Again you can't help but think what a tiny step it is, but at least it's in the right direction.

In the immediate aftermath of the war, the three nations set up separate divisions, but from 1998, the top sides in the Bosniak and Croatian leagues played off for the Bosnian championship. Two years later, it seemed that agreement had been reached on incorporating the Serbs, and the FIFA president Sepp Blatter was invited to Sarajevo for celebrations that were to include a match between a FIFA World Star XI and a multi-ethnic Bosnia. A month before Blatter's arrival, though, the Serbs withdrew, claiming they had not been fully consulted on the format for play-off games. A joint Bosniak–Croat league nonetheless began in 2000; Serb clubs finally joined two years later and the NSBiH is now a truly national body – arguably, in fact, Bosnia-Hercegovina's most national body.

That speaks of a tentative return to the tolerance for which Sarajevo was once famous, but ethnic tensions are never far below the surface. In Mostar, the city whose ancient bridge – for so long a symbol of harmony – was destroyed in the Bosniak–Croat part of the war, for instance, Croats accuse

Muslims of having hijacked Velež, the club that once represented the whole community. 'They took the name because they knew that everybody would have heard of it, but nobody believes it is the same team,' explained Ivan Djorbić, who was so disaffected that he and other Croats resurrected HSK Zrinjski, a team with Croatian roots that had been outlawed by Tito after the Second World War for being too closely associated with nationalism. Luckily for them, the Brijeli Brijeg stadium that had been home to Velež was on the Croatian side of the bridge, so they struck a legally dubious deal with the Croat-run South-West Mostar Municipality to rent the ground for 109 years. Not surprisingly, derbies are hostile affairs. At least, though, there are derbies – or there would be, had Velež not been relegated in 2003 – and Bosniaks and Croats are prepared to compete against each other again.

Just as significantly, in October 2002, the defender Vladan Grujić became the first Bosnian Serb to play for Bosnia-Hercegovina. 'When I heard I was in the squad, I was the happiest man on the planet,' he said. 'It was a real honour for me.' Grujić was born in Banja Luka, the capital of the Republika Srpska, but he insisted all his childhood friends were delighted by his call-up. 'Nobody told me not to do it,' he said. 'Nor did I have any problems or threats from the Serb nationalists. It was simple. People from Banja Luka knew me, they knew my football potential and they all thought I had a place in the Bosnia squad. It was a logical step for me. For me the national team will always be the number one priority.'

Once Grujić had taken the step, others followed. First came the Bochum forward Zvjezdan Misimović, then Semion Milošević, Dušan Kerkez and Siniša Mulina. More will follow, yet Grujić seemed oddly blasé about the political significance of his decision. That may be because he did not want in himself to become a cause, but, given the way his discussion of his international career mingled with the ordinary jargon of football speak, it appeared that he genuinely did just see his call-up as a logical step. 'I had three wishes in my life,' he said. 'I have accomplished one by playing for the Bosnia national team.

'My second is to play in England. What a league! Lots of attractive clubs, you can touch and feel the tradition. That country must be the dream of every football player.

'The third one is the most important for me. I dream of playing for Bosnia in my native Banja Luka. I know the situation is still tense, but I also know a lot of people who want to see the Bosnian national team in Banja Luka's City Stadium. We should break the ice with a Bosnia Under-21 match there first, to see and hear what the reaction is. There are a lot of people who live in Banja Luka who are really happy when the Bosnia team wins a match, but you never know who might come to the stadium to make trouble. It's probably still too early, but I believe the day will come and I am looking forward to it.'

If the opposing parties could come together in Bosnia, the feeling is they could probably come together anywhere in the former Yugoslavia, despite the continuing ill-feeling between and within the other former republics. UEFA tend to treat such things with great reluctance, but support is gradually growing for an Adriatic League such as has existed in basketball since 2001. 'I'd be the happiest man in the world if we could have that kind of league again,' said Varešanović. 'We want to play against Red Star and Dinamo Zagreb – there'd be more quality, more people at the games. If you left it to the sportsmen you could easily manage the league, but for now it's quite impossible. In every former Yugoslav republic there is too much politics.'

It is an enticing prospect, having, instead of leagues in which two sides dominate the rest, a genuine contest with seven or eight major clubs. 'It would be great,' Bilić said. 'There'd be twenty thousand at every game: more money, better games, better football . . . It would not be such a step up in quality for players moving abroad from our league. A foreign manager could come to Split and watch, say, Hajduk against Partizan; it would be a good game and maybe he would pick a player. If he comes for Hajduk against Medimurje, there are a thousand people there, there's no atmosphere, and it's not a great game because of that, so nobody plays well and he doesn't come again . . .'

Quite apart from the benefits for football, it would be a significant symbol of reconciliation – providing, of course, there weren't riots every week, and that is far from guaranteed. Even in basketball there has been crowd trouble when, for instance, Partizan have played in Split, and the size of a football crowd naturally makes security concerns all the more intense. 'It cannot happen,' Blazević said, 'the wounds are too fresh.' Nonetheless, advocates of the plan insist, familiarity would lessen the intensity and perhaps in the future lead to friendship. After all, for centuries, Muslims, Croats and Serbs lived together in Bosnia, with long periods of peace between the brief outbreaks of conflict.

It is not just football that would benefit from greater co-operation. 'We can't sell our shoes to England,' said Bilic, 'so we sell them to our neighbours. I would like the Italians to come to Croatia and say "This is the best coffee in the world", but it ain't gonna happen. We have to deal with our neighbours.' It may not quite be the federal ideal of which Tito dreamt, but at least it is harmony of a kind, albeit one driven by the demands of the market. Football may have played its part in bringing Yugoslavia down, but it also has a part to play in helping its former constituent parts to live alongside each other, perhaps even with each other, once again.

5 BULGARIA

Chaos Theory

Stoyan Georgiev, my fixer in Bulgaria, pulled over on to the hard shoulder and parked on the grass beside an abandoned gypsy caravan. For several hundred yards stretching back towards Pazardzhik, the verges and the central reservation of the dual carriageway were lined by parked cars. This was a special occasion – Hebar, the local club, were at the time a third division team and a Cup quarter-final against CSKA was always going to draw an exceptional crowd – but it must also be acknowledged that Bulgaria as a whole has yet to embrace the car park.

As we walked to the stadium, conveniently located just off the motorway to Sofia, Stoyan offered me a peanut, which I refused.

'But why?' he asked.

'I don't like them.'

'But you must always eat nuts at football.'

He had a point; everybody else in eastern Europe does, at least those who aren't eating sunflower seeds – a peculiarly frustrating habit even to watch: bite off one end, strip the rest of the shell with your teeth, then chew a tasteless sliver the length of a Tic-tac and about a quarter as thick. Given that most fans also smoke, if there is any kind of breeze you come away from games covered in a heavy dandruff of ash and broken husk.

People talk about the FA Cup as something unique – and in terms of tradition and scale it is – but no matter where you are, when a small side reaches the latter stages of a competition, the atmosphere is the same. There was a real sense of festivity about Pazardzhik that day, the babble of fans unused to the attention of the nation and determined to make the most of it. We met a local businessman Stoyan knew from his days doing national service, who admitted he went to, at most, two or three games a season. 'But you are from England,' he kept chuckling to himself, 'and you are here to watch Hebar.'

For him and for other local businesses, the day was about more than football; this was a chance for nationwide publicity. It is not often Pazardzhik plays host to anything of any significance, and it is still best known for a misplaced comma. As the Ottomans carried out reprisals following a failed revolt in 1876, a clerk saved Pazardzhik with a sleight of punctuation, altering orders to 'burn the town, not spare it' to read 'burn the town not, spare it'. Two years later, unfortunately, as the Ottomans retreated in the face of the War of Liberation, the town was torched. Judging from what I saw, the rebuilding hasn't quite finished yet, rusting steel poles still projecting everywhere from the bland concrete blocks.

We were admitted to the press area by an elderly gateman with a face so lined it seemed to have been shattered by the insertion of his eyes; Bulgaria does facial wrinkles exception-ally well. We had to stand – not a particular imposition for me, but presumably a great frustration to the journalists who actually had to file match reports – as the tiny mobile stand that was supposed to house us was filled, as so often in eastern Europe, with leather-jacketed men and their puffa-jacketed, custard-haired girlfriends. They may not be referred to as *nomenklatura* any more, but the phenomenon is the same: the local elite, defined now by financial rather than political preferment, still hold sway, even if it means getting in the way of people trying to do their jobs.

Not being able to see much of the game was probably a blessing, ruined as it was by a dreadful pitch. I know it was a third division ground, but this wasn't even close to respectability, more like something on which you'd graze sheep than stadium turf. It was spongy and drab, pocked with potholes half-filled with sand. Early in the second half a CSKA player, defeated by a bobble, contrived to miss an empty net from six yards. Evgeni Yordanov scored the game's only goal in the first minute, and inevitably it followed a defensive error, a Hebar player stumbling over the ball as it lodged in a penalty-box crater.

So CSKA went through, and, after beating Pirin 1922 in the semi-final, met their eternal rivals Levski in the final. Twenty years earlier, the two had met in the most infamous game in Bulgarian history. Appropriately, the rematch two decades on featured three red cards and a controversial penalty, as Levski ran out 2–1 winners.

At the height of the summer, Bulgaria can become unbearably hot, but 19 June 1985 dawned bright and fresh, the perfect day, it seemed, for the perfect Cup final. A fortnight earlier a Bulgaria side made up largely of players from CSKA and Levski had beaten Yugoslavia 2–1, which, coupled with a 2–0 defeat of France, the European champions, a month before, had taken them to the brink of qualification for the Mexico World Cup. Bulgarian football was in rude health, and the nation, remembering Levski's epic 4–3 victory nine years earlier when the two had last met in a Cup final, was agog.

Levski – named after Vassil Levski, a leader of the Bulgarian independence movement hanged by the Ottomans in 1873 – were officially registered in 1914, having been founded by students from the II Mare High School in Sofia three years earlier. By the time CSKA, the army club, were founded in 1948, they had already won five league titles. Popular as they were with fans, though, Levski, presumably because of their success before the establishment of a Communist government, seem always to have been regarded with suspicion by the regime. Their association with a revolutionary hero can't have helped their standing (a favourite chant proclaimed: 'Levski means freedom') and, in 1950, they were renamed Dinamo Sofia. Eight years later they returned to their original name, but a forced merger with Spartak Sofia, the police club, in 1969 spawned Levski-Spartak, the team of the Ministry of Internal Affairs. Thus was established the classic Communist football duopoly, although CSKA, able to conscript players from across the country, were by far the more successful and, by the time of the 1985 Cup final, they had won twenty-three titles to Levski's sixteen.

In 1985, though, Levski were on the rise. With such players as Plamen Nikolov, Nasko Sirakov, Emil Spasov, and, above all, the hugely gifted and hugely popular Bozhidar Iskrenov, they had already won the league that season, their first successful defence of the title in thirty-five years. Victories over Stuttgart in consecutive seasons, first in the UEFA Cup (although they lost to Watford in the next round) and then in the European Cup, had led many to suggest the 1985 vintage was the greatest in Levski's history.

CSKA, meanwhile, were in transition. Their great generation, which in successive seasons had ended Nottingham Forest's and Liverpool's reigns as European champions, was in decline, but Georgi Dimitrov endured as captain and Plamen Markov continued to pull the strings from midfield, while their side also included the former European Golden Boot-winner Georgi Slavkov and the nineteen-year-old Hristo

Stoichkov. If CSKA drew hope for the final from his emerging talents, they took rather more from the news that Iskrenov would miss the game through injury. It was an absence for which he would later count himself extremely fortunate.

Sofia derbies are always tinderbox affairs, and this one was ignited after twenty-six minutes as Slavkov gathered a long pass from Radoslav Zdravkov and clipped a precise finish past Bobby Mihailov, the Bulgaria national goalkeeper who, incongruously, would go on to play for Reading and gain fame for promoting a brand of hair-replacement therapy. The Levski-Spartak players, believing Slavkov to have controlled the ball with his arm, were incensed, and protested vehemently. Television replays are inconclusive, but suggest they probably had a case. The referee, Asparuh Yasenov, gave the goal, but the mood had turned and his grip on the game was gone. Urged on by a baying, near-riotous crowd, players hurtled into every challenge. Iliya Voinov added a second for CSKA with a deft free-kick eight minutes after half time, and then, on the hour, they won a penalty as Iliya Voinov was fouled.

All composure and self-control gone, Levski's players swarmed around Yasenov and, in the mêlée, Mihailov twice struck him. Amazingly, Yasenov did not send him off and, after some semblance of order had been restored, the goalkeeper saved Slavkov's penalty. From then on the ball was little more than an accessory to a battle, and, after a shocking challenge by Kostadin Yanchev on Spasov, a full-on brawl broke out. A dozen red cards could have been shown, but Yasenov sent off only the two initial protagonists, Yanchev and Spasov.

Sirakov pulled one back for Levski with a penalty seven minutes from time, but CSKA survived the little football that followed. At the whistle, Mihailov ran to confront Yasenov and again hit him, prompting another mass confrontation that seethed for ten minutes before order was restored and CSKA presented with the trophy.

'This is a really bad memory for me,' said Yasenov. 'I tried to be completely fair to both teams, but the pressure on referees in such games is huge. Both the Ministry of Defence and the Ministry of Internal Affairs wanted to prove that they were the more powerful, and the players were given extra motivation from their bosses in uniforms. I probably showed too many cards during the game. There is a truth about matches like this, which is that no matter how strict the referee, if the players want to behave badly, a referee cannot stop them.

'The fatal moment was that first goal. I'm still not sure whether Georgi Slaskov used his hand to score, but after that everything went wrong and the tension was enormous. I think my only big mistake was not to send off Bobby Mihailov. Nobody tried to put pressure on me before the match, but it was always difficult to referee matches between CSKA and Levski. We all knew who was behind the clubs and that we had to be faultless. Sometimes the psychological pressure leads to mistakes.'

If any joy could be taken in such a tainted triumph, it was extinguished the following day as the Bulgarian Communist Party acted against the 'breach of socialistic morals' on both sides. Under the headline 'Let's eradicate unacceptable actions in Bulgarian football' the official Party newspaper, *Rabotnichesko delo*, published a list of draconian penalties.

The two clubs were effectively dissolved, losing their status as the teams of the army and the Ministry of Internal Affairs and being renamed: CSKA as CFKA Sredets and Levski-Spartak as Vitosha. CSKA were stripped of the Cup, and both clubs were disqualified from the league, meaning that Trakia Plovdiv (now returned to their earlier name of Botev Plovdiv), who had finished third, were named as champions. The management of both clubs was dismissed and the two coaches, Manol Manolov of CSKA and Vassil Metodiev of Levski-Spartak, were sacked.

It was the players, though, who faced the severest sanctions.

Four Levski players – Mihailov, Spasov, Nikolov and Emil Velev – were banned for life, as was Stoichkov, for 'a violation of the socialistic moral, and football hooliganism'. Four other players, including Sirakov, received suspensions of between three and twelve months. 'I felt I'd been killed,' said Stoichkov. 'I don't know why I was punished – probably, because I was the youngest. They could have destroyed me.'

The biggest losers were Spasov and Nikolov, both of whom saw the pre-contract agreements they had signed with Porto scrapped by the Bulgarian Football Federation (BFS). Spasov, an elegant midfielder, was particularly unlucky. He had never been booked before that final, and had barely been involved in the brawls. 'At the time I was thirty and the ban was a huge blow for me,' he said. 'I lived in shock for a month. I even tried to talk with influential party leaders to let me go to Portugal, but I couldn't reach them. Two years later Porto won the European Cup . . .'

His ban was lifted the following May as part of a series of pardons delivered by the BFS, as they realised what an embarrassment the World Cup could become if Bulgaria were deprived of several of their best players. Ultimately neither Spasov nor Stoichkov made the squad for Mexico, but Mihailov played in each of Bulgaria's games in the tournament, and went on to win over a hundred caps, while Sirakov scored their late equaliser against Italy in the tournament's opening game. Nonetheless, the severity of the suspensions, which could have crippled Bulgarian football and denied the world the genius of Stoichkov, remains mysterious.

For Levski fans, the overreaction was a sign of conspiracy, of the state plotting against them. 'The aim of the bans was to destroy Levski-Spartak,' said Velev, who worked in a factory during the twelve months before his ban was lifted. 'We had won seven times in a row against CSKA and they wanted to stop us.' Given the damage inflicted on CSKA at the same time, it is not the most convincing argument, but this was not

the first time Levski felt they had been deliberately undermined by the regime.

About fifty kilometres north of Sofia, as the road to Vratsa
hairpins through the mountains, there stands a boulder,
perhaps six feet in diameter, set upon a concrete plinth. It is
usually surrounded by a handful of bedraggled bouquets, for
it was on this spot that, at 11 a.m. on 30 June 1971, Bulgaria's
greatest player was killed. Stoichkov, of course, has good
claim to that title, but in a poll in 2000, it was Georgi
Asparuhov — 'Gundi' as he was nicknamed — who was voted
the best Bulgarian player of the twentieth century.

Asparuhov was born in 1943 in Reduta, a suburb of Sofia.
He showed early promise in football, volleyball, basketball
and gymnastics, but, when he was seven, his father, Asparuh
Rangelov, registered him with the youth section of Levski.
After a two-hour trial, the Levski youth coach Kotse Georgiev
approached Rangelov. 'I can't see what we can teach your
son,' he is reputed to have said. 'He is a natural born
footballer.' He progressed rapidly, and won Bulgarian youth
titles in 1960 and 1961. At the age of eighteen, though, he
had to fulfil his compulsory national service, and so joined the
military school at CSKA. He played in one friendly for them,
after which their coaching staff decided he was not good
enough, and sent him to see out his time with Botev Plovdiv.
It was a huge mistake.

Botev, a club of few pretensions whose sole previous
achievement had been to lose the 1956 Bulgarian Cup final,
won the Cup in 1962, and lost in the final the following year,
when they also finished second in the league. They also
reached the last eight of the Cup-Winners' Cup in 1962–63,
Asparuhov scoring five as Steaua Bucharest were beaten by a
7–4 aggregate in the first round. Botev did what they could to
keep Asparuhov in Plovdiv, but, in October 1963, he returned
to Levski. Asparuhov scored twenty-seven goals in the
1964–65 season as Levski won the title, their first league

championship success in twelve years, and the honours kept on coming. Eusebio described him as 'one of the best I have ever seen' after a European Cup defeat to Benfica in which Asparuhov scored three, and he got another two against AC Milan in the 1968–69 Cup-Winners' Cup. Further league titles arrived in 1968 and 1970, and Cups in 1967 and 1970.

Asparuhov's finest moments, though, came in the national shirt. He played in the final stages of three World Cups and, against Hungary in 1962, scored his country's first ever goal in the finals (although they lost that game 6–1). His most famous goal came against England in a friendly at Wembley in December 1968. Picking up the ball only a few yards inside the England half, he drifted through three challenges and finished calmly to earn Bulgaria a 1–1 draw against the world champions. Strong in the air and blessed with great technical ability, he won fifty caps and managed 150 goals in 244 league appearances for Botev and Levski, but it was his jovial charisma and his loyalty to Levski that made him such a popular figure.

Levski faced CSKA in the final league game of the 1970–71 season, trailing their city rivals by two points, but with a goal difference so inferior that the title was already decided. Tsvetan Vesselinov scored to give them a 1–0 win, but that was of far less significance than an incident in the closing minutes as Plamen Yankov tackled Asparuhov. Most now seem to agree that the challenge was hard but fair, but Asparuhov, uncharacteristically, retaliated, and both were sent off by the referee Aleksandar Shterev. Yankov continues to insist that had Asparuhov not reacted, the game would simply have carried on.

It usually took four days for the disciplinary committee to convene, but the day after the game, a commission met and banned both players for three games. And so, two days before the Soviet Army Cup final, Asparuhov and his team-mate Nikola Kotkov, also an international, left Sofia to play in an exhibition game in the mountain town of Vratsa, where

Botev, the local club, were celebrating their fiftieth anniversary.

Almost an hour after setting off, Asparuhov's famous pale brown Alfa Romeo pulled into a service station near Vitinya. He filled up the tank with 9.20 levs of petrol, but, with typical generosity, did not wait for change after handing over a 10-lev note. The few seconds that would have taken might have saved his life. As he got back into the car, a man approached and asked for a lift. Asparuhov agreed, delaying his departure a fraction. In two acts of generosity, he set in motion the timetable for his death.

A few minutes later, he turned a blind hairpin, and drove straight into an oncoming ZIL truck. The front of the Alfa Romeo was destroyed by the impact, and the car was consumed by flames; all three men inside died instantly. That same day, an accident in space killed three Soviet cosmonauts, and Asparuhov's death did not even make the front page of the sports newspapers. Over 500,000 mourners, though, turned out for his funeral.

A tragedy, certainly, but it is hard to place either Asparuhov's death or the punishments that followed the 1985 Cup final in a conspiratorial scheme that would justify Levski's paranoia. Both, rather, speak of an arbitrary form of justice by a body more interested in being seen to act than in coherence or fairness. In that regard, Bulgarian football is hardly unique, either in the context of eastern Europe or of football's governing bodies.

The 1985 punishments, after all, hit both sides, and, under their new names, both CSKA and Levski struggled initially as they were forced to rely on their youth teams to an unprecedented extent. For Bulgarian football as a whole, the effects, paradoxically, were largely positive, as young players were given their chance much sooner by the big two, while the smaller sides, at last, had a chance at success, making the league far tighter and far more competitive. In the 1985–86 season the teenaged Emil Kostadinov and Luboslav Penev made their debuts for CFKA Sredets while Georgi Donkov, Velko Yotov and Georgi Slavchev got their chance with Vitosha.

Fittingly, though, the main beneficiaries were Beroe, the team from Stara Zagora, who had themselves suffered an irrationally severe punishment from the party. The name Stara Zagora literally means 'Old Town Behind the Mountain', but the actual old town was destroyed by the retreating Ottomans in 1877, and the present city is a weird amalgam: the regimentation of streets laid out to a rigid grid plan offset by a pervading leafiness. My only visit was for a league game in 2002, a dismal 3–0 defeat to Spartak Varna. Beroe's relegation had long since been confirmed, and the ground, a shallow oval of concrete, was all but empty. The only remarkable thing was a vintage fire engine rusting in the long grass behind one of the goals.

The club was founded in 1916, but didn't win promotion to the top flight until 1954. By the late sixties, largely thanks to the attacking trio of Georgi Belchev, Yancho Dimitrov and Petar Zhekov, they had developed into a side good enough to challenge the CSKA and Levski duopoly, even if they continued to operate at a significant disadvantage. Zhekov, for instance, scored 101 goals for Beroe, before, as virtually all good players eventually did, being coerced into joining CSKA, where he scored 144 more to become the top scorer in the history of the Bulgarian league.

Crowds of 35,000 were common when CSKA or Levski went to Stara Zagora, and Levski, in particular, found the trip uncomfortable, failing to win there between 1958 and 1976. It was their meeting in 1970 that will always be remembered. Beroe dominated, and took a sixty-fifth-minute lead through Georgi Belchev. A decisive second eluded them, though, and, in the final minute, Levski won a corner. Sasho Kostov's kick looked simple for Todor Krustev, Beroe's experienced keeper, but as he went to gather, he was impeded by Kiril Ivkov and

Vassil Mitkov, allowing Dobromir Zhechev to force the ball over the line. Beroe protested, but the referee, Boris Trendafilov, gave the goal. As Levski celebrated, Kostov gesticulated mockingly at the crowd, drawing a hail of bottles and other missiles.

The 1–1 result stood, but, a week later, as Beroe blithely prepared for a league game against Dunav Rousse, the party announced its verdict. Most had expected that, at worst, Beroe would have to play some games behind closed doors, but the party took a strict line, expelling Beroe from the top flight and imposing on their coach, Atanas Kovachev, who had been treated with suspicion since an attempt to flee to the USA, a life ban from football. 'I still can't understand why we were punished so severely,' Boncho Merdzhanov, then Beroe's president, said. 'The crowd was wound up by Sasho Kostov's behaviour. He was a great sportsman and you didn't expect gestures like that from him, but that does not justify the crowd's reaction. If there was real justice the fans would have been punished and not the team. Nobody in the team did anything wrong. We tried to defend the club, but there was no overturning the party's decision.'

Nobody was in any doubt that if CSKA or Levski fans had been involved in a similar incident the party's decision would have been very different. Three political leaders from Stara Zagora – General Delcho Delchev, Stoyou Nedelchev and Hristo Shanov – even approached Todor Zhivkov, the General Secretary of the party. He, apparently, admitted there had been an overreaction, but refused to intervene.

A few years later, Krustev was called up to the national side for a game against France. As the squad prepared in Velingrad, they received a visit from Boris Velchev, a Levski fan and, at the time, one of the most influential figures in the party. 'He approached me, and asked if I knew who he was,' Krustev said. 'When I said yes, he asked if I knew who had punished Beroe after the game against Levski. Then he said: "So, be careful. If you play and make mistakes, you will never return to the national squad."' The logic of intimidating your own national goalkeeper is nonexistent, and while there must be a suspicion that Krustev elaborated the story to emphasise his victimhood, the incident smacks more of leaders used to governing by fear, almost instinctively attempting to instil that fear wherever they could.

The season after their enforced relegation, Beroe came back, winning the second division and scoring a record ninety goals in the process. They finished third the following season, and went on to achieve notable results through the seventies, particularly in Europe, where they beat sides of the calibre of Austria Vienna, Athletic Bilbao and Juventus. It was not until 1985–86, though, that they won their first silverware. It is impossible to say whether they would have overcome Levski and CSKA on equal terms, but there can be no doubting that, with such players as Vassil Dragolov, Yordan Mitev, Milan Kashmerov and Tenyo Minchev, they were a formidable side. Others may commemorate 12 April as the date Yury Gagarin completed the first manned space flight, but in Stara Zagora that will always be overshadowed by the events twenty-five years later. As Halley's Comet passed overhead, Vassil Dragolov scored the goal that beat Slavia Sofia and confirmed their only title. Beroe fans eagerly await the comet's return in 2062.

The 1985 Cup final was the first agent of change in Bulgarian football, but there were far bigger upheavals after Zhivkov resigned in November 1989. Although the Communists, under the new guise of the Bulgarian Socialist Party, were returned to government in elections the following year, the atmosphere had changed, and the system changed with it. The punishments imposed in 1985 were overturned, the league title restored to Levski and the Cup to CSKA.

Player sales became the only viable way of surviving as state subsidies disappeared. CSKA made significant gains selling Kostadinov to Porto, Penev to Valencia and Stoichkov to

Barcelona, while Levski sold Sirakov to Real Zaragoza and Nikolai Iliev to Bologna. Previously players had only been able to leave Bulgaria once they'd reached the age of twenty-eight, but with that restriction removed, the summer of 1990 saw an exodus. The result was a generation of players playing regular high-quality football in top-class conditions, and that led to an unexpectedly successful World Cup four years later.

Bulgaria were within seconds of not reaching the USA, but, in injury time against France in the final qualifier in Paris, David Ginola squandered possession, Bulgaria broke and Emil Kostadinov struck a gorgeous winner, qualifying Bulgaria at France's expense. 'God is Bulgarian,' screamed the commentator on Bulgarian television; Gérard Houllier, the France manager, was rather less complimentary about Ginola, and never picked him again.

Still, Bulgaria had been in the finals four times before, and had failed to win a game. An opening defeat to Nigeria suggested more of the same, but Greece, despite having qualified unbeaten (albeit from a group rendered significantly easier by the expulsion of Yugoslavia), proved compliant opposition. They had already lost 4–0 to Argentina, and once Stoichkov had converted a fifth-minute penalty, the only question was how many. Four was the answer again, leaving Bulgaria needing a draw against Argentina to ensure progress as one of the best third-placed sides. They did far better than that.

Argentina had already qualified, and were unsettled by the departure of Diego Maradona, who had failed a drugs test following their victory over Nigeria, but Bulgaria's performance was hugely impressive nonetheless. Stoichkov sprinted clear and jabbed past Luis Islas to give them the lead just after the hour, and, even when Tzanko Tzvetanov was sent off six minutes later, they held their nerve, wrapping up the game with a last-minute Sirakov goal. Only an even later goal by Daniel Amokachi for Nigeria against Greece prevented Bulgaria topping the group.

They went through in second, though, and faced Mexico in the last sixteen, a game ruined by the Syrian referee Jamal Al-Sharif, who showed eight yellow cards and nonsensically sent off Emil Kremenliev and Luis García. Bulgaria eventually went through after a shoot-out, but probably wouldn't have needed it had it not been for a highly suspect penalty from which Mexico had equalised.

And so came the Giants Stadium and Germany, and what their coach Dimitar Penev called, with few dissenters, 'the finest day in the history of Bulgarian football'. Again Bulgaria conceded a penalty, Yordan Lechkov, the tall balding midfielder, tripping Jürgen Klinsmann. Lothar Matthäus, for the second successive quarter-final, converted from the spot. The world sighed, mentally praising Bulgarian pluck and waiting for German professionalism and experience (that side averaged fifty-seven caps per player) to kill the game off. When, with seventeen minutes remaining, Rudi Völler tapped in the rebound after Andreas Möller had hit the post, it seemed they had. He, though, was ruled offside, and, two minutes later, the irrepressible Stoichkov, subdued until then, was fouled by Guido Buchwald and whipped the resulting free-kick into the top corner. Three minutes after that, the turnaround was complete. Zlatko Yankov crossed high from the right, and Lechkov overpowered little Thomas Hässler to thump a header past Bodo Illgner.

Bulgaria could not contain Roberto Baggio in the semi-final and lost 2–1, but the point was made. Stoichkov was a once-in-a-lifetime genius, and with the likes of Kostadinov, Lechkov, Sirakov and Krassimir Balakov, few could dispute that their place in the semi-finals was richly deserved. For all the economic problems at home, the decline of Communism had brought hope to football. It couldn't last.

The changes may have brought money to those clubs with players to sell, and it certainly improved the level of the national team, but the standard of the league plummeted. Between 1975–76 and 1989–90, Bulgarian sides twice reached the semi-finals of European competition, and on four other occasions made the quarter-finals. In the fifteen seasons after that, no Bulgarian side got further than the third round of the UEFA Cup.

As elsewhere, the removal of clubs from state control brought a wave of new owners. At CSKA, Valentin Mihov used the money from the sales of Stoichkov and Kostadinov to sign such foreign stars as Bernardo Redín, who had played for Colombia in the 1990 World Cup. Working with limited resources, Tomas Lafchis coaxed Levski to a hat-trick of titles between 1993 and 1995. For the most part, though, the new owners fell somewhere between opportunistic and incompetent. At Botev Plovdiv, Hristo Danov borrowed huge sums to sign the likes of Nasko Sirakov, Bobby Mihailov, Georgi Donkov and Doncho Donev, but they failed even to qualify for Europe and were soon on the verge of bankruptcy. At other clubs it was a similar story. Grisha Topalov at Shumen, Ivo Georgiev at Montana and Hristo Aleksandrov at Spartak Plovdiv all enjoyed their season in the sun before financial reality bit.

Perhaps the most remarkable, and certainly the most successful, of Bulgarian football's *nouveaux riches*, though, is Grisha Ganchev, a former wrestler who is chairman of Litex, a company that runs a chain of petrol stations across Bulgaria as well as factories producing juice and coffee. Litex's headquarters are on Banat Street in one of the better areas of Sofia. It is not too far from the city centre and the buildings there are reasonably modern, yet Stoyan still had to park on a rough patch of earth running down the centre of the road. In Sofia, cars are stacked everywhere – on corners, on pavements, on central reservations. Life has gone on since 1989, and the city is struggling to keep up.

There is a sense of that too with the architecture. Presented with a city in need of reconstruction after the Second World War, Bulgaria's architects seem to have opted to make their capital as functional and as ugly as possible, despite the considerable aesthetic advantage presented by Mount Vitosha (the 'lungs of the city'), which looms to the south. Although work is being done to restore various historic buildings, Sofia's most characteristic building is the Palace of Culture, a concrete monster of quite staggering awfulness that, to the shame of all concerned, was built as recently as 1981. Everywhere, grey-brown concrete predominates. Litex's offices are no different: nothing in the grim exterior suggests it houses one of Bulgaria's most successful companies.

Inside is a different matter. The walls are practically tiled with paintings, most of them, in a variety of styles, depicting traditional Bulgarian landscapes. Ganchev takes seriously his role as a patron of the arts. In his office, though, football predominated. The walls were dotted with pennants from a host of European clubs, while above the desk was pinned a large poster of the squad.

Ganchev is a short, energetic man, who, even sitting behind his desk, seemed to exude a muscular swagger. He was born in a small village near Lovech, and, in 1996, decided to take over his local club. Until then Lovech had spent most of their seventy-five years puttering along in the second division, changing name with far greater regularity than they did division: founded as Hisarya they went through Todor Kirkov, Torpedo, Kurpachev, Yunak, Osam and Lex before taking the Litex prefix. Why them? I asked. Why not one of the big two? 'It is easy to be a fan of Levski or CSKA,' Ganchev said. 'It is more beautiful when it is your own team.'

Others had gone into clubs with the same attitude, but what set Ganchev apart was that he had no illusions that he could make money from Bulgarian football. 'It's impossible to make a profit at the moment,' he said. 'I invested because I love football and because I wanted to stimulate growth in my home town.'

He did not, though, go in with any sentimentality, immediately sacking every player on the staff apart from Vitomir Vutov, a goalkeeper who was still playing regularly for the club eight years later. His radical approach was successful and Litex were promoted in 1997, finishing six points clear at the top of the second division. They even beat Levski 2–0 in the first leg of a Cup match, only for a controversial late winner from Dimiter Ivankov, the Levski goalkeeper, to rob them of victory in the second leg.

That summer Ganchev declared his ambition to turn Litex into serious title contenders – the empty words of another megalomaniac chairman drunk on early success, many thought – but Ganchev proved as good as his word. He replaced Ferario Spasov, the coach who had earned promotion and whom he had known since their days at sports college together, with the experienced Serbian Dragoljub Bekvalac, but then, apparently from a sense that things just didn't feel right, sacked him three weeks into the season, despite Litex recording two wins and a draw from his three games in charge. Coaches in Bulgaria have a lifespan only slightly longer than that of mayflies, but this, nonetheless, was shocking. 'I believe eighty per cent of success comes from the coach,' Ganchev said, and appointed Dimiter Dimitrov, who had done much to make Naftex Bourgas a force in the mid-nineties. Litex drew their two hardest games, away at CSKA and Levski, and at the midway point of the season were top of the table.

They began the spring season well, but, having signed Radostin Kishishev, who went on to play for Charlton, from the Turkish side Bursaspor, fielded him before he was properly registered. Levski protested, and the two games in which he had played – draws away to Levski Kjustendil and at home to Levski Sofia – were awarded as defeats against Litex. Lesser teams might have crumbled, but Litex were galvanised, and took ten points from their final four games to win the title, the first in their history, by five points. 'In Lovech they partied all night,' said Ganchev. 'There were people still drunk when they went into work the next day.'

After a UEFA Cup defeat to Grazer AK the following season, Dimitrov quit to take charge of the national side, at which

Ganchev turned again to Spasov. If anything, things got even better on the pitch, as Litex hammered CSKA 8–0 on their way to another title. Again, though, Europe was their undoing. Glentoran proved no obstacle in the first preliminary round of the Champions League, and, when Widzew Łódź were beaten 4–1 in the home leg, Litex were already dreaming of a glamorous qualifying-round tie against Gabriel Batistuta's Fiorentina. They conceded three in the second half in Poland, though, and were eliminated on penalties. 'I'm ashamed of our performance and can't cope any more,' said Ganchev, and withdrew from the club. The Albania internationals Alban Bushi and Altin Haxi, and the Bulgaria midfielder Stoicho Stoilov, also left. Litex became plain Lovech again, and the momentum was lost.

A few months later, though, Ganchev returned. 'I love this club, and I love this city,' he said. 'Our main aim will be to entertain the fans; titles are not on the agenda. If we play well, the trophies will come.' The Cup arrived immediately, at which Ganchev restored the Litex name. 'After the run we'd had,' he said, 'the club deserved it.' Success proved harder to come by in his second spell, and it wasn't until 2004 that Litex won another trophy, beating CSKA in the Cup final.

Was the increased competition, then, indicative of a rise in the general standard of the Bulgarian league, evidence that one man with money couldn't buy his way to the title? 'No,' said Ganchev, shaking his head slowly. 'Maybe joining the EU will raise the economic level, but at the moment it will be at least ten years before a Bulgarian side reaches the group stages of the Champions League.'

Whether that will be Litex or not is doubtful. In 2005, Ganchev, in a conscious effort to raise his club's profile, appointed the respected Israeli Yitzhak Schum, who had previously led Panathinaikos in the Champions League. After just six months, though, he departed, muttering grimly about the infrequency with which he was paid. It happens that I know two of the middlemen who helped establish contact between Ganchev and Schum. Needless to say, despite various verbal promises, neither has received a penny for their efforts. Whatever the rights and wrongs of that particular dispute, the general pattern is common enough: good intentions undermined by sharp practice.

6 ROMANIA
Anghels with Dirty Faces

Injury time was approaching when Gavrila Balint headed what he believed was the goal that would give Steaua a 2–1 victory over their city rivals Dinamo in the 1988 Romanian Cup final. As he raised his arms in celebration, though, the linesman raised his flag: offside. What followed has come to symbolise both the madness of football under the Ceauşescu regime and the intensity of the rivalry between Dinamo and Steaua. According to most witnesses, Valentin Ceauşescu, son of Nicolae and president of Steaua, signalled from the Communist Party box for his players to leave the field. 'A crazy day, a show of power,' Mircea Lucescu, the Dinamo coach that day, told me. 'I said to their players, "Come on, please, you are professionals," but they still went off. We were left standing around for half an hour waiting for somebody to tell us what to do.'

Taking some kind of initiative, the Dinamo defender Ioan

Andone dropped his shorts and waved his penis in protest at the Communist Party box, an act for which he received a one-year ban from football. The referee eventually abandoned the match and the Cup was presented to Dinamo. 'We went home,' Lucescu said, 'but the next day they took the Cup off us because Ceauşescu had decided that Steaua had won. Steaua were a tool of the generals and they were afraid that Dinamo had grown too powerful.'

Needless to say, Valentin Ceauşescu's version of events is rather different. 'The players came off the pitch, but it was the coach who ordered them off, not me,' he said. 'My father was sat next to me and he asked me who'd won. I didn't know myself. Dinamo were then given the trophy so I went into their dressing room to congratulate them. Their coach just shouted at me: "You don't decide the result." Then he threw the trophy at me and asked me to leave. In the end it was so ridiculous that I didn't care who'd won.'

Valentin still lives in Bucharest, where he works as a nuclear physicist. He always seemed a little withdrawn, very much the odd Ceauşescu out, the white sheep of the family; so much so, in fact, that it is widely believed he was adopted. These days he is a thin, nervous man, a chain-smoker, his face creased with worry. Having worked at the Nuclear Physics Institute in Magurele and studied at Imperial College, London, he had no intention of pursuing a career within the Communist Party, and, if modern sentiments are to be believed, appears to have been widely admired for his modesty. Where his younger brother Nicu was noted for his flash tastes and travelled in expensive chauffeur-driven cars, Valentin preferred to drive himself in a humble Dacia. He was also a genuine football fan.

In 1983, Steaua were struggling. Five years had passed since they had last won the title, and they were in danger of being eclipsed not only by Dinamo, but also by Universitatea Craiova, who won the league in 1980 and 1981 and, in 1982–83, reached the semi-finals of the UEFA Cup. Concerned, General Constantin Olteanu, the head of the Army

Ministry, which ran the club, appointed Valentin as president, whether in hope of family favour or in recognition of his gifts as an administrative leader, it is hard to say.

Valentin soon became famous for the long hours he worked, despite opposition from his parents. 'They didn't think being head of a football team was good enough for a president's son,' he explained. 'I missed a family Christmas one year because I was on tour with the team and they were very unhappy.' The relationship he built up with the players, though, would ultimately be his salvation: after Valentin's parents had been shot, Marius Lacatus put him up in his apartment in Bucharest. 'Valentin was our friend,' the forward explained. 'I was happy to help him after all he had done for us.' And he had done a lot. Laszlö Bölöni, who has played more times for Romania than anybody except Gheorghe Hagi, maintains that Valentin was 'the best manager I ever worked for'.

In Valentin's first season, Dinamo secured their third consecutive league title. From then on, though, it was a story of Steaua domination. They won five successive championships and, in 1986, became the first eastern bloc side to lift the European Cup. They also effectively became the first club from the East to be run on professional grounds, agreeing a sponsorship deal with Ford. Indeed, had it not been for the intervention of Nicolae Ceauşescu, who decided the plan was too capitalistic, Steaua would have sold Hagi to Juventus in 1988 in return for funding to establish a Fiat car plant in Bucharest. Their critics point out that the military habitually rewarded Steaua players with televisions, video recorders and other consumer goods that were not readily available, but the Securitate, the secret police, were doing just as much to promote Dinamo.

Romania is not an easy country to like, an uncomfortable mix of the appealing and the appalling. Bucharest at night is roamed by packs of stray dogs, the offspring of pets released when Ceauşescu forced families into flats, and there are times, walking down urine-streaked alleys between hideous concrete apartment blocks, when you wonder if it may be the most depressing capital in Europe. Then you turn a corner, and in front of you is a church of exceptional beauty.

Bucharest's most famous landmark is similarly ambiguous. The Casă Poporului (House of the People), an enormous folly built by Ceauşescu as his home and the parliament, is, with a height of sixty-four metres and a surface area of 265,000 square metres, the largest building in Europe. There is no doubting the quality of the craftsmanship of the interior or the impressiveness of the scale, but as a whole there is something monstrous about it. It is estimated Ceauşescu spent $3 billion on his House of the People, while the people themselves rotted in squalid flats. Ceauşescu, believing great capitals had to stand on a waterway, even diverted the Dâmboviţa river to run through Bucharest, but these days the channels run shallow, ugly concrete trenches cutting round the south of the city centre. Everywhere in Romania, the beautiful coexists with the grim.

I have had some very good times in Bucharest, but I have had some very bad. Nowhere have so many people tried to rip me off. It is as though decades under Ceauşescu – probably the most capricious of all the post-Stalin European dictators – has bred a cynicism, a belief that as life is unfair, you might as well take what you can get when you can get it. That said, I have also met with acts of spontaneous kindness; the problem being that you get so used to the cheats that you become aggressively suspicious of people who actually do just want to help. The result is a perpetual sense of confusion and mistrust, and, if the football is anything to go by, with good reason.

Lucescu, warm, affable man that he is – apart from on the subject of the English tomato, which he abhors: 'bland, tough, tasteless, like eating damp cardboard' – is also utterly paranoid, seeing conspiracy at every turn. He was Romania national coach between 1982 and 1986, during which time he led them to a first European Championship finals and would have taken them to the Mexico World Cup had England and Northern Ireland not drawn their final qualifying game 0–0. England were already through; the point meant that Northern Ireland joined them. 'I had a big problem with England and Northern Ireland,' Lucescu said. 'They arranged to draw at Wembley . . .'

This is a regular charge in Romania, and, in fairness, Brian Glanville acknowledges in The Story of the World Cup that there may have been a barely conscious desire on the part of the English players to help a team that was, in many cases, made up of their clubmates, but the accusation that the game was fixed in any organised manner can be refuted simply by watching the video. I tried to point out to Lucescu that Pat Jennings had had a superb game for Northern Ireland, making two outstanding saves, but he was having none of it. 'I know very well what happened,' he insisted. 'I had a big problem with Harry Cavan, who was a vice-president of FIFA and president of the Irish FA. I went to London to arrange the dates, and I said that the last match had to be between the best two sides, Romania against England. We had been at the European Championship in France, and neither of them had, so normally it would be our right, but immediately Mr Cavan said no. He said they had already arranged it, and they put us to play the first match against Northern Ireland for the inauguration of the stadium in Belfast [actually, the inauguration of the new North Stand]. All of FIFA was at Windsor Park – Blatter, Havelange, everybody – and everything was unfair. We lost 3–2, but it was a match of shame because they scored from a penalty and they scored from an offside position.' Not for the only time in Romania, I found the belief in conspiracy shaping the evidence. Northern Ireland's goals that day actually came from an Andone own goal, Norman Whiteside and Martin O'Neill – no dodgy penalties necessary.

Whatever the validity of those claims, in what followed Lucescu seems to have genuine cause for grievance. 'Ten days after they won the European Cup,' he said, 'Steaua came to Dinamo for the derby. Valentin came with a flag to celebrate their success, but we won 2–1. Ten days after that, we played them again in the final of the Cup, and that time we won 1–0. They went mad. In August, Romania played [a European Championship qualifier] against Austria. We won 4–0, but after that they decided to kick me out. The system was like that – I had too much popularity. Valentin wanted it to be only him, nobody else.'

Dinamo, though, were hardly innocent victims before the Steaua juggernaut. Most disgracefully, the Securitate bugged Steaua's offices throughout the eighties. 'They knew everything,' said Colonel Nicolae Gavrila, who became head of Steaua's department of football development in 1985. 'One day General Tudor Postelnicu [the head of the Securitate] told Constantin Olteanu [the Army Minister] everything he had said in a private conversation with Anghel Iordanescu [the assistant coach], just to prove their power.'

Before derbies, it became common practice for the Securitate to try to unsettle the Steaua club captain Tudorel Stoica by having the local police arrest his father, a notorious drunk, in his home town of Galati. Dinamo would also regularly try to obstruct transfers, attempting, for instance, to hijack Stefan Iovan's move from CSM Resita in 1981 by blackmailing him over a woman he had left pregnant two years earlier. Steaua's efforts to sign the defender Adrian Bumbescu from Olt Scornicesti were similarly frustrated for several weeks by the simple tactic of ordering club officials to send Bumbescu to visit his family in Craiova every time Steaua's representatives came to visit.

Scornicesti themselves provide an interesting footnote to the history of political interference in Romanian football. Under Florin Halagian – a coach who has been accused of beating his charges, and would commonly kick under-performing players off the team bus on the way back from away games – the side from Ceausescu's home village miraculously earned three successive promotions in the late seventies. On one occasion they put seventeen past Electrodul Slatina in the second half to win 18–0, having erroneously been informed that their promotion rivals Flacara Moreni, who were 2–0 up at half time, were leading 9–0. Scorniceşti itself, having being selected as one of the flagships of Ceauşescu's programme of collectivisation, whereby rural communities were forced into apartment blocks and their cottages knocked down to increase space for agriculture, is now a concrete mess, but it does boast a 20,000-capacity football stadium, a gift from the dictator to his birthplace. The football team was expelled from the league following the Revolution, but re-formed and now spends most of its time bobbing around the third division.

All the chicanery, though, should not be allowed to disguise the fact that Dinamo and Steaua were two exceptional sides, as Steaua's European Cup triumph proved. 'Each of us knew exactly our jobs, and we had such a perfect idea of where to pass the ball that if the coach had asked us to play with our eyes closed we could have put the ball where we needed to,' Iovan explained. 'We were like a perfect car. Great credit has to go to Bölöni. I don't know how he did it, but he could always find the perfect pass; he was the key to our stability. We were a team that was very attacking and we often forgot about the importance of defending.' Arie Haan, the great Dutch player whose Anderlecht side were hammered 3–0 in Bucharest in the second leg of the semi-final, said he had never seen a side play with such rhythm.

Come the final, though, they found themselves infected by nerves. Given they were playing Barcelona in Seville – an 'injustice' as Lacatus put it – a defensiveness was perhaps only to be expected. Wherever they had played, though, Ceauşescu's restrictions on travel would have ensured Steaua's fans were greatly outnumbered: only 1,000 Romanians travelled to Spain – 200 Steaua officials and 800 Communist Party members. All of them were first vetted by the Securitate, but forty nonetheless defected.

Steaua anyway did not travel well: the away legs in the four previous rounds had yielded only a win, a draw and two defeats. Night-time troubled them, too, and so Steaua spent their final training sessions practising not at the Ghencea, their home, but at the 23 August Stadium, the only ground in Romania at the time with floodlights. To make conditions in Seville as similar to home as possible, they did the equivalent of donning hair shirts by flying their own food out with them – chicken, beef, potatoes and cheese, and some bottles of Jidvei, a Romanian wine. At the last moment a few bottles of Romanian champagne were included, a wise addition.

The longer the final went on, the more frustrated Terry Venables's Barcelona became. Steve Archibald, who had missed the semi-final with a hamstring injury and was a controversial recall in place of Pichi Alonso, was far from his best, and the tensions in the Barcelona squad were exposed as Bernd Schüster, the temperamental German playmaker, stormed straight out of the stadium after being substituted. In contrast to Venables's tribulations, the Steaua coach Emerich Jenei, with seventeen minutes of normal time remaining, pulled a masterstroke, introducing the thirty-six-year-old Iordanescu, who had not played a game all season, for Lucian Balan. The switch steadied them, but Steaua still did not have the resolve to push for a win and the game went to penalties.

Mentally in tatters, Barcelona proceeded to produce the worst sequence of penalties ever seen in a major tournament shoot-out. Mihai Majearu, Steaua's usual penalty-taker, saw his kick saved by Javier Urruti, but the Steaua goalkeeper Helmut Ducadam fisted away José Alexanco's effort. Urruti saved again from Bölöni, then, for Barca, came Angel Pedraza. 'After the first kick, it was a psychological battle,' said Ducadam. 'I was almost sure that Pedraza would go for the same corner as Alexanco, and I was right.' Four penalties gone and all missed, Lacatus dispensed with subtlety, and his powerfully struck shot bounced in off the crossbar. For Ducadam, the mind games continued. 'For the third kick I figured Pichi Alonso would think there was no way I would dive to my right again,' he explained. 'I gambled that he would also place it to my right and he did.' Gavrila Balint made it 2–0, meaning that Marcos had to score. 'The fourth penalty was the hardest,' said Ducadam. 'I wasn't sure if I should dive to my right again or go to the left. I reckoned Marcos would hit it to my left, and again I chose correctly.'

A hero then, but Ducadam soon became a figure of controversy, as he vanished that summer. Truth is an elusive commodity in Romania, and it is still hard to be sure exactly what happened. There were rumours that he had been shot (or, in some versions of the story, had his arm lopped off) by one of Ceauşescu's henchmen, jealous of the car he had received as a bonus for winning the European Cup, but five years later Ducadam returned, briefly – alive and with two arms – to play for Vagonul, a team in Arad. His absence, he said, had been caused by a life-threatening blood disorder that required an intensive course of transfusions. He has always been distinctly uneasy on the topic, though, and there are still those who believe Ceauşescu himself had him beaten up – cruelly attacking the arms that made him great – after he complained at a dinner held in Steaua's honour that a car was not adequate reward for the glory he had brought to Romania.

Steaua's performances in Europe in the following seasons – a semi-final in 1987–88 and a defeat to Arrigo Saachi's AC Milan in the final a year later – indicate just how good a side they were, but it is hard not to sympathise with Lucescu's frustration. Steaua went a ludicrous 104 games unbeaten in the domestic league, and there is no question that they were aided in that run by referees, some games stretching on several minutes over the ninety. That said, neither was it coincidental that three Dinamo forwards – Dudu Georgescu, Rodion Camataru and Dorin Mateut – won the European Golden Boot in the eighties, having been assisted by opposing defenders for the greater good of the Ceauşescu regime. In a 5–4 win over Dinamo, Rapid fans happily highlighted the lunacy of the situation, chanting 'Try harder Camataru, you must score at least twice'.

As Lucescu has it, the fact that Dinamo were able to beat Steaua 3–0 early in the 1989–90 season was a 'sign that the generals were losing their grip'. By December, that grip had gone entirely. On the seventeenth, the Securitate and the army confronted demonstrators in Timişoara as they broke into the offices of the local Communist Party and hurled portraits of Ceauşescu out of the windows. That afternoon, the Executive Political Committee of the Communist Party ordered the army to turn their guns on protesters, and the revolution had its first casualties. Two days later, though, the army in Timişoara went over to the side of the demonstrators. On 20 December, Ceauşescu arrived back in Romania from a state visit to Iran, imposed martial law in Timiş County, and arranged to speak at a large rally in front of the Central Committee building in Bucharest to prove his power remained undiminished. Factories from around Bucharest, as they had often done before, sent their most loyal employees to hear Ceauşescu speak, but when they arrived in the Piaţa Gheorghe Gheorghiu-Dej (what is now Piaţa Revoluţa Revoluţiei) they were told Ceauşescu had changed his mind and that they should go home. Then, though, the factories were told the speech would be given at noon, and that they should assemble more workers. Necessarily, the new crowd was not so carefully hand-picked as the first – perhaps in this instance there was a conspiracy – and Ceauşescu's words were drowned out by booing. Demonstrations continued through the night, and the following morning protesters converged once again on the Central Committee building. Again Ceauşescu tried to speak to the crowd, but this time, as well as the booing, he was pelted with missiles. As demonstrators surged past police into the building, Ceauşescu and his wife escaped by helicopter from the rooftop. They headed first for their villa at Snagov, about twenty-five miles north-west of Bucharest, but, feigning engine trouble, the pilot brought the helicopter down by the side of the main road from Bucharest to Târgovişte. A car was commandeered, but on reaching Târgovişte, Ceauşescu and his wife were arrested. They were tried on 24 December, and executed by firing squad the following day. Five months later, Dinamo did the double.

The intriguing thing about Ceauşescu's escape attempt is that he should try to flee to Snagov in the first place. It seems likely that he thought he could fly by private jet from there to a country willing to offer him asylum, but there were those who saw a Gothic significance in the fact that in the stone church on the island in the middle of Lake Snagov is the tomb of Vlad Ţepeş – Vlad the Impaler – the fifteenth-century Wallachian prince and national hero, who, legend has it, will rise again in his country's hour of need. That is not to say anybody actually thought Ceauşescu, who actively played up an association with Ţepeş, was going to resurrect his political career with an army of the dead, but Snagov was a logical symbolic rallying point.

The undead are pretty much unavoidable in Romania, a land where vampires were an integral part of folklore long before Bram Stoker took the arbitrary decision to set *Dracula* in Transylvania. (Stoker never visited Romania, his first draft was set in Austria and Dracula's castle – which the novel places on the Borga pass and the tourist industry equates with the castle at Bran – was based on Cruden Castle in Aberdeenshire. The common association of Ţepeş with Dracula is just wrong, based on the coincidence that he was nicknamed 'Drăculea' – son of Drăcul – after his father was awarded the Order of the Dragon – 'Drăcul' in Romanian – by Sigismund of Luxembourg in 1431.) Appropriately, it was tracking down the ghoulish tale of a footballer's grave in Craiova that first took me to Romania.

For all Ceauşescu's plans for collectivisation, the south-west of the country remains a rural backwater. Having taken the ferry across the Danube from Vidin in Bulgaria, I caught a train from Calafat to Craiova. It's a journey of only about fifty miles, but it took over three hours as we crawled along, stopping at virtually every field to pick up more labourers, all of whom, it seemed, were ruddy-faced, drenched in sweat and more than a little tipsy from the bottles of beer that were passed around the carriage. It all felt rather as though I'd blundered into a Thomas Hardy novel.

On eventually reaching Craiova, I realised I'd left my notes on the grave back in Sofia. Not the best move, admittedly, but I was confident I knew the name of the graveyard, so I walked out into the car park, located a cluster of taxis, and asked, 'Cimitirul Dorobânția?' The first driver looked blank, and shouted to his mates. Attracted by the thought of an Englishman and his inevitably bulging wallet, a group of about a dozen drivers quickly gathered. 'Cimitirul Dorobân-ția?' I said again. More blank looks.

'*Anglais?*' one asked.

'*Oui, anglais.*'

None of them spoke English. We tried in French (or as close as I get to French), but I didn't know the word for cemetery, or grave, or tomb. One of them rattled through a list of languages: '*Deutsch? Español? Italiano? Russki? Portuguese?*'

'*Nein. No. No. Niet. Não.*'

So I resorted to the universal language of mime, casting dignity to the winds and falling back into the dust, hands pressed together over my chest in the manner of a dead Crusader.

'*L'hôtel?*' the linguist offered hopefully.

I got to my feet and drew with my hands the shape of a cross.

'*L'hôpital?*'

'*Non, après l'hôpital. Après le mort. Je voudrais visiter la place pour les personnes mortes. Je voudrais visiter Florin Piturca.*'

'Piturca', it turned out, was the password.

'Ah, Piturca. Cimitirul Dorobânția.'

'*Comme j'ai dit.*'

The roads deteriorated rapidly as we drove away from the

station, and it wasn't long before they were little more than dirt tracks. We passed the odd donkey-drawn cart, and a couple of kids on battered old bikes, and then, when we had left the town centre far behind, there appeared on the horizon a smudge of dust. As we drew closer, it became apparent that it was a column of people, maybe 200 strong, at the head of which, sombrely swinging a thurible, strode a priest, dressed entirely in black. As we slowed and passed to one side, the procession opened out, and I saw, lying flat on his back on a low wooden trailer, another priest: huge, black-robed, grey-bearded and very obviously dead. As I say, you don't have to go far in Romania to be struck by the macabre.

I had been slightly concerned about finding the tomb once I got to the cemetery, but I needn't have worried. As soon as I walked through the gate I saw Piturca, standing cast in bronze upon his plinth, left arm crooked across his chest, right arm straining backwards, as though to steady himself for a surge on to his right foot. Just by his right foot was a ball, made not of bronze, but of black and white plastic, the original having been stolen in 2000. It looked lightweight, totally out of place, rather as though Roberto Carlos were lining up a free-kick with a penny-floater. Alongside the statue stood the tomb, the size of a small house, marked on one corner with a plaque reading 'Ap. 20' – the number of the apartment in which he had lived in Craiova.

At twenty-seven, Florin Piturca was a well-respected striker for the second division side Drobeta Turnu Severin, nowhere near as good as his cousin Victor would become with Steaua, but a solid enough journeyman nonetheless. On 10 December 1978, he scored in his side's 2–1 victory over Metalul Bucharest, but, on returning home, he told his wife he was feeling ill and went to the bathroom. Ten minutes later, he was dead.

His father, Maximilian, a local cobbler, was distraught, and spent what little money he had in establishing a lasting monument to his son. The night Florin was buried, Maximilian stayed in the tomb. He went on sleeping there every night until his death in 1994. 'That was my husband's house,' Florin's mother, Vasilica, said. 'He worked every day, and every night he went to the cemetery to sleep by his son in the mausoleum.' When I was there Vasilica, a woman perhaps best described as formidable, was trying to get the local council to reverse their decision to refuse her the right to run an electric charge through the statue. 'It is the poor people who stole the ball,' she said. 'If we replace the ball and electrify the statue then everybody knows that anybody who touches it will die.'

She was equally forthright in her beliefs about what happened to her son. 'We wanted to know the cause of his death,' she said. 'We went to the hospital to see the results of the autopsy, and we were advised to go back six months later. When we did, though, they told us it was too late. Some of Florin's team-mates told me that at half time the team doctors gave the players some tea to drink. I believe there were drugs in the tea.' The theory exists that, desperate for sporting success, the Ceauşescu regime used mid-ranking sportsmen as guinea pigs before passing stimulants on to top-level athletes. Whether that is true or not, Zoia Ceauşescu, Nicolae's daughter, was sufficiently upset by the mausoleum on a visit in March 1989 that she decided to have it knocked down, and sent in the bulldozers.

The cemetery's gravekeeper, a short excitable balding man who, when he realised I spoke no Romanian, jabbered on in a composite of English, French and Italian, remembered the night well. 'Maximilian came out,' he told me, 'covered in dust and shaking his fist. "A curse on you and your family," he had cried. "In a year I will be back and you will be dead."' Nine months later, Zoia's parents were executed. By the following March, the tomb had been rebuilt, and Maximilian was back, sleeping alongside his dead son. He fell ill with a heart problem in 1994, but, despite knowing he was dying, chose to stay with his son. 'I have waited for this day for a long time,' he said. 'I am very happy that soon I will see my son again.'

The issue of drugs has never really gone away. Almost quarter of a century after Piturca's death, Romanian football was erecting another monument to another player who died in mysterious circumstances. Catalin Haldan was only twenty-four when, on 5 October 2000, left out of the national squad, he travelled with Dinamo Bucharest to play a friendly against the second division side Oltenita. A few minutes into the second half, he laid a ball off to a team-mate and keeled over. 'He fell first to his knees, stayed there for a second and then fell to the ground,' said Dinamo's goalkeeping coach Gheorghe Nitu, who was the first to reach the stricken player.

Haldan was rushed to a local hospital, and a helicopter arranged to fly him back to Bucharest, but, twenty minutes after collapsing, he was pronounced dead. After an autopsy Vladimir Belis, the director of the Bucharest Forensic Institute, issued a statement saying Haldan had not died as a result of taking stimulants. It was later discovered that Dinamo had not submitted all of his medical records and, more suspiciously, that Haldan had not attended the mandatory three-monthly medical examination the FRF had insisted upon for all players following the death of the Astra Ploiești midfielder Stefan Vraboriu in similar circumstances two years earlier. Belis then found that Dinamo had had all their players checked at the Medsana clinic in Bucharest six weeks earlier, and went to the police to force Dinamo to hand over their records, which showed that Haldan had serious defects to both his heart and his liver. Belis promptly passed the autopsy results on to the National Anti-Doping Commission, which confirmed that Haldan had hepatitis C at the time of his death. The commission's director, Ioan Dragan, subsequently claimed that his symptoms indicated the use of anabolic steroids. Shockingly, Haldan was the fourth Romanian player to die on the pitch in the space of two years, while, ten days before his death, his team-mate Florentin Petre was diagnosed with hepatitis C. Whether he had taken any stimulants or not, the hope in Romania was that Haldan's death and the outpouring of grief that followed would help raise awareness of the problems of drugs in sport. It does not bode well, though, that one of the pall-bearers at Haldan's funeral was Adrian Mutu, who, of course, was sacked by Chelsea for cocaine abuse.

It was only in June 2001 that Romanian football produced its first positive drugs test: the Arges Piteşti forward Adrian Neaga and their reserve goalkeeper Cristian Buturugu failing tests following a game against Rapid Bucharest. Both were later exonerated when it was decided that the entire squad had been 'inadvertently' contaminated by vitamin supplements given them by the club's medical team. It hardly helped Neaga's protestations of innocence, though, that the week before providing his positive test he had become the first player in Romanian history to refuse to give a urine sample, claiming that 'the conditions weren't right to give an accurate result'.

The drugs issue is just part of the mire into which Romanian football has blundered. There may not actually be more match-fixing in Romania than in other countries in eastern Europe, but they certainly do it with more chutzpah. The national side, elevated by such technically gifted players as Gheorghe Hagi, Ilie Dumitrescu and Gica Popescu, may have won admirers for the fluency of their football – the victory over Argentina in the 1994 World Cup stands out – but for most of the nineties Romanian domestic football was dominated by the so-called Cooperativa, a loose cartel of around a dozen clubs who would exchange home wins to ensure that none were ever relegated. It became so pointless for teams from outside the Cooperativa to try to compete that in 2001 Baia Mare, who had won promotion from Divizia B to Divizia A, sold their place in the top flight to Bacau, who had been relegated. The two big Romanian sports papers, *Gazeta Sporturilor* and *Prosport*, for many years fingered Jean Padureanu and Gheorghe Stefan, presidents of Gloria Bistriţa and Ceahlaul Piatra Neamţ respectively, as the ringleaders, but no significant action was taken. Stefan – 'Muttley to Padureanu's Dick Dastardly' as one journalist put it – was also accused of assaulting match officials and intimidating representatives of the league, charges he hardly bothered to refute. 'I believe in a sense of fairness and justice,' he said. 'I always try to defend my team, whatever the circumstances may be. I understand that on occasions I have broken the rules, but when you are emotionally involved in football it's very difficult to keep your emotions in check. When I feel that I and my team have been wronged I believe that I have to make a stand.'

His hold, though, is strong. Those few players who were prepared to speak about the match-fixing seemed genuinely frightened, whispering their responses as though afraid club officials may hear. 'The players are employed by the football clubs and because we're not in a strong position financially it makes it very difficult, if not impossible, for us to reveal things that might jeopardise our careers,' the Ceahlaul defender Leo Grozavu explained. 'We just have to accept that this is the way things are. Only when Romanian football players become financially secure will corruption disappear.'

In July 2000, Stefan finally got some kind of comeuppance as he was suspended for a year by UEFA after an attempt to bribe the French referee Stéphane Moulin with prostitutes ahead of an InterToto Cup third-round match against Austria Vienna. 'We provide hospitality for all our guests,' Stefan blustered, before claiming that Moulin had got the wrong end of the stick and that the four women who had approached him were merely folk singers. 'In the last two years we have hosted teams like Juventus and Mallorca and the referees have been pleased by what they have seen here.'

The response of the Romanian Football Federation (FRF)

was characteristically farcical. Mircea Sandu, the FRF president, who, when he isn't withdrawing his foot from his mouth, seems to spend most of his time washing his hands of important issues, decided it was all Moulin's fault. 'I think Monsieur Moulin is a queer fish,' he said. 'A girl stayed at his table for a second and suddenly he was in a hurry to go back to his hotel.'

That Sandu, a scandal-magnet who, more appositely than might have been thought at the time, was nicknamed 'the Godfather' in his playing days, managed to win four successive FRF presidential elections is little short of miraculous. One night in November 2002, to take only the most notorious incident, his daughter, Raluca, a professional tennis player, was in the Bucharest nightclub Office with her boyfriend Walter Zenga, the former Italy goalkeeper who at the time was coach of National, and a number of other members of National's coaching staff, including the former Chelsea defender Dan Petrescu. At around midnight, the club was raided by police, who made straight for their table, and discovered on the floor two wraps of cocaine – one under the table, and one under Zenga's chair. 'It was fantastic,' said Petrescu, who seems to have found the whole episode hilarious. 'It's the first time I've seen the police do something like this, and it was just like being in the movies. They had their faces covered in black masks and all of them had guns. I was not afraid, as I knew that my wife and I are clean and have never tried drugs. Walter was very nervous but I explained he had nothing to worry about and so he cooperated with the police.' Zenga and Raluca were released without charge the next morning, vehemently protesting their innocence. A police spokesman explained that the raid had been authorised following a tip-off from someone inside the club. Later that day, to the delight of the Romanian tabloids, it emerged that Raluca's ex, the tennis player Ion-Ion Țiriac, had also been in Office that night, with his new girlfriend, the pop star and *Playboy* model Ileana Lazariuc.

Those parts of Romanian football that haven't been written by Edgar Allan Poe, it seems, have been dreamt up by Thomas Pynchon: paranoia is universal. In the bar before the Steaua–Dinamo derby at the Ghencea in March 2002, most of the talk was of whether Chelsea's 3–2 win over Fulham a couple of days earlier had been fixed. To Romanians, a late goal, especially when the other team has just equalised, is always suspicious. I was slightly surprised anybody actually cared about the probity of the English game, but it turned out they were more concerned about their fixed-odds coupons. I recognise that most of the Romanians I know have a background in football, but the habit still seems disproportionately popular. Whenever I was in the Gazeta offices, they seemed to speak of little else, and I still get occasional Friday e-mails enquiring into, for instance, the state of Kevin Kyle's back before they decide whether to put down Sunderland v Gillingham as a home win.

The previous year I'd been to the reverse fixture at the Ştefan cel Mare on a raw April afternoon, a remarkably venomous game in which the local fire services got so sick of dousing flares as they were thrown on to the running track that they turned their hoses on the front rows of the stands. Unyielding, Dinamo fans, numbed by their hatred of Steaua and then by the delirium of a late own goal that gave them an unlikely victory, clung soaking to the wire fencing, hurling coins and abuse at anyone who came within range. Remarkably, in the year that followed, the clubs had managed to ratchet up their mutual loathing another notch.

As I waited for the train to Bucharest on the morning of the game, a tracksuited figure sitting next to me – an off-duty croupier called Ascamio – asked for a light. He was a Universitatea Craiova fan, but he said he was looking forward to watching the game, and hoping, for once, that Steaua would win or at least get a point so that National might take the title. In the previous two decades, only Craiova in 1991 and Rapid in 1999 had broken the Dinamo-Steaua duopoly. 'If

National won the league,' Ascamio said, 'it would show that you do not need money to win. It would show that the days of corruption are over.' With average gates of only around 2,000, National simply couldn't bribe their way to the title as Steaua, Dinamo and Rapid were all accused of doing during the nineties.

He spoke of the 'days of corruption' as though they were a new phenomenon, but it is hard to know when Romanian football was not corrupt. Perhaps there was a brief golden age between the overthrow of Ceauşescu and the hijacking of the game by the Cooperativa, perhaps Dinamo's double in 1990 and Craiova's victory the following year were – amid the chaos of the change of regime – honest, open triumphs, but certainly by the mid-nineties, in thrall to the financial might of the club presidents, football was as bent as it had been when the army and the Securitate were wrangling for pre-eminence. If you walk through Bucharest,' Bölöni said to me, 'you will see many bad things. It is very sad, but the truth is that many people in Romania are very poor. Romanian football is also very poor, so perhaps there is corruption. When I was national coach, if I had found that one of my players was involved in the corruption, I would have expelled him from the side; but it is almost impossible to find out.'

Proof has always been the problem. Senior internationals such as Hagi and Popescu made repeated calls for the FRF to clean up the game, journalists made their accusations, and, for most of his first three terms in office, Sandu continued to mumble sheepishly about a lack of evidence. In November 2001, though, a mishit cross from the balding Slovenia forward Milan Osterc looped over Bogdan Stelea to give his nation victory over Romania in a World Cup qualification play-off. After three successive appearances at World Cup finals, suddenly everybody recognised there was a crisis. The prime minister Adrian Nastase instructed the sports minister Georgiu Gingaras to put the game to rights, and he initiated a police probe into the finances of every top-flight club, pledging the biggest investigation into corruption in Romanian football since 1980, when 130 referees and forty players and club officials were charged with match-fixing.

At the same time, Sandu was re-elected – unopposed – for a fourth term as president of the FRF, and vowed to eradicate match-fixing from Romania before he stood down in 2006. He gathered the club presidents together, and, as though conducting some bizarre (and presumably lengthy) temperance meeting, had them confess their previous crimes. 'It had all got out of control,' he said. 'They said some astonishing stuff in there but no one named any names.' He then declared 'Zero Hour' on match-fixing. 'From the spring, we will shoot corruption dead,' he said. 'This is a war. There is no alternative if we really want to stop the corruption.'

Others were cynical. 'Until the entire leadership of Romanian soccer is changed, the history of corruption will repeat itself,' said Popescu. 'It is like a thief stealing ten times then announcing suddenly he is a reformed man. How are you supposed to believe him?' Sandu, though, was determined to appear adamant. 'We will not await any proof,' he said. 'A fixed match can be seen with the naked eye, and we will punish those who are throwing mud against the cheek of our game.'

And they didn't wait for any proof, docking Dinamo and Ceahlaul Piatra Neamţ three points each for allegedly fixing Dinamo's 2–1 win on the opening day of the spring half of the season. 'They are a mafia,' blustered Stefan. The week before the game, the Steaua coach Victor Piturca had claimed that a Dinamo victory had been agreed as part of the transfer deal that took the striker Costel Ilie to Bucharest over the winter break. 'It will be fixed,' he said. 'It will be a huge scandal. Normally it would be a very open game, and any result would be possible, but everything that people are saying about it not being a fair game will come true. I don't want to accuse Dinamo, but the only time I've seen them play this season was their 2–1 win over Gloria Bistriţa, which was a very strange game.' Within three months, though, Dinamo's punishment was overturned on appeal.

A Steaua coach attacking Dinamo, of course, was nothing new – nor were accusations against Gloria and Ceahlaul – but the tensions between the two Bucharest giants were given an added spice by the increasing involvement of Giovanni Becali, by far the biggest agent in Romanian football. It is alleged that before the Revolution he carried out a series of robberies and frauds across Europe with another Romanian, Dan Albanu, who was killed in a car crash in 1990. The pair followed the Romania national team whenever they played away, and became well known to players. Accordingly, he was ideally placed to become an agent when the markets opened up following the collapse of Communism. His company, International Sports Management, acted for a number of high-profile players, among them Hagi, Popescu and Stelea. Until 1999, he was also a firm friend of Victor Piturca.

What happened that autumn is far from clear, but Piturca and Becali became sworn enemies. Piturca, at the time, was national coach, and, in 2000, he led his side, which included the ageing Hagi, to the finals of the European Championship. Quite reasonably, he insisted that those players who had played in all the qualification games should receive larger bonuses than those – Hagi among them – who had missed the vital away win over Portugal. Hagi protested, Piturca refused to back down, and, having committed the ultimate sin of offending Hagi, Piturca was sacked before the finals and replaced by Jenei.

The two, it was fairly well known, did not get on. Piturca had been, if not the star, then at least the leading scorer of Steaua's European Cup-winning side, but, in that 1985–86 season, a nineteen-year-old Hagi, then at Sportul Studentesc, beat him to the top-scorers' title by a single goal. Hagi joined Steaua on a one-match loan for the European Super Cup final against Dynamo Kyiv later that year, but, after scoring the winner with a deflected free-kick, never went back. Valentin

Ceauşescu has always insisted that he never wanted to sign Hagi, saying he was 'too much of an individual', but he nonetheless became the fulcrum of the team built by Iordanescu, who had succeeded Jenei that summer. Piturca's team became Hagi's team, prompting rumours of jealousy, and matters were hardly helped when Piturca led the goalscoring charts by one going into the final game of the following season, only for Hagi to rack up an unlikely six to take the title.

Even allowing for that, though, Hagi's complaint was odd enough that questions began to be asked. Why would Hagi, who is noted for his generosity, quibble over a sum that, alongside the wealth he has accumulated from the game, could have meant little to him? Could it be, people wondered, that Hagi was put up to destabilising Piturca by somebody with a deeper agenda, by, for instance, Giovanni Becali? Shortly after Piturca's appointment as coach of Steaua, the conspiracy theorists noted, Becali declared himself a Dinamo fan and initiated the spending spree that saw, among others, Ovidiu Stinga, Florin Pirvu, Bogdan Lobont and Dorin Semeghin join the club.

Giovanni Becali's cousin Gigi was, at the time, the majority shareholder of Steaua, and, just to add another strand to the tangle of interrelationship, Hagi was once close enough to him to serve as best man at his wedding. Hagi, of course, is a Steaua legend, and, since ending his playing career, has regularly made clear that he would love to return to his former club as coach, something that would have left Giovanni Becali with a significant influence over Romania's two biggest clubs. That season, Hagi had repeatedly attacked Gigi Becali, Piturca and the other major investor, Viorel Paunescu. 'They won a title, but we all know how that came about,' he said. 'In Europe they did nothing. Steaua is a team that is honoured throughout Europe. Three men cannot simply turn up, invest a few dollars and think the club is theirs.'

As Steaua's form slipped after Christmas, and fans began to call for Piturca's head, Hagi stepped up his attack. It was after a goalless draw against National, who had been reduced to ten men with half an hour remaining, that matters came to a head as fighting broke out among frustrated fans. 'Even when they have an extra man, Steaua cannot win these days,' Hagi said. 'The team is nothing, and the fans are upset so they called for the coach and the directors to resign. Fans all over the world do that if they are angry with the performances of their team. It's a democratic means of expressing an opinion and it must be respected. But what I saw against National when the crowd started whistling and jeering was truly amazing. I saw fans being beaten by Gigi Becali's men. How can you beat a fan because he doesn't like how the team plays? In the Bernabéu, if 100,000 fans were waving their white handkerchiefs to protest about the performance of their team, can you believe that the Real Madrid president would send in gorillas to beat them up because the coach doesn't like to see the fans criticising him or the players?'

Steaua, of course, categorically denied the claims. 'I don't understand where this attitude against me has come from,' said Gigi Becali. 'He is godfather to my children, but that doesn't stop him having something against me. I still love him, because I understand he is just a weapon in the hands of others. Maybe nobody else will ever be born with his talent, but it seems now that he wants to be president of the country, run all of football and have people look at him as God. The only place he would ever beat me is on a football field. It would have been better if he had stayed out of this storm and held on to his crown as the king of football. I will not be evicted from Steaua, not by a hundred Hagis or by NATO troops.'

Amid all the sniping, the form of both sides suffered. Dinamo went on a run of one win in seven games, while Steaua took just four points from six home games. In Romania, though, there is no such thing as poor form, and

Gigi Becali blamed Nicolae Grigorescu, the head of the Romanian Referees' Commission, whom, he said, had had it in for him since a night in a casino when he refused to lend him £7,000. 'I used to think he was an honourable man,' he said. When Grigorescu dismissed the allegations, he went further. 'I would never have believed he could be such a good actor,' he said. 'Perhaps he missed his calling by becoming a referee.'

Piturca, meanwhile, decided those members of his squad who had signed up to Giovanni Becali's agency were to blame, and, calling them 'traitors', dropped the defenders Iulian Miu and Valeriu Bordeanu and the forward Ionel Danciulescu. 'Giovanni wants to ruin Steaua and make it easy for Dinamo to win the title,' Gigi Becali said. 'Anybody on his books is for Dinamo and against Steaua. He says he just wants to help players move abroad, but that is a lie. I know of players who have refused to sign for Steaua because Giovanni wants them to sign for him.'

Ostracised by Steaua, Danciulescu decided to return to Dinamo, whom he had left in acrimonious circumstances in 1998. His efforts against Manchester United in the third qualifying round of the Champions League in 2004–05, when he was denied a goal only by Mikaël Silvestre's determination to bundle the ball over the line himself, marked the final stage of his rehabilitation, but, back in 2002, Dinamo fans were deeply suspicious. A month after the derby, following some particularly vicious barracking during an away game at Bacau, he drove his jeep off the Ciurel Bridge and into the River Dâmboviţa. Luckily the vehicle landed the right way up, and he was able to swim to safety. Newspaper reports later claimed he had been drunk and that hospital staff had provided a urine sample for him; he maintained he was simply distressed.

At the derby itself, Danciulescu was booed by both sets of fans as he jogged out to warm up, setting the tone for an evening of needle and controversy. The game finished 2–2 and featured ten bookings and two red cards, but, in the bar afterwards, two incidents dominated conversation: Dinamo's opener, which followed a gratuitous foul by Claudiu Niculescu on the Steaua goalkeeper Martin Tudor; and a second-half handball that could have given Steaua a penalty. The referee, Cristian Balaj, everybody told me, must have been bribed, so that Dinamo would win the title. I pointed out that, while Niculescu's foul was obvious and really should have been given, the penalty appeal was a joke, the ball having been lifted into a defensive hand from a matter of inches. What about the game the day before, I was asked, when National drew disappointingly with Sportul Studentesc? Wasn't it obvious that the fixers had been in, that little National had been paid off? Well, not really, I said: National had hit the woodwork twice, and it seemed to me that they'd just had one of those days. I didn't understand, I was told: I was a naïve foreigner. In Romania, teams don't have just one of those days.

Three weeks later, National lost their final game of the season 2–1 in Craiova, while Dinamo beat Braşov 4–0 to take the title by two points; if their punishment for match-fixing against Ceahlaul had not been overturned, National would have been champions. Ceahlaul were relegated in 2004, suggesting the grip of the Cooperativa is weakening, and Rapid won the title again in 2003, but, essentially, by hook or by crook, the domination of the big two continues.

7 THE CAUCASUS

Wandering Rocks

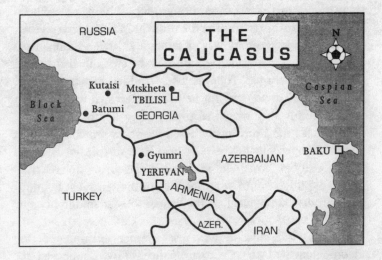

i Georgia

On 23 May 2001, as he did every day, Levan Kaladze took a taxi to the Tbilisi Railways Hospital where he was training to be a doctor. On this particular morning, though, as he walked from the cab to the hospital door, he was approached by three men in police uniform. There was a brief altercation, and then the men dragged him to their car, a white Niva, bundled him inside and sped off. Police later traced them as far as Mtskheta, just to the north-west of Tbilisi, but then the trail ran cold. That night, Kaladze's aunt received a telephone call directing her to a drop where the kidnappers had hidden a letter written by Levan. In it, he said he would be freed for a ransom of $600,000. Levan, whose brother Kakha had left Dynamo Kyiv for AC Milan four months earlier, has not been seen since.

The Ministry of the Interior believed Levan was being held

in the Pankisi Gorge, a lawless area of Akhmeta, north-east of Tbilisi, long identified by Russia as a bolt hole for Chechen rebels, and by the USA as an al-Qaeda stronghold. Three Red Cross volunteers and two Spanish businessmen were taken hostage there in separate incidents in 2000; none have ever been found. In Levan's case, though, for a couple of years at least, the kidnappers remained in touch. 'There were several telephone calls and anonymous letters,' Kaladze explained to me through Zaza Tsuladze, who was onefootball's correspondent in Georgia. 'Then they sent a video in which Levan was blindfolded, begging for help. I was terrified that I would say something that would stop us getting Levan back.'

Eventually the kidnappers offered a deal, by which Kaladze's father Karlo was to deliver $65,000 in cash to a wood near Khobi, a city in Samegrelo, in the west of Georgia, an area that has seen a huge influx of refugees from the separatist fighting in Abkhazia. Karlo went to the rendezvous at midnight, but when he asked to speak to Levan, the kidnappers panicked. For Karlo, the episode was just another example of the incompetence of the Georgian police. 'I was supposed to deliver the money, and the police were supposed to be waiting,' he said. 'But they failed, and they have never told me why.'

Kaladze's frustrations grew to the extent that he considered renouncing his Georgian citizenship to become a Ukrainian. His father threatened to set himself on fire in front of the Georgian parliament, calling it 'a disgrace' that the Italian prime minister Silvio Berlusconi – at the time, the president of AC Milan – seemed more interested in the case than the Georgian authorities. Two years after Levan's kidnapping, his family agreed to pay the kidnappers $200,000, plus an extra $100,000 if he was released within twenty days. They paid out the first instalment, but Levan is still missing.

Georgia is a dangerous, volatile place. I was fortunate that when I was there in June 2001, Georgia's relationship with its separatist regions had entered one of its less fraught periods. A

The young Siniša Mihajlović sporting the curls that earned him the nickname 'Barbika' (Barbie) after joining Red Star Belgrade in 1991; Zvonimir Boban and Robert Prosinečki line up ahead of Yugoslavia's World Youth Cup semi-final against East Germany in 1987.

Zlatko Zahovič and Srečko Katanec celebrate after beating Ukraine in a play-off to qualify for the 2002 World Cup; Red Star fans celebrate a goal in the derby against Partizan.

Georgi Asparuhov, the legendary Bulgarian, with his son in Sofia.

Restored after the revolution, the statue of Florin Piturca still stands alongside the mausoleum where his father used to sleep.

A statue in the wall of the Hanrapetakan Stadium, Yerevan.

Having displaced Stalin, Mother Armeni stands guard over the capital.

Sunflower seeds and cigarettes.
Traditional match-day fare in Tbilisi.

Anatoly Banishevsky, Azerbaijan's most
famous player and a keen amateur
photographer.

The Armazi Stadium,
home of WIT Georgia Tbilisi,
Georgian
champions in 2004.

Valentin Semiglazov in action for Neftchi against Dinamo Tbilisi.

Eduard Streltsov.

group of journalists who went to Tbilisi in March 2003 to cover Georgia's European championship qualifier against the Republic of Ireland, though, were held up at gunpoint on their first night and spent the rest of the trip holed up in their hotel. That is a shame, for Tbilisi is a lovely city, more Levantine than Soviet in feel, its hodge-podge of pleasantly shabby streets dotted with palm trees. That said, there is something unsettling about a place where the proprietor of a twenty-four-hour Internet café leaves his semi-automatic pistol lying on the counter. Most of my time in Tbilisi passed in an alcoholic haze, which is probably the best way to experience the Caucasus. Perhaps it is a need to assert their values given the proximity of the Muslim world, perhaps it is simply that there isn't much else to do, but Georgians have elevated drinking into a way of life, and, while there, I lived their way.

I went to Tbilisi partly to visit Zaza and his wife Natya, who translated for him, and partly to cover WIT Georgia Tbilisi's InterToto Cup-tie against SV Ried of Austria; the idea being to discover whether there was anywhere in the world that the competition had a purpose. WIT were forced to switch the game to the vast Boris Paichadze Stadium in central Tbilisi, after UEFA decided their usual home, the Armazi Stadium, was unsuitable. This kind of thing usually irritates me: clubs, I think, have a right to play at home, and if that means millionaire fancy-dans for once having to change in a concrete outhouse with only two showers and a cracked urinal for comfort, well, so be it. So, when, after a visit to the cathedral at Mtskheta with Zaza and Natya the day before the game, I discovered that the Armazi lay just off the road back to Tbilisi, I insisted on going to have a look. I hold my hands up: UEFA were absolutely right.

There was a set of goalposts at each end, and there were white lines wobbling through the grass, but, that aside, the only thing to mark it out as a stadium was a sliver of cracked concrete terracing, no more than six or seven steps deep, that staggered along the bank by one touchline. Empty football grounds, haunted by voices that echo back through the generations, can be profoundly melancholic places, but the Armazi didn't even feel empty. There was nothing to contain the nothingness: no stands, no terraces, not even a fence to act as a line of demarcation. It was just one field among many, devoid of cows, admittedly, and with slightly shorter and less patchy grass than the fields surrounding it, but essentially just another block of green in a rough swathe stretching all the way to the hill on which the church of Jvari perches. It was an undeniably beautiful spot, but it wasn't a football ground.

We hadn't been there long when the groundsman, clad incongruously in a shiny white Liverpool away shirt, scuttled up to see what we were doing. Natya explained I was a journalist, at which he stretched his arm towards the rutted, puddled pitch, and grumbled about a lack of resources. If the surface at the Armazi is typical, it is hardly surprising Georgians have a reputation for being superb dribblers who never pass the ball. I felt a little embarrassed for the groundsman, and would have left, but he insisted on showing us inside the concrete shack that served as dressing rooms. There were the odd trappings of professionalism – training bibs and cones strewn on the floor, a magnetic tactics board propped against the wall – but it's hard to imagine many British schools still put up with such spartan conditions. The groundsman led us into the showers, and, with a mighty yank, turned a lever on the wall. From two of the six shower-heads thin streams of water dribbled on to the concrete floor. I held my hand out, and wasn't at all surprised to find the water was cold.

The Paichadze, if anything, is an even sadder place than the Armazi. WIT – who are named after their sponsors, a company that, among other things, produces pet food – have never been anything. They are a small club with no history and no fans and the fact they play in a no-stadium is, although depressing, at least logical. The Paichadze is a different matter. It is one of those vast concrete bowls so beloved of the Soviets, constructed for Dinamo Tbilisi in 1976 as they approached the height of their powers. When Dinamo beat Liverpool in the European Cup in 1979, it is estimated that 110,000 fans, many of them uniformed police and army, squeezed on to the low wooden benches. These days, the benches lie in disrepair, splintered and broken, and replaced in the only part of the ground that is open by a few thousand desultory plastic seats. Downstairs, on the concourse, set into one of the massive struts that support the stand, is a photograph of Dinamo's 1981 Cup-Winners' Cup-winning side. With such talents as David Kipiani, Vitali Daraselia, Ramaz Shengelia and Alexander Chivadze, that was a great side – capable of fluid, technical football of the highest order. Two decades later, a case study in post-Soviet corruption and the perils of privatisation, they were struggling to survive.

Dinamo were founded in November 1925 by a merger of police, army and navy teams, and were run by the Interior Ministry, who believed a football team would help to promote fitness in the secret police. Stalin was a Georgian, and Lavrenty Beria overtly supported Dinamo, but that was not the advantage it might have seemed. It was not until 1964, eleven years after Stalin's death and Beria's subsequent execution, that Dinamo won the title for the first time, a failing that many Georgians believe to have been politically motivated. Boris Paichadze, after whom the stadium is named, was the great star of Dinamo in the years around the war, an elegant forward who earned the nickname 'the footballing Caruso' after a particularly impressive tour of Romania. Three times he inspired Dinamo to second place in the Soviet championship, three times to third, and three times he played on the losing side in Soviet Cup finals. 'Once I said to Beria that it would have been better if people could have said that Dinamo had been champions of the USSR several times,' Paichadze wrote in his memoirs. 'He went mad, and screamed that the champions could only be from Moscow or Kyiv, and said that we should just accept coming second.'

It was not until the late seventies that Dinamo enjoyed a sustained spell of predominance. Strongly supported by Eduard Shevardnadze, then the head of the Georgian Communist Party and later the president of an independent Georgia, and coached by Nodar Akhalkatsi, they won two Cups, the League and the Cup-Winners' Cup in the five years that followed the construction of the Paichadze. West Ham fans who were there still speak in awe of Dinamo's 4–1 win at Upton Park in the Cup-Winners' Cup quarter-final in March 1981. Dinamo went on to win the competition that season, and reached the semi-finals as defending champions, but, later that year, Daraselia, who had scored the winner against Carl-Zeiss Jena in the 1981 final, was killed in a car crash (Kipiani, who had provided the assist, died in a similar way twenty years later), and their period of achievement came to an end.

Independence, though, brought immediate success, as Dinamo dominated the Georgian championship, becoming the first European side to win ten successive league titles. There may have been triumph on the pitch, but off it affairs were sliding into chaos. Dinamo were privatised in 1992, with the Ministry retaining a tenth of the club through the Dinamo Sports Association, a further tenth going to Merab Zhordania, a former player who was appointed president, and the remaining 80 per cent to Merab Ratiani, the president of Bermukha, a company specialising in transportation and the manufacture of chocolate. He was a member of the Mkhedrioni, the nationalist paramilitary and political organisation established by Jaba Ioseliani in 1989, which, presenting itself as a modern equivalent of the Georgian guerrilla groups that fought against Persian, Ottoman and Russian rule – the word translates roughly as 'horsemen' – was instrumental in deposing Zviad Gamsakhurdia as president and replacing him with Shevardnadze in 1992.

The first scandal wasn't long in coming. It wasn't until

1993 that the champions of the independent Georgian league were admitted to European competition, by which time Dinamo had already won four Georgian titles. Their run in the Champions League, though, consisted of a single qualifying round tie against Linfield, after which they were expelled from the competition for having attempted to bribe the Turkish referee. That, of course, cast doubt on the integrity of their championship successes, but in a country where corruption had become a way of life, nobody seemed particularly concerned. Financially, meanwhile, Dinamo seemed hugely successful, operating, as Dynamo Kyiv had, effectively as an import-export business, tax breaks having been secured for them by the Mkhedrioni. 'The Georgian mafia at Dinamo concealed $28million from their budget,' the reformist politician Givi Targamadze later claimed. 'They imported oil and grain to Georgia and paid no tax on it.'

Certainly something curious was going on with the club's finances, because, despite several significant player-sales, they declared themselves bankrupt in 2000. Ioseliani had by then been arrested, while Zhordania, having become president of the Georgian Football Federation (GFF) in 1998, had given up the presidency of Dinamo Tbilisi. Suspicious of the import-export business, the Ministry of Internal Affairs began to investigate the club, despite effectively owning 10 per cent of it. Ratiani was arrested in July 2000, after allegedly attempting to divert a significant slice of the fee from the sale of Georgi Demetradze to Alania Vladikavkaz into his own bank account. He was released in December 2000 after paying a £45,000 fine.

After Ratiani's arrest, the focus turned to Zhordania, who, it was alleged, had a secret bank account in Switzerland into which he creamed off a share of the transfer revenues received by the club. When police went to interview Zhordania late in October 2001, though, they discovered he had left the country a couple of weeks earlier. The general secretary of the GFF, Valery Cholaria, insisted he was merely away on holiday, admitted he had no idea where, but said Zhordania would return in the first week of December. By November, Georgian police announced they were preparing to launch an international manhunt, only for Zhordania to reappear, as Cholaria had said he would, at the beginning of December. He had been – and, bearing in mind his banking arrangements, it would take a face of stone not to raise an eyebrow – in Switzerland. 'I haven't committed any crime,' he said. 'I wasn't hiding anywhere, and I have nothing to hide. I was on vacation, but now I've come back, and I'm ready to answer all questions. These accusations are absurd. No secret account exists at the Finanz Bank and none ever did. Everybody knew about that account. I was president of Dinamo Tbilisi at that time and I personally opened that account, as UEFA had requested, in order to receive financial help from them.' He spent forty-five days in prison in 2003, but was released when he repaid $350,000 into club funds. He finally resigned as president of the GFF in April 2005, after again being arrested, this time on charges of embezzling $10million from Dinamo between 1997 and 2000.

It had been long established that something was seriously amiss, and in February 2001 FIFA banned Dinamo from any transfer activity after an investigation revealed that not a penny from the sales of Levan Kobiashvili, Levan Tskitishvili and Alexander Iashvili to Freiburg; Rati Aleksidze to Chelsea; Khaka Kaladze to Dynamo Kyiv; and Demetradze and Mikhail Ashvetia to Alania, had ended up in club accounts. That was when the Georgian fourth division side Mretebi saw fit to mention that, according to the deal by which they had sold Georgi Kinkladze to Dinamo in 1993, they were owed 8.5 per cent of the £2million for which he had joined Manchester City in 1995.

At that stage, it appeared, with Dinamo in desperate need of new investors, that a consortium headed by Revaz Arveladze, a former Georgia international and the brother of Archil and Shota Arveladze – themselves both internationals and, at the time, of Cologne and Ajax respectively – would take over, but, with financial investigations ongoing it was decided to put the club completely under the control of the Ministry of the Interior. '[Revaz] Arveladze came to me with a plan,' Targamadze, then the Minister of the Interior, explained, 'and they had a foreign investor who would take care of the club. I don't doubt his honesty, but there are serious criminal organisations who stole millions of dollars from the club. The Ministry of Internal Affairs was investigating the case, and so it was appropriate that they should take charge of the club.'

Later in 2001, the Ministry sold 90 per cent of the club to Sport World Partnership, a company registered under British law in Gibraltar and owned by Badri Patakartsishvili. Born in Tbilisi in 1953, he had worked in the Maud-Kamvol textiles factory before moving to Moscow in 1991, where, through dealings in the auto trade, he became an associate of the Russian oligarch Boris Berezovsky. Having been welcomed into the so-called 'Family' of wealthy businessmen that surrounded President Yeltsin, Patakartsishvili invested in such companies as Logo Vaz, Aeroflot, Lada, ORT and TV6 – all large organisations undergoing hasty privatisation.

Until 2001, he and Berezovsky also jointly owned 50 per cent of shares in the oil giant Sibneft, the rest of the company belonging to Roman Abramovich. Berezovsky claims that the two of them were forced to sell their half of the company to Abramovich for $1.3billion – a figure he believes to be between a third and half the true value – or face seeing Sibneft destroyed by the new Russian president Vladimir Putin, who had by then begun his crackdown on the Family. Soon afterwards, the Russian Prosecutor General's Office issued a warrant for Patakartsishvili's arrest after he repeatedly failed to report for questioning over his part in an attempt by Nikolai Glushkov, a former deputy general director of Aeroflot and another Berezovsky protégé, to flee the country. Offered asylum by Shevardnadze, Patakartsishvili fled to Georgia. Having liquidated his Russian assets, he initiated a series of projects, buying health resorts in Ureki and Kobuleti in the west of Georgia, beginning construction of a harbour on the Black Sea at a cost of $1 billion, founding the TV company Imedi, and investing in Dinamo, to whom he promised Champions League football within four seasons.

That always seemed a ludicrous boast, but Dinamo, their finances stabilised, did at least win the league again in 2003, ending three years of dominance by Torpedo Kutaisi. It was WIT, though, who, extraordinarily, given their evident poverty, took the title in 2004, beating Sioni Bolnisi in a championship play-off that took over three hours to complete because of crowd trouble in which two fans were stabbed. Sioni were subsequently banned from competing in the 2004–05 UEFA Cup, and their assistant coach suspended for attacking the referee.

That at least speaks of passion, of which there was conspicuously little at the InterToto game against SV Ried. Most of the crowd seemed to regard the game as little more than an inconsequential backdrop to their consumption of sunflower seeds. WIT won 1–0 despite having a man sent off, but none of the 6,000 crowd seemed that bothered. Yet 6,000 is a large attendance for Georgian football; we may mock the InterToto, but it is one of the highlights of the Georgian football calendar.

With a couple of minutes remaining, Zaza abruptly left his seat and went to talk to a balding man sitting a few rows in front. He came back and muttered something to Natya, who proudly announced that Rezo Dzodzuashvili had granted us an interview. He, I was vaguely aware, had just been sacked as joint national coach after his co-coach David Kipiani had resigned, and had responded with a rant at Zhordania. The details were far from clear in my mind, but it seemed senseless, not to say rude, to turn him down, so, when the final whistle blew, we went to meet him at the front of the stand.

It was one of those desperate interviews in which you

realise early on that your interviewee is not being helpful and that you can think of only about two questions to ask him. All journalists must have experienced the awful sinking sensation – if they haven't, it simply means they've never interviewed Darius Vassell, the king of the monosyllable – and there's really nothing you can do other than blunder to as swift a conclusion as you can, while still retaining some shred of dignity. At least I had the time it took Natya to interpret, to think.

'So, can you explain the circumstances surrounding your dismissal?'

'I have not lost my job. I am coach of Torpedo Kutaisi.'

'Yes, but your dismissal from the job of national coach?'

'I am no longer coach, but I'm sure the team will continue to prosper.'

'How is your relationship with the Georgian Football Federation?'

'Fine.'

And so it went on – going nowhere. When, after a couple of minutes I glanced round for inspiration, I became aware for the first time that behind me had gathered a jostling crowd of probably around fifty people, all straining to hear Dzodzuash-vili's words of wisdom while Zaza attempted to keep them at a reasonably discreet distance. At that, I lost all self-control, thanked Dzodzuashvili sincerely and snapped off my Dicta-phone. I later checked what he'd said when he'd first been sacked, and discovered he'd claimed that Kipiani and Zhorda-nia had picked the team for defeats to Italy, Hungary and Romania, whereas he'd been in charge of the victory over Lithuania.

That night, I had dinner with Zaza and Natya and a group of their friends in a fantastic hill-top restaurant overlooking the city. We were to eat, we were told, in the traditional Georgian manner, which, for all the sophistication of the local cuisine, basically means with lots of wine and a fair amount of vodka. Zaza was appointed *tamada*, putting him in charge of the toasts. In theory, how much you down from your glass indicates how heartily you agree with the toast, but in practice it's very hard not to down the lot every time. How, after all, can you show any reserve in drinking to the hospitality of your hosts, or the beauty of Mother Georgia, or even, when raised in an effort to be accommodating, the good health of the Queen? At least the glasses offered a choice: if we'd really been doing it properly, I was told, we'd have been drinking from hollowed-out horns, which can't be put down until they've been drained. The final toast, drunk with large glasses of vodka to underline its importance, was to football, and its ability to draw people together. Trite and sentimental, perhaps, and wholly disregarding of the rampant corruption, but at the time nothing had felt truer.

ii Armenia

When they made the trip to Armenia to face Dinamo Yerevan in September 1949, Dinamo Moscow were on their way to a fifth league title. After thirty-five minutes, though, they found themselves 3–0 down, and, despite pulling one back two minutes before half time, there was still a real possibility of a shock that could have derailed their championship charge. That, clearly, wouldn't do, so General Blinov, deputy minister of the Ministry of State Security, telephoned the government room at the stadium and ordered the Armenian Minister of the Interior, Comrade Grigoryan, to take measures to ensure victory for Dinamo Moscow. Hearing the conversation, one of the heads of the Sports Committee of the Armenian Republic, an apparatchik whose name survives only as Simonyan, is said to have gone pale and whispered, 'The people will not understand.' Grigoryan, though, went to the Yerevan coach, Boris Apukhin, and explained the situation. He responded by replacing one of his experienced defenders with a youth-team player. Even worse, when the teams came out for the second half, a sinister figure in a black coat took up a position behind the Yerevan goal, every now and again hissing 'Miss!' when the goalkeeper went to gather a shot. Dinamo Moscow, not surprisingly, came back to win 4–3. Dinamo Yerevan's next game was away to Stalinabad (now Dushanbe), a trip that necessitated a flight via Moscow. On arrival in the capital the players were thanked by General Blinov, and each given a gift of 2,500 roubles.

Were they cheated? Were Dinamo Tbilisi prevented from winning the title? Were Dynamo Kyiv really opposed by Moscow? When everybody accuses everybody else, it is hard not to conclude that conspiracy is just an easy excuse. That tale has obvious elements of mythology, but the gist is probably true: no nation has been so put upon as the Armenians. In his final public speech, delivered in Liverpool in 1896, William Gladstone spoke of them as 'a martyred people' and said, 'Of all the nations of the world, no history has been so blameless as the history of the Armenian people'. The following century brought massacres at the hands of two different enemies and a devastating earthquake; suffering has become a national characteristic.

The first thing that struck me about Armenia was how much smoother the road became once I'd crossed the border from Georgia. The second, when our minibus stopped by a low hut just before the road wobbled into a steep-sided cutting, was that the smell of damp woodsmoke mingling with coffee steam is the greatest known to man. That was a chilly morning, the cloud squatting low over the Caucasus and casting everything in soft focus, but, sitting outside on a rough-hewn bench, eating lamb freshly grilled over an open fire, was one of those moments when all seems perfect with the world. That journey from Tbilisi to Yerevan is one of the most beautiful I have ever made, seven hours of rocky crags, deep gorges and mist-shawled valleys. Even the border post, by a bridge strung high above a frothing river, was spectacular, the view itself well worth the $20 bribe I had to pay for a visa.

Yerevan, itself, is a strikingly unusual city, constructed almost entirely of pink stone, and dominated by Mount Ararat, which looms on the horizon, just over the border with Turkey. There was something weird about the sun there as well; just as the light seems somehow thinner in northern cities such as Gothenburg or St Petersburg, so in Armenia it seemed thicker, as though what I were seeing was not the city itself, but the city as it would look in an over-coloured postcard from the sixties. That first evening I wandered up through Victory Park towards the huge statue of Mother Armenia that glowers down from the plinth on the hill where Stalin used to stand, past the fountains that, at the time, the government couldn't afford to run, and paused on the way back for a beer or two. On the wall of the tennis club opposite, I noticed, there were three huge photographs of Andre Agassi. That seemed a little odd, but then again, I reasoned, it was a tennis club. As I walked back towards the hotel, though, I became aware that Agassi was everywhere – his face on billboards, his name scrawled in graffiti.

Agassi is, as the receptionist in the hotel told me, 'Armenian by blood'. So, too, are Youri Djorkaeff and Alain Boghossian, both of them members of the France squads that won Euro 2000 and the World Cup two years earlier. Invaded variously by Persia, Turkey and Russia, mass migrations have been a regular part of Armenian history, and the diaspora has been so accepted as a fact of life that it is a point of pride that there is an Armenian community in virtually every country in the world. There is a curious sense in examining Armenian football that Armenia is not the place to start.

Certainly Djorkaeff, brought up in Décines near Lyon, is highly sensitive to his dual background. 'My first country is France,' he explained, 'but I would never forget that I have a very strong Armenian streak, and that when I speak up for that, I am speaking not just for a cause that is mine, but also my grandparents'. That runs in my blood.' He is Armenian through his mother, while his father, Jean, who also played for France, is a Kalmuck, one of an ethnic group based on the north-western shore of the Caspian Sea.

Djorkaeff first visited Armenia in 1999 to play for France in a friendly. It was a trip that clearly left a lasting impression. 'My father was the only one who had been to Armenia,' he said. 'When I set off I was there to win a match, but now I recall faces, images. I saw Lake Sevan and Echmiadzin [the religious capital], and of course I liked them, but I wasn't there to be a tourist. I walked in the street and met people. It really was extraordinary. They treated me like a head of state. I'd had no idea how they saw me in Armenia. President Kotcharyan gave me an Armenian passport, which is a symbol for my family, our history, Décines and the Armenians of France. I want to share these honours with all the Armenians I represent. When I was champion of Europe or the world, it was the Armenians of France who were champions of the world.'

There is a sense, not merely from Djorkaeff, that to be an Armenian is something that transcends national boundaries, that there is something that binds all Armenians, wherever they live. Djorkaeff spoke of a strength drawn from a common sense of adversity, of a will to survive that is passed on through the generations. 'All people who have suffered draw strength from their misfortune, and the trace of their trials is without doubt registered in the genes,' he explained. 'When you have grandparents who have suffered, who have lived through things through which you will never live, you don't have the right to complain, but there is a lesson to be learned, and it can really become a strength. My grandparents never complained and that has served as an example to me.'

In that context it is perhaps not surprising that it was at the Armenian Theological Seminary in Calcutta, the destination of one of the earliest migrations, that, in 1890, the first Armenian football club was established. By 1900 there were two Armenian clubs in the Turkish port of Izmir (or Smyrna, as was) and, before long, Tork and Araks were founded in Istanbul (then Constantinople). Armenians also had significant parts to play in the development of the game in various parts of the Russian empire. Martin Merzhanov, the founder of the seminal magazine *Football-Hockey Weekly*, for instance, although born in Nakhichevan-na-Donu, was of Armenian heritage, as was the Kuban-born Abram Dangulov, who managed Krylya Sovetov and Spartak Moscow and discovered a number of greats including Nikita Simonyan. It was not until 1920 that the first official game was played on Armenian soil, Kumayri (which became Leninakan in Soviet times and is now Gyumri) beating Yerevan 3–1 in the English Garden in the capital.

The first Armenian championship was established in 1936, and was won by Dinamo Yerevan, with Spartak Yerevan finishing second. Both applied to the Supreme Council for Physical Culture to be admitted to the Soviet Supreme Championship. The request was met, but in a typically puzzling way, with Spartak being placed in Group D (the fourth division) and Dinamo in Group E (the fifth); the result, according to Ghazaros Teknejyan, Spartak's goalkeeper at the time, of lobbying by Nikolay Starostin, the chairman of the Spartak Voluntary Sports Society. It was only after the Second World War and the forced repatriation of hundreds of thousands of Armenians that football really took off in what remained the smallest of the Soviet republics. Even then, though, Armenian clubs seem never to have been taken particularly seriously, to have been there primarily to make up the numbers and reflect the greater glory of those clubs preferred by the state.

Ararat Yerevan would become the great Armenian team, but Dinamo Yerevan were the first to play in the Soviet top flight, earning promotion in 1948. Success, though, was denied them by the usual tangle of Machiavellian intrigue and the fact that they weren't very good. There is, for once, clear evidence of interference, although it seems less that Armenians were targeted than that they were considered exploitable. Inspired by their goalkeeper Sergey Zatikyan – who kept twenty-seven clean sheets that season, including twelve in succession – Spartak went unbeaten through the 1954 season to finish top of one of the three parallel second divisions, and reached the Cup final, where they had realistic hopes of upsetting Dynamo Kyiv. Unfortunately, 1954 was the 300th anniversary of Ukraine's unification with Russia, and so, at least if the Armenian version of the story is to be believed, the authorities in Moscow decided it would be fitting if a Ukrainian side won the Cup, a gesture the noted Russian referee Nikolay Latyshev, who took charge of the 1962 World Cup final, supported wholeheartedly enough to disallow an apparently legitimate Spartak goal, deny them two penalties and then allow a Dynamo winner from an offside Mikhail Koman. As if Latyshev's performance weren't bad enough, Axel Vartanyan, the doyen of Soviet football historians, later uncovered a document from a conference of Soviet football doctors the following January in which the Dynamo Kyiv physio Yuriy Bezyinnyi admitted his players had habitually used illegal stimulants that season. Vartanyan, it should be added, despite being of Armenian blood himself, is extremely doubtful of claims that that Cup final was fixed.

The sense of grievance in Yerevan, though, was only to intensify. Spartak finished fifth of six in the promotion play-offs that year and so remained in the second division, but the following season they were on course to finish top again (this time the second flight was split into two rather than three groups), when they met Dom Ofitseov Sverdlovsk, an army team and their main challengers, in Yerevan on 9 October. With five minutes remaining, and the scores level at 2–2, Haroutiun Karajyan scored what seemed to be the winner Spartak needed to go top of the table, only for the Moscow-based referee, a Comrade Shvetsov, to rule it out, igniting a near-riot in the Hanrapetakan Stadium. As the disorder spread into the streets, players and officials had to be secretly transported from the stadium. The leadership of the Armenian Sports Committee was dismissed, but a protest was sent to the Section of Soviet Football (SFS) nonetheless, and they ordered the game to be replayed in Odessa. Very early in the rematch, Sverdlovsk were awarded a penalty, which they converted to secure their promotion.

Spartak Yerevan did finally win their promotion to the top flight in 1959, but it was Ararat Yerevan who gave Armenian football its greatest moment. They took their place in the Supreme League in 1966 and never relinquished it, and, with such players as Eduard Markarov and Arkady Andriasyan – not to mention Sergey Bondarenko, a player who scored so often with long-range drives that it became a common joke to say that 'he had scored from the fish shop' that stood a couple of miles down the road from the Hrazdan Stadium – became one of the dominant forces in Soviet football in the early seventies. The golden year was 1973, when, under Nikita Simonyan, they did the double. 'It was much harder to win the league with Ararat than it was with Spartak Moscow,' Simonyan told me. 'We had some good players, but essentially we were a provincial side. I had to change my personal style, because the players had a different mentality. We had two Ukrainians in the side, but they had lived in Yerevan from childhood, so they had adopted the spirit of the people. Players from the south are more skilful, more technical, even if it is bad for the team as a collective. You have to stick them to each other.'

Ararat, named after a mountain that most Armenians believe should lie on their side of the Turkish border, even more than Dynamo Kyiv, became a locus for nationalism. 'In Ukraine there were five teams,' Simonyan said, 'but in Georgia or Armenia only one, so these really were the teams of the republic. They were financed from the budget of the republic, and the politicians paid a lot of attention to the performance of the team.'

Fans would chant 'Haya-stan, hoop-tor' (Come on, Armenia') or simply 'Hayar' ('Armenians') followed by three short claps, both refrains that were taken up by the independence movement. That nationalist spirit had its most obvious outpouring on the night of the Cup final in 1973, when Ararat, facing Oleksandr Sevydov's Dynamo Kyiv, had the chance to avenge Spartak's defeat to the same opponents nineteen years earlier. It was, by all accounts, an outstanding game, which, with two minutes remaining, Dynamo were leading 1–0. Sevydov then decided to withdraw Oleh Blokhin and Victor Kolotov, two of his best players, and, a minute later, the Ararat number eight Levon Ishtoyan broke into the box and slammed an equaliser into the top corner. In extratime he added a second to the disbelief and delight of the 15,000 Armenians in the Luzhniki. Back in Yerevan, car horns were sounded through the night, nationalist songs were sung and, in tribute to Ishtoyan, the number eight was painted on the back of the Lenin monument in Republic Square.

The paint was soon removed, and Lenin too has now disappeared, the place where his statue stood marked only by a patch of dead grass. Ararat, similarly, are not what they once were. Now that independence has been won, there is no need to use their games as a stage to protest for it, and their crowds have slumped to only a few hundred; perversely, Armenian football is now suffering because they have stopped being persecuted. Ararat were even suspended from competition for the 2003 season after their head coach, Arkady Andriasyan, refused to allow one senior and four junior members of his squad to join up with the Armenia squad for training matches in Israel, concerned, he said, over safety. Ararat's sponsors reacted by dismissing Andriasyan and merging Ararat with another team they backed, Lernagorts from Kapan. They appointed a new coach and director, but Andriasyan's suspension was lifted on the eve of the thirtieth anniversary of the double success, and he was reappointed coach at the beginning of 2005. With the emergence of powerful sponsors from the diaspora – the American businessman Hrach Kaprielian and Vardan Surmakesh, the president of the Swiss company Frank Müller – they welcomed Andriasyan's return with bullish noises about restoring the team to its former glory. Whether that is possible, given the apathy that independence has brought, is doubtful.

About sixty miles north of Yerevan is Tsakhadzor, which was once a state-of-the-art Soviet Olympic training complex, and now operates as a half-hearted tourist resort. The name means 'Valley of the Flowers', and when I was there, it seemed the flowers were reclaiming their valley. It was an eerie place, set high in the mountains, the wind whistling through its emptiness as though it were a lost Inca city, abandoned in a moment at some unknown catastrophe. It was there, in 1987, that Robert Emmiyan set the European long-jump record with a leap of 8.86 metres, which, at the time, was the second-longest jump in history. A decade and a half later, though, the sandpit was waist-high in rosebay willowherb. A few yards away, across a cracked and faded running track, was an overgrown football pitch. Climbing a little through the pines, I came to the swimming pool, empty but for a sludgy covering of dark-green weed. Just above that was the gymnasium, on the wall of which, beneath a stylised mural of a gymnast, was written the Olympic motto: Citius, altius, fortius. Bleak irony was a particularly Soviet trope.

The catastrophe here, though, is not unknown. On 7 December 1988, Armenia suffered a massive earthquake that claimed over 30,000 lives and destroyed huge numbers of buildings. The quake was centred near the northern city of Spitak, but it is estimated that a third of the country was affected. The economy was further destabilised by the war with Azerbaijan over the disputed region of Nagorno-Karabakh, which led to the influx of several hundred thousand refugees. By 1993, many Armenians could survive only with the help of relatives from abroad, while electricity was often available only for an hour or two a day. Conditions got so bad that around a million Armenians left the country in the five years following independence. Investing in sport would have been a ludicrous extravagance.

In football, the first years after independence, as they were elsewhere, were marked by confusion over the league structure, withdrawals, walkovers, bankruptcies, and politicking within the federation. Presidents arrived and disappeared almost as regularly as match-fixing was alleged. Remarkably, the first independent championship was won jointly by Shirak Gyumri, a team from the area worst affected by the earthquake. Poignantly, the brochure they produced ahead of that first season contained the pictures of three players – Albert Akimyan, Sargis Sahakyan and Gevork Vardikyan – who had been killed in the disaster. Led by their controversial president Garnik Khachatyan, they were the only team to compete in each of the first twelve championships, winning three of them, despite paying wages of only around $50–100 a month and refusing to sign any foreign players. They finished bottom of the eight-team first division in 2004, but retained their place in the top flight not, the Football Federation of Armenia announced, 'as indulgence to some particular team, but as the first step of planned enlargement of the league to fourteen clubs'.

It is Homenetmen, though, whose progress is most representative of the chaos of the Armenian league. By the second season they had acquired a sponsor and were known as Homenetmen-AOSS, and the year after that they became ASS-SKIF. They were back to plain old Homenetmen for the transitional 1995 spring season, by which time Homenmen, an entirely different team, had emerged. Homenetmen then became Pyunik (which translates as Phoenix) and won the championship in 1995–96, retaining it the following season.

In 1999 (the seasons having reverted to spring–autumn), Pyunik's founder, Ruben Hayrapetyan, withdrew his financial backing, and the entire playing staff joined Kilikia. They then lost a relegation play-off, but Homenmen, who were by then known as Erebuni, withdrew from the following season's championship along with FK Yerevan, allowing Kilikia to retain their place. They played the following season without incident, but in 2001 were expelled from the league for non-payment of fees after playing a single match. Confusingly, that match was a 3–2 defeat against a side called Pyunik. They had been restored by Hayrapetyan, and took their place in the first division after Armenikum, one of the promoted sides, were disbanded by their sponsors. The new Pyunik went on to win the next four championships, including a run of fifty-nine games unbeaten between October 2002 and November 2004. The excellent rsssf website, in an exasperated footnote, explains it has taken the decision to refer to this new entity as Pyunik [II].

The first three of those championships were won at a canter, but, gradually, other teams are beginning to challenge their dominance. Banants, for instance, who finished third in 2004, show how clubs can regroup after financial difficulties. They were founded in 1992 by Sargis Israelyan, who demanded his side should play open, attacking football. That May they were rewarded with victory over Homenetmen in the first independent Armenian Cup final, but, three years later, they went out of business. Israelyan refounded the club in 2001. 'The team of the nineties was better equipped technically and played more romantic football,' Israelyan said. 'Nowadays our teams are more athletic and rely on pace and the functional qualities of players. That it is now a prerequisite for success.' The club also now runs a football school – 'an economic necessity', according to Israelyan; pragmatism is replacing romance, and the traditional, free-spirited Armenian style is disappearing.

Perhaps it was because I'd significantly overpaid him, but the taxi driver who brought me back from the cathedral at Zwartnots was hugely friendly. He knew about a dozen words of English, and I about half that in Armenian, but he gave me some apricots, bought from an old woman by the side of the road, and then, after I had somehow explained that I wrote about football for a living, he insisted on taking a detour. 'No extra, no extra,' he assured me. As he turned a corner, I saw, looming ahead of us, the new national stadium, itself a symbol of Armenia's economic upturn. Modern stadia tend to follow a similar pattern from Manchester to Mali – all functional concrete and coloured steel – but the Hanrapetakan was a welcome exception, featuring, midway up the main stand, a number of archways in which stood bronze statues of figures from classical mythology.

I wandered admiringly up and down the car park for a while, then the driver beckoned me to a gate at one end of the stand. It was locked, but between the hinges and the wall there was a gap, through which, after much badgering from the driver to overcome my nervous reluctance, I squeezed. Inside, the ground was decorated in a more orthodox fashion, although the normal rounded rectangle was pressed out at one side to accommodate the 100m track, so from above it would have resembled a giant omega. After drifting aimlessly around for a bit and trying out a few seats, I realised that once the adrenaline rush has passed, there's not a lot you can do after breaking in to a national stadium, so I broke out again.

The next morning, I took the misguided decision to have breakfast at the hotel. A wizened old man in a stained maroon uniform slapped a plate of limp salad and tough cheese down in front of me, and then gave me a thimbleful of thick orange-coloured juice. I drained it, and asked if I could have some more. The waiter looked at me, snapped 'No', turned away and wandered off to be surly elsewhere. The Soviet hangover, clearly, has not entirely gone.

Generally, though, Armenia, like a Pyunik, is on the rise. The water features leading up to Mother Armenia are working again, the Northern Avenue – designed by the great Armenian architect Alexander Tamanyan in the 1920s but never built –

is finally being constructed and the roads have been improved so the journey to Tbilisi takes only four and a half hours. Tsakhadzor is being restored, and Republic Square now boasts 2,750 fountains. The football, too, is improving, and great hope rides with Edgar Manucharyan, a talented young forward who joined Ajax in the summer of 2005.

If international success remains a long way off, there are at least signs of clubs establishing themselves on pragmatic, businesslike lines; although it would be naïve to imagine that that does not also probably mean the involvement, at some level, of Armenia's criminal oligarchies. 'Football is like grape juice,' the Armenian writer Armen Nikoghosyan put it. 'From this, young wine can be prepared, or, if you wait a while longer, a stronger wine. You can take from this, spirit for the production of vodka, or distil the spirit one more time, pour it into oak casks and wait until it has become cognac. The more effort and money we spend, the more Armenian football will develop, but at the moment we can speak only of a positive tendency after years of fermentation.'

True as that may be, Armenia's greatest contribution to world football remains in having provided the cognac with which Valeriy Lobanovskyi pickled himself.

iii Azerbaijan

On the Tuesday, the sky was blue, the weather was warm and the sun shone. Azerbaijan and an England World Cup qualifier seemed a very pleasant way to earn a living. Baku, though, is not known as the city of the winds without reason. By the Wednesday morning, the sky was sepia and 70 m.p.h. gusts and squalls of rain were pummelling the town. This, Richard Williams of the *Guardian* discovered with remarkable alacrity, was the Khazri. Covering England seemed suddenly a dreadful punishment dreamed up by a malevolent god. There was a roof on the press box at the Tofik Bakhramov Stadium, but given the wind was blowing straight across the pitch, driving the rain horizontally, it hardly mattered. There was water on the desks, there was water on the chairs, and there was water in our laptops. The marquee where the post-match press conference was supposed to be held blew down.

It was so windy that even when there was a phone signal, which wasn't often, it was virtually impossible to hear the person at the other end. The *Financial Times* had to send me my wordage by text. Then, just as I was panicking about how to file, an Azerbaijani man in a beehive hat turned up and gave everybody a cable to connect to the local Ethernet, which, miraculously, worked perfectly. It didn't stop the cold, though. My hands were a pale mauve by the time the game came to an end, but I'd got enough of my match report done that, once the crowd had thinned, it seemed safe to nip off to the toilet. It wasn't the best convenience I've ever used, a badly tiled hole in the ground that was full to the brim and more, but it was only after I'd finished that the real flaw in the design became evident: as well as a bolt on the inside of the door, there was one on the outside, and somebody had locked it. I hammered on the door, to which a child's voice replied: 'Ten dollar'.

In retrospect, given there was urine and worse slopping about my feet, it doesn't seem that bad a deal (particularly if I could have got a receipt off him to claim expenses), but, quite aside from the fact that I had no money on me, after three hours of shivering frustration I wasn't about to be held to ransom, so I attacked the door with fury. Much pounding of fists and several screamed threats later, I realised that the kid had slipped the bolt. At that moment, though, a battalion of the Azerbaijani army decided to leave their positions around the perimeter of the pitch and return to the car park by a route directly between the toilet and my laptop. As I stood on a concrete outcrop watching the soldiers stream from a vast pool amassed behind one goal, the FT rang. I explained I'd file as soon as the army had got out of my way, and held up the phone. I don't know how many of the 1,500 pairs of feet they heard tramping past, but by the time the last soldier was out of the way, they'd hung up.

It was, I confess, a huge relief to get back to the hotel and warmed up that night, but by the morning I was feeling very sorry for Azerbaijan. The fans who had packed the press stand in the belief the roof might somehow keep off the horizontal rain had been remarkably good-humoured. They greeted every thirty-yard drive (and there were many) from an Azerbaijani forward with a sharp intake of breath as though it had skimmed just wide, before laughing uproariously because sometimes it hadn't even reached the goal line. The antics of Jakhangir Gasanzade in the Azerbaijan goal – unorthodox, bordering on the inept – were treated almost as a form of stand-up comedy. Yes, everything surrounding the match had been chaotic, but it was hardly anybody's fault that the Khazri had sprung up at just the wrong time and ruined what was probably the biggest match ever to be played in the country.

Actually, it wasn't just the wind. David Beckham had done his bit to take the lustre off the game, first by flying into a challenge with Ben Thatcher in the qualifier against Wales the previous Saturday and fracturing a rib, and then by charging into him again moments later, manufacturing a booking so that he served a suspension while injured and thus wiped his disciplinary slate clean. Everything leading up to the Azerbaijan match was dominated by Beckham's admission that he had deliberately engineered the yellow card; the match became a mere side issue to yet another Beckham saga. Sir Geoff Hurst said he had brought the nation into disrepute and should be stripped of the captaincy. Sven-Göran Eriksson, normally so placid and diplomatic, finally snapped in a press conference: 'Jesus,' he said to yet another question about on-field ethics. 'I'm not a schoolteacher or the father of a Sunday school.' It was all great copy and all great fun, particularly as nobody really took Azerbaijan seriously.

The people who missed out, though, were the Azerbaijani fans. Walking through the old town of Baku on the morning of the game, I was accosted by three kids, probably eight or nine years old, knocking around a saggy red football. In the small square beside the Maiden's Tower, we had a quick kickabout while they, apparently delighted to have met a real live Englishman, rattled off the names of most of the England squad. Then one of them, with a look of hurt, said, 'Why no Beckham?' I tried to explain, clutching my ribs and waving imaginary yellow cards, but rather wished I'd followed the example of Matt Dickinson from *The Times* who, asked the same question that evening, opened his mouth as if to launch into a full account, then thought better of it, and simply said: 'It's a long story.'

Azerbaijan had played Italy two years earlier, but it seemed that the arrival of England had been even more keenly awaited. That was partly because recent draws against Northern Ireland and Wales had fostered a belief that Azerbaijani football was on the rise, but more because Azerbaijan's greatest moment in football is inextricably linked to England's. The national stadium in Baku is named after Tofik Bakhramov, the linesman who judged that Geoff Hurst's shot on the turn ten minutes into extra-time in the 1966 World Cup final had bounced down off the bar and over the line, putting England 3–2 up against West Germany. Crassly, English fans have spent four decades being grateful to a 'Russian' linesman.

All technological evidence now suggests that Hurst's shot came down on rather than over the line, but it would be a brave man to say that in Azerbaijan. When Gamid Gamidov, the sports editor of the *Azeri Echo*, suggested Bakhramov had got his most famous decision wrong, he was deluged with letters accusing him of, to use Hurst's phrase, bringing the nation into disrepute. Arguably Bakhramov did that himself with a comment he is supposed to have made on his deathbed. Asked by a reporter, desperate to have his final thoughts on the controversy, how he could be sure the ball had crossed the line, Bakhramov apparently answered with a single word: 'Stalingrad.'

Gamidov may have his doubts about that decision, but when I suggested to him that naming a stadium and erecting a statue (Hurst was in Baku to unveil it) of a referee and linesman was perhaps a little unusual, he looked at me uncomprehendingly. 'No, no,' he said. 'He was a very good referee.'

That's as may be, but the lionisation of Bakhramov also speaks of a dearth of very good players. Azerbaijan's best was probably Anatoly Banishevsky, who is famous mainly for scoring with a header from forty yards in a friendly for the USSR against Brazil in 1965. The following year he was the inspiration behind the Neftchi side that finished third in the Soviet Supreme League, the highest position achieved by an Azerbaijani club. Truly, 1966 was Azerbaijani football's *annus mirabilis*. That season, over 40,000 would regularly turn out for home games, but, whether because of the relative lack of success or because of the large number of Russians working in the oil industry on which the club was based, Neftchi never seems to have had a nationalist focus. Azerbaijani football's nadir is equally obvious: the spell between May 2002 and May 2003, when the championship was suspended.

The Azerbaijani Football Federation (AFFA) was founded in 1992 under the leadership of Fuad Musaev, who had run football in the republic during Soviet times. He was, by all accounts, tough, passionate, charismatic and forthright. He oversaw AFFA's affiliation to UEFA and FIFA and secured funding for the building of an 8,000-capacity stadium in Baku. He had only two flaws: he was widely believed to be embezzling AFFA; and he showed blatant favouritism to Safa, who played in the stadium he had built.

It was in the 2001–02 season that matters came to a head. Several newspapers reported – although without, it must be said, much in the way of hard evidence – that Musaev had diverted $35million of UEFA and FIFA subsidies into a personal bank account in Switzerland. On the playing side, the championship was sliding into disarray. Virtually every club seemed to be in financial difficulty. The Ministry of Finance sold Dinamo Bakili's ground without their consent. Araz Nakhichevan – who had initially been suspended from the league for non-payment of their subscription fee, and had only been reinstated after another club, Vilas Masalli, were dissolved shortly before their opening match of the season – withdrew from the league after finishing the first part of the season in the lower half of the table and so being condemned to the relegation play-offs. 'The system is unacceptable,' their director Sudzhethan Novruzov suddenly decided. 'Playing for the bottom six places is absurd and we can't afford to waste money on it.'

It was on 2 April that farce became crisis. Going into injury time, Khazar University were holding out for a goalless draw away to Safa in the second round of games in the championship play-off. Injury time, though, went on, and on, and on, until finally – the official record says after five minutes, others claim it was after as long as twenty-seven – Safa were awarded a controversial penalty, which they converted to win 1–0.

The president of Khazar at the time was Hamlet Iysahamli, who remains director of the university. I met him in his office on campus, a large, book-lined room noticeably devoid of football memorabilia. He could, he told me, have become a professional chess player, but chose instead to become a professor of mathematics. With his soft, slightly high-pitched voice, gently crinkled face and attitude of benign detachment, he is an unlikely rebel, but it was he who brought down Musaev. Others saw Musaev as a corrupt tyrant, but Iysahamli spoke of him almost as a student who had disappointed.

'Under his presidency,' Iysahamli said, 'the federation was not run according to any rules but by what was in his own mind. He was in general a kind person, eager to develop football, but at the same time his ideas were untidy, and he had been one of the secretaries of the Communist Party in

Soviet times so he was used to getting his own way. He had some ideas about which teams should be first and second. Safa was his team and he had the idea that if most of the good young players could be put into that club, it could provide some kind of a base for the national team.'

The idea in itself was not a bad one. In Latvia, Skonto have effectively served as a nursery for the national side, Dynamo Kyiv provided the base of the USSR team in the seventies and eighties, and the great Hungary side of the 1950s was forged at Honvéd. The problem, though, was that a lot of talented young players preferred to play for Khazar University, where they could study for a degree as well as playing football. 'Our team was a little better, more disciplined and a little brighter,' Iysahamli said, 'and he didn't like it.'

There had been numerous allegations of match-fixing and a 'refereeing mafia' before, but it was events at the Safa Stadium that forced Iysahamli to act. 'It was o–o at ninety minutes,' he said. 'There had been five minutes added at the end of the first half, then five minutes added at the end of the second, and then again five minutes. Then in the twenty-seventh minute of added time, one of their players went down in the box, no contact – penalty – 1–0.' He shook his head as though still baffled by the obviousness of the scam. AFFA's disciplinary committee initially ordered the game to be replayed, but that decision was overturned on appeal. 'So I said that after that we could not continue to play in the league,' Iysahamli went on, sounding almost apologetic. 'Musaev said that it wasn't him, but that the referee was crazy and stupid and so on, but everybody understood. Then I rang my colleagues at the other clubs and invited them to come out with me. All of them stopped playing in the championship.'

On 12 April, the only game played in the championship play-off was Safa's o–o draw at home to Kapaz. By 4 May, with Neftchi taking the lead in the revolt, a new championship had been convened outside of AFFA's jurisdiction and without Safa. UEFA, whose policy in such instances is always to support the national association, refused to ratify it. Although Khazar joined the new competition, Iysahamli insisted he thought it was a bad idea and always sought reconciliation. 'It became a struggle for power,' he explained. 'Other people wanted to be president and Musaev used that to his advantage. So we had three groups: the president, the Neftchi faction who wanted their own league without any federation, and those like us who wanted one championship under the flag of the federation but with different rules.'

By the following November, the league had not restarted, so Neftchi organised an eight-club tournament – without Khazar – to celebrate their 65th-anniversary. Karabakh-Azersun Agdam took the title, beating Neftchi on penalties in the final. If that raised hopes that the league could be reconvened in some form, though, they were dashed four days later, when FIFA imposed a blanket ban on Azerbaijani clubs taking part in international competition, and, bewilderingly, decided that only Musaev had the right to lift the ban – as and when he decided that the situation had stabilised. The wrangling continued, with Musaev countering threatened votes of no confidence by insisting he could not call elections until the championship was under way again.

Even when, in January, the six regional football federations and eleven clubs took legal action against AFFA demanding the formation of a new association, Musaev seemed untroubled, but then the Ministry of Taxes began proceedings against AFFA to recoup a deficit of £300,000, apparently tax owed on gate receipts and TV revenues from the Euro 2004 qualifier against Italy. AFFA insisted they owed only £60,000, but their property and the Safa Stadium were seized, and the apartment of Oktay Zeynalov, the director-general of the federation, searched. He was arrested at the beginning of April, and immediately blamed Musaev for the shortfall. Iysahamli, who was a member of the executive committee throughout, explained how every time issues of accounting were raised, Musaev would say he was just about to have everything audited by a major Western company.

On 4 March, frustrated by the continued support given by UEFA and FIFA to Musaev, the eleven rebel clubs agreed to return to AFFA, on the condition that elections be held. AFFA replied with a list of fourteen requirements for each club to meet before the championship could be resumed, many of which were considered unreasonable. That led to another unofficial tournament, ten clubs taking part in the optimistically named Unity Cup, which was won by Neftchi.

By that stage the Ministry of Justice had begun proceedings against AFFA on the grounds that, as elections for the presidency should have been held the previous May, it was in violation of its charter. That finally moved the executive committee of AFFA to act, and on 7 April they attempted to hold an extraordinary general meeting. Musaev, knowing he would be forced to resign if fourteen of the twenty-one members of the committee voted against him, countered the threat by denying them access to the AFFA headquarters. The delegates held their meeting on the street outside and resolved that the championship should start on 20 April, and that a conference to elect a new president should be convened for 30 April. As only eleven members of the committee voted, though, leaving them three short of a quorum, Musaev declared their resolution void and dismissed the two vice-presidents who had organised the meeting.

A week later, the clubs and AFFA finally reached an agreement of sorts on the start of a new championship, determining both the format of the competition, minimum squad sizes, and registration fees, but the next day FIFA disqualified AFFA, an action in which they were soon followed by UEFA. Members of AFFA's executive committee responded by writing two letters: one to Musaev, encouraging him to open dialogue with his opponents; and another to the presidents of FIFA, UEFA and the Russian Football Union explaining the details of their dispute (when in doubt, it is still to Russia that the former Soviet republics turn).

UEFA responded in time-honoured fashion by establishing a committee, of which Iysahamli was a member. A new constitution was drawn up, and the championship finally began on 17 May. Musaev agreed to hold elections before the end of the year, but, filibustering magnificently, he managed to put them off until 29 December, when the Neftchi president Ramiz Mirzoev, who was also president of Azeri Neft Ianaga – the former state oil company – was elected, apparently on the assumption that, being independently rich, he would be less drawn to corruption.

The first impact of Mirzoev's appointment was to make the government more kindly disposed to football. Banks, factories and oil refineries have all been persuaded to sponsor clubs, while in the city of Yevlakh a group of businessmen got together to set up their own team, Karvan, in the summer of 2004. They were immediately admitted to the Premier League as it expanded to eighteen teams. There have been casualties, though. The league table is still riddled with asterisks denoting name changes as sponsors come and go and clubs shift from city to city. Khazar Sumqayit, promoted in 2003, have disappeared completely, while Safa withdrew from the league during the winter break in 2004–05 citing financial difficulties.

Referees are now paid five times what they were in Musaev's time, and the result is that they too seem less prone to accept financial inducements. Just as important, from both a coaching and a symbolic perspective, in February 2004 Carlos Alberto Torres, he of the thunderous right-foot shot that rounded off Brazil's 4–1 victory over Italy in the final of the 1970 World Cup, was appointed as national coach. The money to fund those two initiatives, though, had to come from somewhere, and it seems at least in part to have come from the pool for paying the national team's bonuses. In Musaev's day they used to get $3,000 to play, but even if they'd beaten England the players would have received only $2,000. That, inevitably, caused resentment among certain players, most notably the goalkeeper Dmitri Kramarenko. He announced the week before England arrived that he would not play for the national team again while Mirzoev remained president of AFFA – which at least gave the crowd the delights of Gasanzade's manic flailing.

His team-mate at the Russian second division side Baltika Kaliningrad, Emin Agaev, withdrew in sympathy. Others, though, just seemed happy that Azerbaijani football was up and running again. Kramarenko, after all, had a history of absentee-ism. Nobody else has been the victim of so many late strains, family crises and mysteriously cancelled flights. In August 2001, puffed by a move to Dinamo Moscow, he rejected a call-up for World Cup qualifiers against Moldova and Macedonia FYR, citing the poor standard of Azerbaijani football. A year later, having been persuaded back into the side, he failed to turn up for a Euro 2004 qualifier in Helsinki, claiming that thieves had broken into his car and stolen his passport. Most fans I spoke to in Baku seemed to acknowledge he was significantly the best goalkeeper in the country, but regarded his loss as an acceptable, perhaps even inevitable, sacrifice.

There were changes too at Khazar University, with Iysa-hamli stepping down as president as the International Bank of Azerbaijan invested in the club, which has been renamed Inter Baku. As elsewhere, money (some legal, some not), finally, is talking. 'In the new situation it was impossible for the university,' he explained. 'When I understood that under the new situation four or five clubs would have a budget of one million US dollars, we had to change. When my team was set up our budget was one hundred thousand dollars. So now they have more money and I'm sure they'll do very well.' I was just wondering whether there was a note of regret in his voice when he laughed. 'Actually, at the moment,' he said, 'they're only twelfth.'

*

By the time Azerbaijan arrived in Newcastle for a World Cup qualifier in March 2005, Kramarenko had returned, but the optimism had evaporated, its last traces dispelled by an 8–0 defeat to Poland the previous Saturday. The top scorer in the Azerbaijani league, Zaur Ramazanov, had just been suspended for attacking a linesman; Carlos Alberto had fallen out with most of his creative midfielders, while the irregularity of his visits to Baku was becoming a source of concern. 'He is picking the team by remote control,' moaned Rasim Kara, the coach of Khazar Lenkoran. Carlos Alberto resigned soon after.

Most of the criticism, though, was reserved for Mirzoev. 'He is lazy,' Iskender Javadov – one of the legends of Azerbaijani football – said in calling for his resignation. 'Mirzoev should visit regions, meet with representatives of the clubs. He believes he did a great thing in appointing Carlos Alberto, but it was only self-promotion. They spoke of qualifying for the World Cup, but now only fools can dream of it.'

Speaking of dreaming fools, AFFA attempted to put together a bid to host Euro 2012, which, given the problems in Azerbaijani football, falls into the category of running before you can crawl. Quite aside from the extinction of several clubs, allegations of match-fixing have resurfaced, leading Mubariz Mansimov, the owner of Khazar Lenkoran and the biggest investor in Azerbaijani football, to threaten to withdraw his club from the league.

Yet, as Iysahamli pointed out, for Azerbaijan the present situation represents an improvement. 'I don't think the situation is really excellent,' he said. 'We still have many problems, but now we have some kind of rules and people are following them. There is a lack of tradition, though, and this country has many problems that inevitably influence football. The rule of law is not always there, but I believe the situation is better than it was.'

8 RUSSIA
Fallen Idols

When Eduard Streltsov arrived at the dacha of Eduard Karakhanov on 25 May 1958, he had the world at his feet. He was twenty, widely recognised as one of the best footballers on the planet, and handsome to boot. He was as near as the Soviet Union got to a celebrity. A fortnight later, on the opening day of the World Cup, the USSR drew 2–2 with England in Gothenburg. Streltsov wasn't there. The finals would be dominated by Brazil, and by the emerging talents of the seventeen-year-old Pelé. In Russia they believe it could have been Streltsov's tournament, but he was in jail, awaiting trial for rape. He was convicted and sentenced to twelve years in the gulag. His guilt, though, remains questionable, and there are those who believe he was set up.

What happened at Karakhanov's dacha that night is the grand mystery of Russian football. There are a million explanations bound up in a million conspiracies, and the testimonies of those who were there have been skewed by time and drink, and possibly by deliberate falsification. There is even a campaign posthumously to clear Streltsov's name, led, incongruously, by the former world chess champion Anatoly Karpov and Yury Luzhkov, the mayor of Moscow.

If you want to know about Soviet football, at least a dozen people had told me, you must talk to Axel Vartanyan. Born in Tbilisi, he worked for many years as a schoolteacher, but is now the prime archivist of football in the Soviet era. I went to meet him at his apartment in an eastern district of Moscow.

Vartanyan is a not a tall man, and, with his thinning bouffant of snowy hair and his well-filled waistcoat, there is something of the hobbit about him. We chatted in his study, a room crammed with books and files, newspaper cuttings and photocopied documents, all meticulously annotated in his tiny, crabbed Cyrillic. The advent of computers seemed to have passed him by. After about three hours – by which time our conversation had drifted to my pet theory that a glut of great wingers in the early fifties (Matthews, Finney, Shackleton, Robb, Astall ...) had contributed to England's tactical Luddism – he asked his wife to bring a pot of tea and some marzipan cake (he doesn't drink coffee – bad for his heart), and then we talked some more. Poor Vladimir, formerly onefootball's correspondent in Russia, who was acting as my fixer and translator, looked exhausted. We spoke of many things, but, mostly, we spoke of Streltsov. 'For me,' Vartanyan said, 'Streltsov is a weakness. I had no idols but him. Not just for his skills, but as a person, for what he represents.'

Before I met Vartanyan I had half a notion that Streltsov represented something quite profound. After talking to him, I was convinced of it. Streltsov, I would argue, has immense symbolic value. I would say he has come to stand for nothing less than the unblemished soul of Russian football. In a world of intrigue and state oppression, Streltsov was heroically independent.

*

While others remember the 1952 Olympics as the first flowering of Hungary's *Aranycsapat*, in the USSR it is recalled for causing the break-up of what was arguably the greatest club side Russia ever produced – CDSA (or CDKA, as they were until 1950), the army side. In seven seasons they won five Soviet titles and three Cups, playing a brand of dashing but organised football that, along with their military ranks, earned them the nickname 'the Lieutenants Team'. They were coached by Boris Arkadiev, whose book *Tactics of Football* became a bible for coaches across Europe in the years immediately after the war. An eccentric who would take his players on tours of art galleries, he stands in the direct line from Chapman and Meisl, alongside Guttmann, Bukovi and Sebes, as one of the great pioneers, developing the W-M in Russia and becoming, in 1940, the first coach to experiment with two full-backs and two centre-backs. It was he who, at Dinamo Moscow, encouraged players to switch positions ('organised disorder' as it was quickly dubbed) and developed the *passovotchka* style with which the Dinamo tourists bewildered Britain in 1945, although he had been sacked a year earlier after a Cup defeat to Zenit Leningrad (now Zenit St Petersburg). Dinamo's loss was very much CDKA's gain.

Understandably, it was CDSA players who made up the bulk of the USSR side in Helsinki. Bulgaria were beaten 2–1 in the preliminary round (Great Britain's amateurs, incidentally, lost 5–3 to Luxembourg at the same stage), but the first round proper paired the USSR with Yugoslavia, silver-medallists four years earlier. The Soviet authorities had always been uneasy about games against foreign sides – when CDKA lost twice on a three-match tour of Czechoslovakia in 1947, it led to a two-year moratorium on games against foreign opposition – but the pressure to beat Yugoslavia was even more extreme. Tito, playing off East against West, had led his federation into a position of non-alignment with Moscow, and, as a consequence, Stalin was desperate to see Yugoslavia defeated. The Best Friend of Sportsmen had previously paid football little attention – although a half-hour demonstration match between Spartak and Spartak Reserves put on for him in Red Square in 1936 was extended to forty-three minutes because he seemed to be enjoying himself so much – and when he did for once take an interest, things went badly. The USSR came from 5–1 down to draw 5–5, forcing a replay, which Yugoslavia won 3–1. 'It was not a football match, it was a political game,' said Stjepan Bobek, who scored Yugoslavia's second goal in the replay. 'I remember seeing the headline: TITO 3 STALIN 1'. Stalin was furious, and disbanded CDSA 'for damaging the prestige of the Soviet state'. Three players – Konstantin Kryzhevsky, Anatoly Bashashkin and Konstantin Beskov – were suspended for life, and even they were probably grateful their fate hadn't been any worse. After all, Konstantin Schepotskyi of Dynamo Kyiv had been arrested in 1938 and tortured for seven years to try to make him confess to being a Polish spy, and his only crime had been not to wear a medal given him to commemorate the twentieth anniversary of the Revolution.

Stalin's death in March 1953 eased the pressure to an extent, CDSA were re-formed as CSKA and Kryzhevsky, Bashashkin and Beskov were all able to resume their careers; but football in the USSR was still a precarious business in desperate need of a tonic. How, after all, could Soviet players have performed at major tournaments knowing the potential consequences of defeat? Streltsov, cocky, charismatic and preternaturally gifted, suffered no such fears. He seemed the answer to their prayers. 'His influence on us I would call a hypnosis by individuality,' his biographer, Alexander Nilin, wrote. 'He had a magic that made us expect the impossible . . . the boy came to us from the land of wonder.'

It was in April 1954 that Streltsov made his debut for the first team at Torpedo Moscow – a club based on the ZIL car plant – becoming, at the age of sixteen years, eight months and twenty-four days, the youngest goalscorer in the history of the Soviet league. The following season, he finished as the league's top scorer and earned an international call-up for a friendly against Sweden in Stockholm. Too young said the doubters, but Streltsov got three in a 6–0 win, becoming the first player to score a hat-trick on his debut for the USSR. That game has since taken on a mythic status in Russia, a glimpse of what might have been; three years later, without Streltsov, it was to Sweden that they lost 2–0 in the World Cup quarter-final.

Streltsov had that happy knack of always turning it on when it really mattered, and he was the undoubted star of the 1956 Olympics. The USSR beat West Germany in the first round, Streltsov scoring the winner, then needed a replay to see off Indonesia in the second, setting up a semi-final against Bulgaria, who, having received a first-round bye, had reached the last four by beating Great Britain 6–1. The Soviets struggled against the fresher Bulgarians and matters got even worse when their right-back Nikolay Tyschenko broke a collarbone. With substitutes yet to be sanctioned for official competition, he had the injury set in plaster and returned to the field, but could do little other than trot around on the right flank trying to avoid confrontation. It was still goalless at ninety minutes, but Bulgaria took the lead through Ivan Kolev early in extra-time. By then, Valentin Ivanov was also hampered by injury, leaving the USSR effectively down to nine men and trailing.

The day before meeting Vartanyan, I had met Konstantin Kleshchyov, the editor of the Russian sports weekly *Sovetsky Sport*. A confirmed cynic, he is well aware that the Streltsov myth has benefited from his arrested potential, that by not playing during what would presumably have been the peak of his career, Streltsov was spared the possibility of disappointing his public. Even he, though, seems not to doubt that Streltsov is the greatest talent Russian football has known. 'He was a player who could stand like this for ninety minutes,' he said, putting his hands on his hips, 'then score the crucial goal.' In Melbourne he not merely did that, equalising after 112 minutes, but also laid on the winner for Boris Tatushin four minutes later.

Bizarrely, Streltsov was then dropped for the final against Yugoslavia because the USSR coach Gavriil Kachalin liked his strike-pairing to play together at club level. With Ivanov, his team-mate at Torpedo, injured, Streltsov was replaced by the thirty-year-old Spartak Moscow forward Nikita Simonyan. Anatoly Ilyin scored the only goal of the game, condemning Yugoslavia to their third silver in successive Olympics and giving the USSR their first success in international football.

Simonyan is one of the most successful figures in the Soviet game. He won four league titles and two cups as a player, and four cups and two league titles as a coach. 'The Olympics was the highlight, no doubt about that,' he said when I met him at the RFU building near the Luzhniki Stadium. On the wall of his office was a photograph taken on the boat on the way home from Australia (twenty days to Vladivostok, then eight more on a train to Moscow), the triumphant eleven who played in the final standing squinting into the sun, arms wrapped around each other's shoulders. As if prefiguring the days when the authorities would deliberately airbrush him from history, Streltsov is not there. 'They wanted only those who had won medals,' Simonyan explained. In those days if you didn't play in the final, you got nothing. Simonyan, recognising Streltsov's contribution in the semi-final, offered him his medal, but Streltsov refused. 'He said to me,' Simonyan recalled, '"Nikita, I will win many other trophies."' Streltsov did gain some reward, though, as every member of the squad was awarded the Merited Master of Sport degree (ZMS), the highest honour that could be bestowed on a Soviet sportsman, and something that guaranteed a higher wage.

The first cracks emerged later in that 1956 season. A natural target for opposition defenders, Streltsov began to collect bookings as he took his retribution. Then, on 11 April 1957, in a league game between Torpedo and Spartak Minsk played in Odessa – it was common for spring matches to be staged in the south, away from the worst of the weather – provoked by a series of bad challenges, he was sent off for the first time in his career, having lunged two-footed, studs up, at the opposing number five, Vyacheslav Artemiev. Vartanyan has studied both articles in newspapers and the official referees' reports and believes Streltsov was more sinned against than sinning. 'During games he was regularly kicked,' he said. 'There were dirty tricks against him and he was tackled from behind, but as a rule he would not react. Sometimes he did get wound up and he did react, but he would always do it openly – walk up to his opponent and hit them, no dirty tricks.'

Fair play is one of Vartanyan's hobby horses; he insists that he cannot recognise Diego Maradona as a genius because of the handball against England in the 1986 World Cup, and laughed off my suggestion that Terry Fenwick's brutality in that quarter-final surrendered any English claim to the moral high ground. He is critical also of Valeriy Lobanovskyi, whom he is convinced fixed games. Oleh Blokhin, he says, has admitted as much to him, while the party themselves reprimanded Lobanovskyi after a televised goalless draw between Dynamo and CSKA Moscow in Kyiv in May 1987.

Despite the occasional disciplinary problems, Streltsov remained a formidable player. He married in June 1957, and celebrated by hitting thirty-one goals in twenty-two games between 21 July and 26 October, a little under a hundred days. The following month, though, Streltsov and his Torpedo team-mate Ivanov missed a train from Moscow bound for the East German city of Leipzig, where the USSR were to play a World Cup qualifying play-off against Poland. The railway minister – for nothing, of course, could be done without the involvement of politicians – ordered that the train be stopped in the Moscow suburb of Mozhaisk, where the players, who had taken a taxi, joined the rest of the squad. That incident might have been forgotten, particularly as Streltsov scored in a 2–0 win, but a few days before a USSR trip to China in

January 1958, he was involved in a brawl with police near the Dinamo metro station. He was convicted of 'minor hooliganism' and sentenced to three days in jail. The All-Union Committee of Physical Culture (VSFK) met on 4 February, and, at the request of both Torpedo and the USSR national side, stripped him of his ZMS. He was also withdrawn from the USSR squad, and took his place in an initial forty-man party for the World Cup only after making a public apology.

Preparations for Sweden began with a training camp at Spartak's base at Tarasovka, a few miles north of Moscow. On the evening of 25 May, the final day of training, Tatushin, Streltsov and their team-mate Mikhail Ogonkov left the camp for a party hosted by Eduard Karakhonov, an army officer recently returned from the Far East. On the way, they were introduced to two women – the twenty-year-old Marina Lebedeva and her friend Tamara Timkina. Most witnesses seem to agree that Marina seduced Streltsov, and they almost certainly spent the night together. The next morning, Lebedeva sent a brief letter to the Moscow public prosecutor: 'On 25 May 1958,' it read, 'in a dacha next to the school in the village of Pravda, I was raped by Streltsov Eduard. I ask that he be brought to justice.' Timkina wrote a similar letter, accusing Ogonkov.

Only Ogonkov and Tatushin made it back to Tarasovka. 'Strelstov never turned up at the camp that morning,' Simonyan said. 'There were rumours that something had gone on, then the police came. They told us what had happened. We had been in the training camp for a long time, and that morning we were going home.' By then Streltsov had already been arrested. Ogonkov and Tatushin were picked up later that day and by mid-afternoon all three were being held at the Butyrka jail in Moscow. When news of the arrest broke, 100,000 workers at the ZIL factory threatened to march in protest, but their demonstration was called off when it was revealed that Streltsov had confessed.

On 27 May, the VSFK imposed on Streltsov a life ban from

football. The same day, Timkina withdrew her accusation, and Ogonkov and Tatushin were released the following morning. On 30 May, Lebedeva sent another letter to the public prosecutor: 'I ask that the criminal proceedings against Streltsov Eduard Anatoliyevich be stopped, because I forgive him,' she wrote, although the implication of that is still that she had been raped. Then she had another change of heart, and withdrew the second letter. A day later, the USSR's final twenty-one-man World Cup squad was delivered to FIFA. Streltsov was not on the list, and neither were Ogonkov and Tatushin, both ostensibly left out for having missed training. Streltsov's case was rapidly brought to court, and, on 24 July, three days after his twenty-first birthday, he was convicted and sentenced to the gulag.

Was he, though, guilty? His confession is not the conclusive evidence it might seem, because it quickly became apparent that he made his statement only after being told that he could go to the World Cup if he admitted his guilt. For Vartanyan, and for many others, there is evidence that there had been a campaign against Streltsov for over a year before the incident at Karakhanov's dacha.

That he drank is indisputable. Ivanov was three years older than Streltsov, and seems obsessed by his former team-mate's death from throat cancer in 1990, when he was fifty-three. 'In life he was too good and kind,' he said. 'It was the fans who killed him. Everybody wanted to drink with him, and he got more and more fans. He was playing for the factory team . . . working class, you know . . . and they would come after work and say "let's drink". If he had refused they would have said he had snubbed them, and of course that had an impact on him.' Vartanyan, equally, put Streltsov's early death down to his good nature rather than the more obvious cause of smoking. 'He was exposed to radiation in the camps,' he said, 'and then in 1986 he played in an exhibition game in Chernobyl after the disaster, and that pushed him over the edge.'

Streltsov also seems to have been something of a woman-iser. Again, that in itself probably would not have been a problem, had it not been for his relationship, if indeed there was one, with the daughter of the Culture Minister Yekaterina Furtseva, the only woman ever to become a member of the Politburo. Svetlana Furtseva was sixteen, and apparently besotted with the nineteen-year-old Streltsov. Her mother, a favourite of Khrushchev, met Streltsov early in 1957 at a reception at the Kremlin to celebrate the Olympic victory. She mentioned his probable marriage to her daughter, to which he replied, 'I already have a fiancée and I will not marry her.' As if that weren't humiliating enough, he was later heard to say to a friend, depending which account you believe, either 'I would never marry that monkey', or, 'I would rather be hanged than marry such a girl'. From then, if the conspiracy theorists are to be believed, his card was marked.

Certainly the reaction to his sending-off in Odessa that April appears excessive. The headline in *Sovetsky Sport* read: 'This is not a hero' and several letters were printed, supposedly from members of the proletariat, condemning Streltsov as an example of the evils of Western imperialism. The practice was common enough for dissident writers and politicians, but for footballers it was unheard of. Vartanyan has analysed all the sendings-off between 1954 and 1958. 'Of forty-five dismissals,' he told me, 'twenty-eight were for fouls worse than Streltsov's, but eleven of those cases were never mentioned in national newspapers. In fifteen, the papers simply stated such-and-such was sent off. Only the two cases involving USSR internationals got any attention, but neither of them provoked the criticism Streltsov got. There can be no doubt there was a campaign against him.'

Well, perhaps. It is difficult to know exactly how he can rate the severity of fouls – particularly in the absence of video evidence – and the actions of a celebrity naturally draw an exaggerated attention. A few days after the match, though, Streltsov was called before the Section of Soviet Football (SFS), and his ZMS withdrawn. On only one other occasion during Streltsov's career was such a serious punishment imposed, and that on a player who had head-butted an opponent. On 20 April, though, the decision was rescinded, and Streltsov was instead banned for three games. Again, though, it does not require plotting in the Kremlin for bureaucrats to make an example of a popular, high-profile player.

The SFS seems never to have warmed to Streltsov. An internal memo even criticised the timing of his wedding. 'We found out before the important friendly against Romania that he had married,' it read. 'This shows how weak the educational work at Torpedo is.' Communist Party archives, similarly, reveal a degree of distrust, and Streltsov, having attracted the interest of clubs in France and Sweden following tours with Torpedo, was marked down as a possible defector. 'Streltsov,' his file reads, 'according to a verified source, said to his friends in 1957 that he was always sorry to return to the USSR after trips abroad.'

And then there is the matter of why Karakhanov asked the players to his dacha. He was, at best, an acquaintance of Tatushin, and, while it is certainly possible that he just liked the idea of having three footballers at his party, there are those who see something more sinister in his invitation. It is suspiciously convenient, they say, that he had returned from serving in the Far East a matter of days earlier.

All that, though, is circumstantial. More concrete evidence of a plot comes from an interview Kachalin gave Vartanyan shortly before his death. 'When I tried to help Streltsov,' he said, 'I was told by police that Khrushchev himself had been informed about the case. I then dashed to a regional Communist Party committee headquarters and asked the First Secretary to suspend the case until the end of the World Cup. I was told that nothing could be done, and they pointed meaningfully upwards. I understood then that it was the end. I heard that Furtseva had it in for Streltsov, but who knows exactly what happened?'

What is incontrovertible is that something did. 'They went to the dacha . . . ' Ivanov said. 'It's a dark story. Who raped whom, it's hard to say. I think if a girl goes to the suburbs for a night . . . then a guy is waiting for her as it were . . . and she is the same . . . but I don't believe it was a set-up, no. Maybe it was the host of the dacha. I don't know who raped her, but she said it was Streltsov. So it's a dark story.'

Perhaps significantly, none of the players to whom I spoke were prepared, even now, categorically to defend their team-mate. Viktor Shustikov joined Torpedo six months before Streltsov's arrest, and went on to make a record 427 appearances in the Soviet league. 'Streltsov was good-natured and simple,' he said. 'He always helped the younger players, and it was always easy to play alongside him because the other teams would send players to mark him.' Age, though, had caught up quickly with Shustikov, and he struggled to recall his playing days with any great clarity. Asked about the rape and the conspiracy theory, he simply spread his hands. 'I don't remember,' he said, 'but I did hear that he had refused to marry Furtseva's daughter.'

Most odd, though, was Simonyan's reaction. 'What happened with Streltsov you cannot explain,' he said. 'It is a mysterious thing. He wrote to his mother saying he was taking the blame for someone else. It was the system that punished Streltsov. I don't know for sure if there was a rape on the part of Streltsov, but he and the girl slept together.' He shrugged. 'He was young, a bachelor, unmarried . . . '

Actually, of course, Streltsov had married just under a year before. Perhaps that is an indication he didn't take his vows particularly seriously, perhaps Simonyan's memory is just faulty. As he broke off, Simonyan reached into a drawer in his desk and took out a book. He opened it and removed a photograph which, without a word, he then handed to me. The print showed four images. Two were of a dark-haired young woman – Lebedeva. In one, she was lying back on what appeared to be a hospital bed, apparently asleep, her eyes ringed with bruises. The other two were of Streltsov. In the more striking, his face, captured in profile, was streaked from nose to cheekbone with three parallel scratches. There is, of course, the possibility that the photographs were doctored, or the injuries inflicted at a later date, but Soviet justice rarely required quite such damning evidence.

Lebedeva herself has disappeared, the last sighting of her coming in 1997, when, the day after the annual ceremony held by Torpedo at Streltsov's grave, a club director called Yury Zolotov went to the cemetery to tend the flowers that had been left. As he approached, he saw a woman kneeling by the graveside, weeping. He recognised her as Lebedeva, but as soon as she became aware of his presence, she rushed away.

Guilty or not, the machine soon went into action against Streltsov. That June, amid stories from the World Cup in Sweden, the official newspaper *Komsomolskaya Pravda* reported an incident that had taken place on 8 November the previous year, a fortnight before Streltsov and Ivanov had missed the train to Leipzig. 'He burst into a flat that was unknown to him,' the article read. 'He scared those who were sleeping in it and began furiously to smash plates and glasses.' Streltsov's friend Galina Chupalenkova, though, gave a rather different account. She said that somebody came up to Streltsov, and smacked him in the face. Streltsov then gave chase, and ended up running into a basement flat. Although there was a disturbance, nothing was broken, and he reached an out-of-court compensation settlement with the occupants.

That aside, Streltsov's history was quietly erased. An official football directory from 1959 lists the five goals he scored for Torpedo in 1958 as having been 'scored by other players', while his part in the 1956 Olympic squad was expunged. *Komsomolskaya Pravda*, the story of the smashed crockery aside, mentioned Streltsov only once in the years immediately following his conviction, and that was a clumsy character assassination. 'Streltsov,' it claimed, 'is less than a primitive man. His incompetence in the simplest matters provoked amusement and smiles among his friends in the team. He openly thought that the city of Sochy [a Black Sea resort where Soviet clubs often held their pre-season training] was on the Caspian Sea. He thinks that sea water is only salty because herring swim in it.' He may – although it seems scarcely credible – have been confused about the location of Sochy, but the jibe might seem more convincing if the second allegation weren't lifted straight from Chekhov's short story 'Examine'.

Streltsov's first months in the gulag at Lesnoy were tough, and he appears to have struggled to come to terms with his sudden fall from grace. 'In his first year in the camps he never stopped believing that they would come and set him free,' wrote Nilin, 'that there was somebody in Moscow working on his behalf. That's why he wasn't hard, why he wasn't inventive about fighting for survival.'

An eighteen-year-old thug who went by the nickname of Repeinik (a kind of burred grass) took against Streltsov, and taunted him at every opportunity. Before long, Streltsov snapped, and he attacked Repeinik, who, it later emerged, was an informer for the authorities. The other prisoners held a meeting in the camp boiler room, and decided that, in their terminology, Streltsov had to be 'set on the clock', that is, killed. He was badly beaten – the prison report says 'either with an iron bar or the heel of a shoe' – but survived, whether because of his robust constitution or because the camp guards couldn't countenance the death of such a noted figure is unclear.

After his recovery, Streltsov was moved to another camp, and gradually life became easier. While the suggestion that he was excused from the main labour of chopping down trees to entertain guards with his ball skills seems implausible, it certainly is the case that he earned a respect in prison because of his reputation as a footballer. 'At Torpedo we never forgot about him while he was in prison,' said Shustikov. 'Our coaches sometimes visited him, and once I drove his mother to see him after he had been moved to a camp at Tula [about 130 miles from Moscow]. We would always tell him about Torpedo, about the team.'

It is what happened after his imprisonment, though, that makes Streltsov truly remarkable. He was released in 1963 after serving five years of his twelve-year sentence and, prevented from returning to top-level football by the VSFK's ban, he began playing for ZIL's Department of Technical Supervision (OTK) in the factory league. Not surprisingly, they won all eleven of their games that season, and Streltsov began to be sneaked into increasingly important fixtures.

A petition signed by a thousand factory workers was sent to Leonid Brezhnev, then the secretary of the Communist Party, asking him to rescind Streltsov's suspension. The Ideological Section of the Party Central Committee, though, opposed the move. 'In contravention of the suspension,' they wrote, 'the heads of the factory sports organisations have twice – in May and June 1963 – let Streltsov play for Torpedo's reserve team . . . and once in a friendly match in Gorky [now Nizhny Novgorod]. Before the match in Gorky it was deliberately announced on the public address system at the stadium that Streltsov would play. When the directors of the Central Council of the Sports Societies Union tried to stop him, the majority of spectators chanted "Streltsov, to the field", until it was decided to let him play to avoid crowd trouble. This was all done to publicise Streltsov and have him readmitted into the first team. We therefore propose that the request to lift the ban on Streltsov be rejected.'

Brezhnev marked the letter 'Agreed', but, after ousting Khrushchev in October 1964, he sanctioned Streltsov's return. 'He didn't play for a year after being in prison,' Shustikov said. 'He worked for the factory, and played for a factory team. But sometimes we would take him to away matches. The club management was concerned that the fans would boo him for what he had done, but on the contrary I remember something that happened when we took him to a game in

Kharkiv. He sat in the stand and the public went mad insisting
we should field him. After the match, to mark the occasion,
they drew a circle in chalk around the chair in which he had
sat.'

Ivanov similarly remembered the warmth with which
Streltsov was greeted. 'After he returned to Torpedo, we
travelled and in every town we met somebody who had been
in prison with him,' he said. 'That was another thing that
killed him. They all wanted to drink with him. So what with
the fans and those people, all wanting to drink . . . That is why
he retired a little earlier than the rest of us.'

That first season back was spectacular. Torpedo were a
decent side, and had won the title without Streltsov in 1960,
but he made them brilliant. Prison, according to Ivanov,
hadn't changed Streltsov. 'It only made him bolder,' he said.
'He still had his health, and talent is talent. He was the best
player in the USSR.' Torpedo lost only two games in that 1965
season and claimed the second league title in their history.
Streltsov returned to the national team, scoring twenty-five
goals in thirty-eight games, and in both 1967 and 1968 he
was named Soviet Player of the Year. He added a Soviet Cup-
winners' medal in 1968.

It might not have been quite the level of success of which
he had boasted to Simonyan in 1956, but after losing almost
seven years of his career, it was remarkable enough. Perhaps
the metaphor is too easy, but it isn't difficult to see why
Russian football is so drawn to a talent who withstood state
oppression and emerged triumphant. Certainly that is how
Vartanyan views him – as a glorious martyr. The problem, of
course, is that that interpretation requires him, despite the
scratches, to be innocent.

Conscious that Vartanyan and I had rambled on for the best
part of six hours, that night I bought Vlad dinner as a thank-
you for interpreting. You might have thought that a day spent
discussing the dangers of drinking in Russia would have
taught me a lesson, but no. There was beer and there was

vodka, and, while I certainly hadn't had a skinful, by the time I got on the Metro to go back to my hotel, I'd had enough that the warmth of the train, after the cold of the night, sent me to sleep.

(The Moscow metro, incidentally, is fantastic, its only fault being the general reluctance of passengers ever to raise their eyes. There was a glitch in a football game I had on my Commodore-64 whereby two players running square into each other would stick, feet pedalling furiously and shoulders wobbling, but neither able to slide past the other. Muscovites on the metro are pretty much the same, all bowed heads and shoulders tensed for impact. It also perhaps says something about the Russian psyche that where the indicator boards on the London Underground give you something to look forward to by counting down to the next train, the clocks in Moscow count up, showing by how much you missed the last one.)

I was awakened by a soldier at Shchyolkovskaya, the last stop on the purple line, at around 2.30, by which time I'd been relieved of my wallet and my phone. I still had my metro pass, but the trains had stopped running for the night, leaving me stranded, approximately ten miles from my hotel with fourteen roubles (about 28p.) in my pocket and the temperature significantly below zero. It occurred to me even at the time that the situation was not unlike that faced by Michael Douglas in The Game, but given his immediate reaction, as far as I could recall it, was to run about randomly in a flouncy shirt, I realised I was on my own, and so, asking the soldier for directions, I set off to walk and/or hitch. After about a mile I met a couple who spoke enough English to take pity on me and pay for a taxi back to the hotel. Sometimes all of us are reliant on the kindness of strangers, and to them I am immensely grateful. Certainly the next time I meet a distressed Russian blundering around Wandsworth in the early hours, I will do all I can to help.

*

The following day we headed up to Tarasovka, where Spartak still have their training base. Spartak are by some distance the most successful Russian club of all time, having won twelve Soviet championships, and nine of the first ten Russian league titles. More recently, though, they have had their problems, being left behind as big business and the oligarchs' discovery of their love for football has elevated the likes of CSKA and Lokomotiv.

Spartak, despite much grumbling, still play at the Luzhniki, the stadium that hosted the opening and closing ceremonies at the 1980 Olympics. I first saw it in 1992, as I headed south on a bus across the Steppes towards Tambov (annoyingly, a few days later it was there that Spartak beat Liverpool 4–2 in the Cup-Winners' Cup, but school trips rarely take account of such things). Back then, it loomed through the November sleet as something unspeakably Soviet: imposing, forbidding and concrete. It was still known as the Lenin Stadium, and it still looked essentially as it had in 1982 when it was the scene of what many consider football's worst stadium disaster.

Almost a decade later, I returned for Spartak's derby against CSKA to find it transformed, a new roof glinting splendidly in the spring sunshine, bright plastic seats replacing the old benches, and the desks in the press area vast and topped with mock-marble. Lenin still shook a Communist fist by the main entrance, but there were few other reminders of 1992. On the pitch too, there was a sense of the old order being overturned. With Rolan Gusev, that most frustrating of wingers, outstanding, Spartak were picked apart, and were fortunate to lose only 3–0. That night, as I walked back past the Bolshoi Theatre to my hotel, a shaven-headed CSKA fan reeled up to me. 'We kicked their asses,' he belched in a fog of vodka-breath. 'Ten years we have waited, but the revolution has begun.'

At the time I was sceptical – CSKA, after all, had beaten Spartak 4–1 in 1998 to little effect – but the fan was right. That season CSKA lost the title to Lokomotiv in a play-off, with Spartak eleven points adrift in third; in 2003, as CSKA took the championship, Spartak finished a lowly tenth; and in 2004 Spartak were only eighth. The years of Spartak domination are over, and Russian football has entered a more competitive, brighter age. Spartak, nonetheless, remain Russia's most popular club thanks to their reputation for having maintained their independence in Soviet times. Like Streltsov's, though, the preservation of their reputation has required some discreet pruning of the actuality.

In the entrance hall of the training base at Tarasovka hangs a photograph of an old man. Russia is full of photographs of old men, but this one, more than most, is worthy of reverence. It is Nikolay Starostin, the man who took MKS – a club based on a catering firm – restructured and refounded them as Spartak in 1935, was sentenced to ten years in the gulag and returned to lead the club as they became the most successful Russian side in the USSR.

Life wasn't easy for Starostin. He was left as his family's main breadwinner when his father died in the typhoid epidemic of 1920, but managed to support his mother and three brothers by playing ice hockey in the winter and football in the summer. All of his brothers – Alexander, Andrey and Pyotr – played for Spartak, while Nikolay ended up captaining the USSR at both sports.

If those who eulogise him are to be believed, his downfall had its roots in a game in Georgia in the mid-1920s in which he outplayed the opposing left-half, Lavrenty Beria. As head of the secret police, Beria went on to become, after Stalin, the most feared man in the USSR. His position made him, *ex officio*, president of Dinamo Moscow, although his first love remained Dinamo Tbilisi. Whether being nutmegged really turned Beria against Starostin is impossible to say – there is no evidence beyond Starostin's word that the game even took place, and Beria certainly never played at a top level, but Spartak's success certainly irked him. They won the championship in 1938 and 1939, and, even worse, in 1939 beat Dinamo Tbilisi 1–0 in the semi-final of the Cup, thanks to a goal from Andrey Protasov. Dinamo protested that the ball had not crossed the line, but the VSFK allowed the result to stand. Spartak then won the final against Stalinets Leningrad, only for the VSFK – Starostin suggests on Beria's orders – to decide that the semi-final should be replayed after all. Spartak this time won 3–2, Georgy Glazkov scoring a hat-trick, and were named Cup winners.

Three years later, Starostin was arrested. To Spartak fans, the delay was caused by the fact that it was only under the cover of war that such a prominent figure could safely be put on trial. In his autobiography *Football Through the Years*, Starostin says that during interrogation at the Lubyanka he was accused of having plotted to assassinate Stalin during the forty-three-minute exhibition in Red Square in 1936. This, of course, was a ludicrous charge, the only evidence being a photograph found in his flat, showing Starostin and his team-mates in a car that passed close to Stalin as they arrived for the game. Besides, two referees – Vladimir Stripikheyev and Vladimir Ryabokon – had been shot in 1937 over similar allegations; if there had been a shred of evidence against Starostin, he would surely have been interrogated then. Nonetheless, Starostin and his brothers were each sentenced to ten years in the gulag – another example, the modern mythology would have us believe, of the machine crushing an individual, and doing down Spartak as it did so. 'My brothers and I did not exist by ourselves,' Starostin wrote. 'People saw us as embodying Spartak. Beria was dealing not just with four men, but with the passions of millions of ordinary Soviet people.'

His book, though, is not exactly a document of unadulterated veracity. Starostin, for instance, claims he came up with the name Spartak after reading a book about a Roman gladiator, even though there had been sporting clubs called Spartak from the mid-twenties, long before he became involved with MKS. Equally, if Beria really were fixing games, he must have been extraordinarily bad at it, given that Dinamo Tbilisi did not win a single trophy until eleven years after his death. Nor does Starostin's relationship with the football authorities seem ever to have been so bad as he made out; it was his influence that saw Spartak Yerevan admitted to the fourth division of the Soviet League in 1937 while Dinamo Yerevan, who had finished above them in the Armenian championship, were consigned to the fifth. Equally, it is likely that the truth behind his imprisonment was rather more prosaic, that he was jailed for a simple fraud. (I have seen documentary evidence to support this claim, but for legal reasons I cannot reveal what.)

Starostin, anyway, was not above offering inducements to help his side. Towards the end of the 1969 season, when he was head of the club (the term 'president' was frowned upon), Spartak had to play CSKA twice in quick succession. They won one game and drew the other and, as a consequence, took the title; a few weeks later, several CSKA players moved into new apartments provided by Moscow City Council, with whom Starostin had always maintained excellent relations.

Starostin's version of the legend nonetheless endures, and so does the persecution complex of Spartak fans. The day before I watched CSKA beat Spartak, I met Oleg – one of the most strident voices in the chat-room on the club website – in a Czech bar near Moscow Zoo. He was a huge man in his early forties, muscle just beginning to run to fat. His hair was cropped short and neatly parted, and he wore the sort of wide-lensed gold-framed glasses that mark people out as either computer technicians or violent nutters. As it turned out, he was both.

He ordered a glass of wine – his doctor had told him to cut back on the booze – and unzipped his navy and red Russia tracksuit top to reveal a green T-shirt on which was printed a picture of a pig and a set of scales. 'This is my club,' he said. 'The 100kg Club. There are fifty-two of us, Spartak fans from across the globe – Calgary, Berlin, Dallas, Melbourne – and we go to all the Champions League games. We were on the beach at Estoril one year and one of us said, "Hey, we are all big guys. We could all eat 100kg of meat." That is why we are called the 100kg Club.' Meat is very important to Spartak fans. They have now appropriated the term, but for years opposing fans would taunt them with chants of 'Meat, Meat', a supposedly insulting reference to their origins in the catering trade.

Oleg began supporting Spartak as a boy, when he spent six years at their football school near his home in the north-east of Moscow. Locality in Moscow, though, usually has little to do with affiliation. With a few notable exceptions – Zenit represent St Petersburg, and Anzhi certainly stand for the Caucasian south – the same is true of most of Russia. After all, even if you count only European Russia (it is rare for Siberian teams to take a place in the top flight, although Tom Tomsk were promoted in 2004 along with, pity the schedulers, the Chechen side Terek Grozny), the country has an area of seventeen million square kilometres. Fans who live in Arkangelsk to the north or Perm to the east lie around 1,000km from the nearest top-flight side which, in distance terms, is like living in London and supporting Sparta Prague. The selection of clubs is thus more to do with ideology than geography.

Of course, those who worked in the railways tended to support Lokomotiv, and those with military connections favoured CSKA, but, for many, Spartak – funded loosely by the trade unions but essentially independent – represented a welcome alternative, free of the state, and for that they were persecuted; that at least is the romanticised version. The fact that they won twelve Soviet league titles suggests that, certainly once Stalin had died and Beria been executed in 1953, the repression was minimal. It is even harder to take them seriously as a club of dissent when fans proudly count among their number Konstantin Chernenko, who succeeded Andropov as president in 1984, and died to be replaced by Mikhail Gorbachev a year later.

Not, of course, that I dared say any of that to Oleg, who, despite nine league titles in ten years, still insisted on a cosmic conspiracy against Spartak. His prime target was Moscow Council, whom he blamed for forcing Spartak to use the Luzhniki. In that, he had a point. The Luzhniki, magnificent as it is, is an absurd setting for Russian league football. It is shared by Torpedo and Spartak, but whichever side is at home it is rare that more than 15,000 of its 80,000 seats are filled. It, like everything in Moscow, arguably like Russia itself, is just too big. Even for the derby against CSKA when there were 50,000 there, the stadium felt empty and any atmosphere was dissipated. Those are the practical, modern reasons for wanting to leave, but for Spartak fans the Luzhniki was the setting for the darkest moment of their past.

On 20 October 1982, an unusually cold night even by the standards of the Russian autumn, Spartak beat the Dutch club Haarlem 2–0 in the second round of the UEFA Cup. Only 10,000 turned out to watch, so police crammed them into one section of the stadium. With Spartak leading 1–0 and the game heading into injury time, hundreds of fans made for the exits, only for Sergey Shvetsov to add a second. Many of those already on the icy steps behind the stand turned back to join the celebrations, but ran into a wall of other fans on the way out. Police refused to open any other exits, and with supporters stumbling and slipping in the darkness, dozens were trampled or crushed to death.

Some estimates suggest as many as 340 were killed, but the official death toll stands at sixty-six, a figure the late Leonid Romanov, a former head of the Spartak fan club, believed to be reasonably accurate. With Brezhnev ailing fast and Andropov not yet installed as his successor, the USSR could not countenance such a tragedy, and so a cover-up was put into effect. While many suspected something awful had happened, it was only in 1989 that the full story became known. By the morning after the disaster, the bodies had been removed, and, to try to play down the scale of the horror, families, monitored by police, had to pay their last respects forty minutes before the dead were buried in a mass funeral.

Spartak, understandably, want a home of their own, but plans to build their own stadium – of a more realistic size and without the running track – have persistently been blocked by the city, which doesn't want to lose the rent that Spartak pay to use the Luzhniki. It doesn't help the conspiracy theories that Luzhkov, the mayor, who is in his sixties and, in Vlad's words, 'bald, like Lombardo', plays football twice a week with Yury Belous, the president of FK Moskva. 'Luzhkov is the centre-forward, of course,' Kleshchyov told me, 'and Belous, the playmaker.'

Belous, a successful entrepreneur, somehow persuaded Luzhkov that Moscow council, in order to promote the city, needed to buy half the shares in what, when it first splintered from Torpedo Moscow, was Torpedo-ZIL, and, after a couple of seasons as Torpedo-Metallurg, is now FK Moskva. Five clubs from the capital, apparently, just weren't enough. I saw FK Moskva beat Zenit 3–2 in the Petrovsky Stadium in St Petersburg, a game that effectively ended Zenit's chances of qualifying for the 2005–06 UEFA Cup. They were one of those sides you love to see as a football tourist, packed with players you vaguely remember from elsewhere who, when you're sitting alone in a freezing press box exhausted after a fretful sleep on the night-train, are as welcome as old friends.

There was the diminutive former Steaua Bucharest midfielder Pompiliu Stoica, surprisingly but effectively converted into a left-back; there was Mariusz Jop, last seen at Wisła Krakow, dominating the centre of defence alongside Jerry-Christian Tchuisse, who was born in Cameroon but is now a naturalised Russian, and would have played for the national side had it not been for objections from right-wing groups; and, there, providing a cameo distillation of his career by coming on with three minutes to go to slice a chance horribly and then get booked, was Amir Karič, signed by Ipswich after Euro 2000 when Slovenians were indispensable accessories for any self-respecting mid-ranking club, but never good enough to be fielded by them in a league game.

What is enticing for the outsider, though, is not necessarily good for Russian football, and with their Romanians, Poles, naturalised Cameroonians and Slovenians – not to mention a Moldovan, a Bosnian, a Lithuanian, a Ghanaian and an Argentinian – FK Moskva are typical of Russia's modern footballing problem: the mediocre league of nations. There are mumblings about the stifling of young Russian talent, but the clubs that have money – and a lot of them now do – continue to buy foreign. It might not quite be so ludicrous as it was when Arsenal Tula sent Yevhen Kucherevskyi to Brazil to sign a team, but the preference is still for off-the-shelf exoticism.

The other effect of such cosmopolitanism is the erosion of the 'Russian style'. It was never so obvious or so defined as the hard pressing of the Ukrainians or the dribbling of the Caucasian states, but from the days of Arkadiev onwards, Russian football has been neat and technically precise, and has usually featured a sweeper. Those days are disappearing, flat back fours are becoming more prevalent and the football is becoming increasingly similar to that played in the West. That matters little from anything but an aesthetic point of view, and perhaps a gut recoil from the prospect of globalised homogeneity, but it is symbolic of a wider shift in the Russian attitude.

FK Moskva did not exist when I met Oleg, and while it's safe to assume he would not approve, it's also safe to assume the bulk of his hatred would still be directed at CSKA, whose victory in the final Soviet championship he insisted on seeing as evidence that they were favoured by the old regime. The fact that it was only their second title since the disbanding of the Lieutenants Team cut little ice. 'If we lose the championship,' he said (and back then such a thought was scarcely credible), 'I don't mind so long as we beat CSKA.'

He wasn't just talking about football. 'Hooligans have regular fixtures,' he told me. 'We arrange a place and meet outside town. Last year there were three hundred of us and three hundred of CSKA and we won. It's OK, there are rules; everything is organised now, with the Internet. You can use fists, or bottles, but no knives. It's getting more difficult these days, though, because the police have started using undercover agents. The best thing is fighting with police in other countries. You throw things at them and then they run at you, and you fight.'

Spartak have had a hooligan element since the seventies, when shaven-headed thugs in their red-and-white colours would rampage through city centres and daub their slogans on walls – further evidence, to those who are looking for it, of the club's renowned independence. The day after I met Oleg, there were 149 arrests at the derby.

That game was the first definitive evidence of Spartak's declining status. That is partly the result of the increased wealth of Russian football and the willingness of companies like Sibirsky Aluminium (SibAl) and Yukos to sponsor clubs, but Spartak themselves have declined. Oleg Romantsev, once simultaneously their coach, their president and the national coach, was largely responsible for their rise, but he also has to take most of the blame for their fall. The club were less dependent on state support than others, but in the early nineties Spartak still benefited hugely from Romantsev's policy of scouring the former Soviet republics for young talent he could develop and sell on. Players such as Alexander Mostovoi, Igor Shalimov, Dmitry Radchenko and Valery Karpin passed through Spartak on their way to western Europe and, at one point, player sales accounted for 70 per cent of their annual budget.

'He was hard on everybody,' the Spartak midfielder Yegor Titov said. 'He was always demanding, but he was a fair man. As a coach or a manager I'd put him on a level with Lobanovskyi. People ask if it was hard to motivate ourselves in the years when we won the championship every season, but not with Romantsev. Every draw was tragic for us, because as a punishment he would lock us in here in the camp.'

Romantsev became coach of Spartak in 1988, elected by the players after Konstantin Beskov was ousted following a dispute with Starostin, over, it is alleged, Beskov's unbending opposition to match-fixing. Five years later Romantsev was appointed president after a vote of no-confidence – largely by players whose contracts were about to expire – in the incumbent Yury Shlyapin. He was highly successful, and, in 1998, after a string of dire results led to the dismissal of Anatoly Byshovets, he was named national coach for the second time.

The strain of occupying three roles, though, took its toll, and Romantsev's drinking became more pronounced. 'He's from Krasnoyarsk,' Kleshchyov said. 'Siberians are big, strong people and when he was young he could drink two bottles of vodka a day, but as he got older it began to affect him.' He then told me about a Champions League game away to Lyon in 2001 when Romantsev, after a heavy night, turned up at an afternoon press conference very much the worse for wear. 'He didn't know what he was saying or doing,' he said. 'And when the players see that, they lose respect.' Romantsev's drinking continued at the 2002 World Cup, when Russia, having beaten Tunisia in their opening game, lost their next two group matches and were eliminated. After the defeat to Belgium, the midfielder Alexander Mostovoi was asked jokingly if he'd had a vodka to ease his disappointment. He responded by shaking his head. 'That's just for those upstairs,' he said. Romantsev has since given up alcohol, and shed several pounds, but the damage to Spartak was done.

In 2000, Lukoil, one of Russia's largest oil companies, agreed a sponsorship deal with the club worth $3million a year, but that only made things worse as Romantsev sold his shares to the senior Lukoil director Andrey Chervichenko, a man Kleshchyov described as being 'one hundred per cent incompetent in football'. The main beneficiaries of that incompetence were agents. In 2003, Spartak had eighty senior players on their books, including seven goalkeepers. The main loser was Dmitry Sychev, a scorer in that World Cup defeat to Belgium, and the latest in a line of young forwards to have been promoted as the saviour of Russian football. As an eighteen-year-old he earned $800 a month, but when he came to negotiate a new contract, he asked for a raise to $5,000. Given most of the rest of the first-team squad at the time earned between $10,000 and $15,000, that might not have seemed unreasonable; Chervichenko, though, not only refused, but also added a $6million buy-out clause to his existing contract. Understandably frustrated, Sychev turned to the civil courts, an act which, in itself, earned him a six-month ban. During his suspension he signed a pre-contract agreement with Dynamo Kyiv, but eventually joined Marseille for $3million, half of which Chervichenko ended up paying to his agent. Like so many Russians abroad, he flopped dreadfully, scoring just five goals in two seasons, and returned to Moscow with Lokomotiv in 2004. Back home, he blossomed again, and hit fifteen goals as Loko won their second title in three years.

After Romantsev's departure, Titov, having helped them to six of their nine league titles, was left as the great symbol of Spartak, the most potent reminder of the golden years. He, though, missed the entirety of the 2004 season through suspension, having tested positive for bromantan (a stimulant developed in Moscow to enhance alertness among Soviet troops in Afghanistan) after Russia's Euro 2004 play-off against Wales. When I met him at Tarasovka in the final week of that season, he insisted he was innocent. 'I don't know why it was positive,' he said. 'Nobody knows. The sentence anyway was not fair. I was banned for a year and you see other players who are only banned for a few months.'

When I spoke to him Titov was still at Spartak, so his protestations of innocence and ignorance were perhaps to be expected. It is hard, though, to believe that nothing was going on, and, in May 2005, following a lengthy investigation by *Sport Express*, the RFU launched a full inquiry. According to *Sport Express*, RFU tests found traces of bromantan in samples given by Titov and the defender Yury Kovtun in early September 2003, and as a result both were left out of the final Euro 2004 qualifier against the Republic of Ireland (officially, Titov had a minor strain and Kovtun a stomach upset). At the same time, three Spartak players − Roman Pavlyuchenko, Alexander Pavlenko and Alexander Belozyorov − were withdrawn from the Under-21 squad. Five days later, Spartak fired their coach Andrey Chernyshov, his assistant Serhiy Yuran and a club doctor, Anatoly Shchyukin − none of whom had been at the club for more than three months. Chervichenko insisted it was because of 'a lack of mutual understanding with the players' (and they had just lost 5−2 to Lokomotiv) but he also spoke mysteriously of having a 'nasty surprise'. Another doctor, Artyom Katulin, was banned for two years by the RFU, although that suspension was later halved.

When it became known that Titov had tested positive, journalists began to recall other odd episodes. In Spartak's 3−2 defeat to Dinamo in August 2003, for instance, the defender Maxim Demenko, having been substituted, went and sat on the wrong bench for several minutes. 'Everything was a blur,' he said. 'I saw them put up the board with my number and I applauded the fans, but after that I was oblivious to everything. Then our players asked me why I'd gone to the Dinamo bench, and I didn't know what to say.'

The former Dynamo Kyiv captain Vladyslav Vashchyuk, who came on for Demenko, spoke of players being given white pills, which they were told were 'salts' or 'minerals'. After the Dinamo game, he said, he saw several players shaking.

'Afterwards, when I found out about the doping, I understood what had happened,' Demenko went on. 'I'd been tense, but I hadn't known why. Night came, but I didn't want to sleep. It went on for five days. Lots of the guys were complaining about it. We were on the verge of nervous breakdowns. After the Dinamo game, I was vomiting, so I went to Katulin. He said they'd given us nothing illegal and it was just because of the pressure. How were we supposed to know? I missed all the 2004 season because of the doping. My body stopped feeling pain and I ruptured the ligament in my knee.'

Both Vashchyuk and Demenko expressed sympathy for Titov. 'He was just a scapegoat,' Demenko said. 'He paid for somebody else's mistake.'

Perhaps Titov too, in time, will become another martyr to the system. Certainly Kleshchyov, cynical as ever, believes he differs from other sportsmen only in that he was caught. 'I think, I hope, [he names a leading Russian swimmer] is clean,' he said, 'but I have always been a romantic.' His last comment, I presume, was intended as irony; if Kleshchyov counts as a romantic in Moscow, then Russian football truly is doomed.

Desperate to regain their pre-eminence, Spartak paid a Russian record fee of £7million to sign the Argentinian forward Fernando Cavenaghi from River Plate in the summer of 2004. Typically for the way their fortunes have turned, he scored just once in his nine appearances that season. Even were he firing, though, Spartak could never dominate as they used to; these days they are just one team among many. 'It's tough for us,' Titov said. 'We got used to winning and now we have to recognise it is a different world. We knew that the money would make it harder for us, but we didn't realise how much it would change things.' The CSKA fan who accosted me outside the Bolshoi that night was right: there has been another revolution.

The Spartak of the nineties were a very good side, and they might have enjoyed tangible international success had Romantsev not been so focused on his policy of develop-and-sell. In 1995, for instance, Spartak won all six of their group games in the Champions League, beating Blackburn, Rosenborg and Legia Warsaw, but then sold Viktor Onopko, Stanislav Cherchesov, Serhiy Yuran and Vasily Kulkov over the winter, and lost tamely to Nantes in the quarter-final. That said, their route to pre-eminence was eased by the chaos that existed in the rest of Russian football as clubs tried and, for the most part, failed to cope with the changing financial climate and privatisation.

Asmaral, perhaps, provide the most bewildering example. For a long time they had ticked along as Krasnaya Presnya, an unassuming second division side whose only claim to any kind of notoriety was as the club where Romantsev began his coaching career. In 1990 they were bought by Khusam al Halidi, an Iraqi businessman. He renamed the club using the first syllable of the names of each of his three children and appointed Konstantin Beskov as coach. The club finished seventh in the inaugural season of the Russian championship in 1992, but Beskov resigned the following year and Asmaral were relegated. Three years later, they slipped into the third division and were disbanded.

Clubs appeared, clubs disappeared, and, Spartak aside, the old hierarchies were overturned. Historically Lokomotiv were always Moscow's fifth team – 'the fifth wheel of the cart', as other Muscovite fans taunted them – but in 2004 they became only the second team to win two Russian titles, aided by the Railway Ministry, which paid for their impressive new stadium and training base. Typically, the minister who sanctioned that outlay, Nikolay Aksyonenko, was deposed in 2002 after being accused of fraud. For all Loko's on-field success, though, it is CSKA who sit at the head of the oligarchs' table. They won the league title in 2003 and then, in 2005, became the first Russian winners of a European competition, beating Sporting in Lisbon to lift the UEFA Cup.

Having won the final Soviet championship, CSKA's early years in the Russian League were something of a non-event. Their comfortable but dull mid-table existence, though, came to an end when the Defence Ministry sold the club in January 1997. Within weeks, the new shareholders had fallen out and two different CSKA ice-hockey teams applied for membership of the league; the dispute eventually being settled when one of the warring parties, Alexander Tarkhanov, sold his shares to Shakhrudi Dadakhanov, a Chechen businessman. The following year Dadakhanov was at the head of a Chechen consortium that bought 49 per cent of the club. He was named club president, and persuaded Oleg Dolmatov to leave Chernomorets and take over as coach. The move initially seemed inspired, as CSKA won their final twelve games of the season – including that 4–1 win over Spartak – to finish second. Having budgeted for Champions League football, though, they came only third the following season and lost to the Norwegian side Molde in the second qualifying round of the Champions League.

With the club facing financial ruin, the Defence Ministry began a struggle to regain ownership, accusing the Chechen shareholders of supplying arms and money to rebels in Chechnya. Dolmatov's wife vanished – she has never been found – and then, in 2001, Dadakhanov's nephew, Aslanbek, was arrested in Moscow after police claimed to have found $25,000 in counterfeit notes and videotapes of Chechens shooting Russian soldiers in his flat. Dadakhanov insisted the arrest was part of a plot to undermine his leadership of the club, but eventually surrendered his shares, allowing a takeover by the ministry, a Russian investment group called AVO Capital, and Bluecastle Enterprises, a company based in Stevenage. Bluecastle theoretically own only 49 per cent of the club, but would have a controlling interest if there is any truth in reports of their links to AVO, who bought 26.8 per cent. When I checked in August 2004 – after Chelsea had drawn CSKA in the Champions League – Bluecastle's nominal director was Aman Antoinette Khan, who was charged with representing the company to Macasyng Holding BV, a Dutch-registered shell company managed by the Rijnhove Group. They specialise in running beneficial trusts, which are often a way of disguising ownership. There is nothing illegal in any of that, but it is odd.

When, in March 2004, Sibneft, the oil company Roman Abramovich sold for $13billion in September 2005, agreed a three-year sponsorship deal with CSKA worth US$54million, the Moscow rumour mill began to turn, particularly when it emerged that one of Macasyng's directors was Oleksander Garese, a Ukraine-born, France-based businessman who, in 1999, served on the board of Omsk Bacon, a subsidiary of Sibneft.

There are those who saw the Sibneft deal as a sop thrown by Abramovich to Russian public opinion, which is at least in part outraged by the transfer of wealth drawn from Russian natural resources into the pockets of the likes of Juan Sebastián Veron and Hernán Crespo. Luzhkov even accused Abramovich of 'spitting on Russia' when he invested in Chelsea. Sibneft's CEO, Eugene Shvidler, who is often seen alongside Abramovich at matches, insisted the sponsorship deal with CSKA was a 'social responsibility', nothing more than an extension of the policy by which they invest $10mm a year in the ice-hockey team Avangard Omsk and sponsor the international biathlon championships in Khanty-Mansiisk.

There were others, though, who saw the formation of a network of clubs. The theory, admittedly, is backed only by circumstantial evidence, and feels at times like the kind of batty global conspiracy that would usually involve the Knights Templar, the Rosicrucians and lizards disguised as Henry Kissinger; but it is undeniable that there are a lot of coincidences. Chelsea already had strong links to Benfica and PSV Eindhoven, and, particularly in the wake of Jiri Jarošik's move to Chelsea, the suggestion was that CSKA could be used as a conduit to move the best players from eastern Europe to Stamford Bridge. With Europe covered (aside perhaps from Italy), the next logical move was a bridgehead in South America.

Sure enough, in November 2004, a London-based group called Media Sports Investments bought into the Brazilian club Corinthians. Again the waters are muddy, but Berezovsky, having previously worked with Kia Joorabchian, the Anglo-Iranian fronting the company, while denying direct involvement with MSI, soon announced he would be investing in a new stadium for the club. Given Berezovsky and Abramovich's bitter falling-out over the Sibneft buy-out, that only makes it all the more baffling that Abramovich's yacht, the *Grand Bleu*, was booked into the Puerto Madreno marina in Buenos Aires when Corinthians bought the young Argentinian forward Carlos Tevez from Boca Juniors for £10.5million – a truly startling sum in South American football.

Then there is the fact that soon after the takeover, Corinthians signed a cooperation agreement with Dinamo Tbilisi. Their president, Alberto Dualib, insisted the deal was completely separate from the MSI investment, but given that the Dinamo owner, Badri Patakartsishvili, was once a co-owner of Sibneft with Berezovsky and Abramovich, it is hard not to start drawing conclusions. Abramovich, it should be stressed, has always denied any involvement with either Bluecastle or Joorabchian.

However, the outcome is the same. Russian football, like pretty much everything else in the country, was once in the hands of vast, state-run organisations, and is now in the hands of a small group of very rich men. Shvidler is not the only link to Russian football's elite among Abramovich's coterie. German Tkachenko, vice-president of SibAl and president of Krylya Sovetov, is also a regular at Stamford Bridge and was even there with the agent Pini Zahavi when Abramovich agreed to buy Chelsea. The oligarchs' investment has lifted Russian football, not quite to the levels of the sixties perhaps, but certainly above any other league in eastern Europe. Kleshchyov, uncharacteristically sanguine, believes this can only be for the good, not merely in terms of financing the signing of top players, but also because football to the oligarchs is 'just another toy'. As he sees it, they have so much money already there is no incentive to throw games and little point in fixing matches to ensure a slice of, say, UEFA Cup advertising.

Football, anyway, has become an accepted part of Russian business, a way of smoothing along deals. The agent and businessman Sergey Falkov bought the second-flight side Zhemchuzhnaya to gain access to the mayor and governor of Sochy, where he wanted to build a hotel. When the hotel was built, he sold the club. To him, the deal made perfect financial sense: the hotel project cost around £10m, while the budget of the club was only £200,000. Where there is football, there is money, and, in Russia, generally speaking, where there is money there is corruption.

In his playing days, Yury Tishkov was one of Russia's brightest forwards, top scorer in the UEFA Cup when Torpedo Moscow reached the quarter-finals in 1990. Several foreign clubs took an interest in him and he would have joined Sheffield Wednesday in 1994 but for a failed medical. A series of niggling injuries forced him to retire in 1998, but he remained in football, coaching Torpedo's youth team and becoming an agent (something at which he was, by all accounts, extremely good, gaining respect for his shrewdness while remaining popular). 'He was,' Ivanov said, 'a good guy in a dirty world.' In January 2003, aged thirty-one, he was stabbed to death outside his home in Moscow.

His killer was never caught, but there are few who do not link the murder to the deal Tishkov had brokered a few weeks earlier that took the highly promising midfielder Dmitry Smirnov from Torpedo-Metallurg (now FK Moskva) to Spartak. Smirnov had for a while been threatening to leave, having gone unpaid for several months, but when Norilsk Nikel took over the club and cleared the debts (and changed the name from Torpedo-ZIL), his grievance seemed to have gone. When he then departed anyway, it left a bitter taste, and not just at Torpedo-Metallurg. CSKA believed they had first option on the player, and their sense of indignation was hardy helped when Tishkov described their conduct during negotiations as 'idiotic'.

The idea that Russian football has suddenly become clean is laughable. My last visit to Russia coincided with an assault on the FIFA referee Nikolay Ivanov, who was beaten up near his home in St Petersburg shortly before taking charge of a game between Krylya Sovetov and FK Moskva.

Earlier in the month a newspaper in Kaliningrad printed the transcriptions of tapes indicating that Baltika, the local club, had attempted to fix matches against Chernomorets and Spartak Moscow. The club insisted the tapes had been faked.

Perhaps there is a positive in the fact that the newspapers are now investigating corruption and doping, but even Vartanyan, who really is a romantic, is sceptical. 'Our football has never been independent,' he said. 'Once the influence came from the party, and now the influence is from big business.'

Only Streltsov, the flawed but eternal martyr, stands aloof.

EPILOGUE

Igor Akinfeev dives to his left and pushes away Moutinho's drive. The ball bounces to Tello and he drills it back the box, towards Liedson and Rogério, who stand unmarked, onside, and two yards from an open goal. Rogério jabs a leg at the cross, and 48,000 in the Estadio José Alvalade rise to greet the equaliser. The ball, though, flicks his shin, cannons on to the post, and rolls along the line into the arms of the prone Akinfeev. The goalkeeper stands, looking almost bewildered that it is not 2–2, then hurls the ball sixty yards into the path of Daniel Carvalho. The Brazilian, racing down the left, outpaces the hapless Joseph Enakarhire, and crosses. Ricardo, the goalkeeper, comes to gather but is defeated by the whip of the delivery, leaving Vágner Love to lash the ball with gleeful abandon into an empty net. What should have been 2–2 has become 3–1, and CSKA Moscow have become the first Russian winners of a European trophy. The next day *Sport Express* proclaims that Russian football will henceforth be divided into two periods: Before and After Lisbon.

It is easy to read too much into results in a single competition, but that success is nonetheless indicative of a general rise in Russian club football. Six days earlier, a deal was announced taking Costinha and Maniche from Porto to Dinamo Moscow for £14million – that is, two European Cup-winners, who could easily have found teams in the Premier-ship, opted instead to move to a club who can hardly even class themselves among the Russian elite, having at the time not won the league for twenty-nine years. Wherever the money has come from, it can hardly be denied that Russian football is in more robust health than ever before. CSKA,

Dinamo, Lokomotiv, Spartak, Zenit St Petersburg and FK Moskva all have hugely wealthy sponsors willing to invest in players, and willing to offer wages high enough to entice those players from the West. The Russian league is now as polyglot as the Premiership, which raises inevitable concerns about the development of Russian players, but I doubt many Russian fans would swap their situation with that of any other post-Communist country. Where there are proven incidents of match-fixing and intimidation these will probably be forgiven, and when society has problems as endemic as it is does in Russia, their presence in football can hardly be helped.

Exceptional generations of players can make mugs of us all, but elsewhere the situation is far worse. Poland and Hungary seem almost to have given up – a sign, perhaps, of nations no longer desperate enough to require validation through football, and not yet comfortable enough to invest it with the faintly ludicrous importance it has in England today. Serbia and Romania wonder how they can have fallen so far, so quickly. Georgia and Armenia ponder the point of football when there are no Muscovites to upset. Bosnia-Hercegovina slowly puts itself back together after war. Everybody has their specific concerns: railing against corrupt owners, mercenary players or a feckless football association; but everywhere outside of Russia, the basic problem is money. There is very little, and what there is has often been come by illegally. Those who are prepared to invest often see the club as little more than a laundry. How, then, can Eastern clubs compete? How can they build the facilities for the modern development of players? How can they stop their best players leaving? How can they ever build a side when they know any player who shows any talent will be tempted away?

The answer is simple: without the help of an Akhmetov or a Sibneft, they can't. Perhaps the pace has increased, but this is a reality clubs have faced domestically for years. Dnipro Dnipropetrovsk players moved to Dynamo Kyiv, Beroe players moved to CSKA Sofia and Vojvodina players moved to Red

Star, just as surely as Crewe players moved to Liverpool. The difference now is that the pyramid has become internationalised. An Armenian forward joins Ajax, who hope in a few years to sell him on to Barcelona. Karpaty Lviv sign a Nigerian, and look to pass him on to Germany, England or Spain. That is the market.

The disaster for eastern Europe is that their clubs were at their weakest just at the time when the advent of the Champions League and the Bosman ruling was increasing the gulf between rich and poor, with the result that the standard of football in the Premiership or la Liga is now far, far better than it is in Croatia or Poland. Turkey, the Netherlands, France and, particularly, Portugal have challenged the hegemony of England, Spain, Italy and Germany of late, but essentially the big four expect to divide the European silverware among themselves. Russia, perhaps, will join that list, but to fans of, for instance, Steaua Bucharest, a second European Cup success is as far away as a second league title is for Ipswich. They play their football at their level, and then they turn on the television and watch the big clubs, with their legions of foreign players, contest the big prizes.

National teams are a different matter. Great generations of players can emerge anywhere at any time, and globalisation actually probably aids the smaller, economically poorer nations in that their players, once sold abroad (and settled – young talents can be ruined by being transplanted too early from their natural environment), benefit from better training facilities and a higher level of competition than they would enjoy in their homelands. It may even be that regular first-team football is not essential: Greece, in 2004, certainly benefited from the fact that their players were on the whole fresher than the bigger names from France, England, Italy and Spain. With varying degrees of nationalistic feeling also playing their part, in fact, international football seems to be becoming increasingly competitive.

*

Symbolically at least, Novy Arbat is the heart of the new Russia. It is tacky, bright, brash and loud, a relentlessly, soullessly vibrant, neon-lit strip of bars and clubs. It is not, in all honesty, my natural habitat, but I am there to watch Chelsea, that other great symbol of the new Russia, play Everton in one of the sports bars that have sprung up across eastern Europe over the past decade.

As I go in, I have to pass through a metal detector. As the doorman says, where there is gambling, it is better there are no guns. Downstairs, the huge dark vault is split in two: to the left, a casino with roulette wheels and blackjack; to the right, a disorienting array of televisions showing sport from across the world. In one corner, a group of British expats watch Wales play South Africa at rugby, in another two tall blond men gaze dispassionately as Djurgården celebrate winning the Swedish Cup final. In the middle, in front of the largest screen, is a blue-shirted horde. With stilted inflection, they sing Chelsea songs, and then, having cheered a 1–0 victory, they roar on Crystal Palace as they gamely hold Arsenal to a draw.

It is not just because of Abramovich. In the manner of fans everywhere, most of those in blue insist they had nailed their colours to the mast long before Chelsea became the grandees they are today. 'You started to see people in Chelsea shirts and scarves from 1992 when [the goalkeeper] Dmitry Kharine went there from CSKA Moscow,' Valery Petrakov, the head of the Moscow Chelsea Supporters Club, tells me. 'And lots of people chose Chelsea because of their reputation for violence.'

The following day, I watch the Manchester derby in the *Bobby Dazzler*, a faux-Irish bar that is home to the Moscow Manchester United Supporters Club. Needless to say, they despise the Ivan-come-latelies who have latched on to Chelsea. The arguments, in other words, are the same as those in which their English counterparts engage. I have been in similar bars and heard similar arguments in Warsaw, Bucharest and Kyiv. Given there is an ironic kudos to be gained from supporting smaller clubs (particularly when they happen to wear the same colours as the local team), I have even, God help me, in a bar in Ljubljana, discussed the form of the Yeovil forward Phil Jevons.

Clubs look abroad, and so, increasingly, do fans. Local football will never wholly die, for certain clubs have an emotional hold, and the market, anyway, requires a nursery for new talent, but this, I suspect is the future: football globalised almost to homogeneity. That may, in time, lead to decline in corruption, but an indefinable something will have been lost.

BIBLIOGRAPHY

Babeshko, Oleksiy and Andriy Babeshko, *Shakhtar* (Diaprint, 2003)

Bali, Janos, 'Ferencvaros, Hungary, and the European Champions League: The Symbolic Construction of Marginality and Exclusion' in Gary Armstrong and Richard Giulianotti (eds), *Fear and Loathing in World Football* (Berg, 2001)

Bowler, Dave, *Winning isn't Everything: A Biography of Sir Alf Ramsey* (Victor Gollancz, 1998)

Charles, John, *King John: The Autobiography* (Headline, 2003)

Connelly, Charlie, *Spirit High and Passion Pure: A Journey Through European Football* (Mainstream, 2000)

Downing, David, *Passovotchka* (Bloomsbury, 1999)

Dougan, Andy, *Dynamo: Defending the Honour of Kyiv* (Fourth Estate, 2001)

Foer, Franklin, *How Soccer Explains the World: An Unlikely Theory of Globalization* (HarperCollins, 2004)

Freddi, Cris, *Complete Book of the World Cup 2002* (CollinsWillow, 2002)

Freeland, Chrystia, *Sale of the Century: The Inside Story of the Second Russian Revolution* (Little, Brown, 2000)

Garton Ash, Timothy, *The History of the Present: Essays, Sketches and Despatches from Europe in the 1990s* (Allen Lane, 1999)

Giulianotti, Richard, *Football: A Sociology of the Global Game* (Polity, 1999)

Glanville, Brian, *Champions of Europe: The History, Romance and Intrigue of the European Cup* (Guinness, 1991)

The Story of the World Cup (Faber and Faber, 2001)

Glover, Jonathan, *Humanity: A Moral History of the Twentieth Century* (Pimlico, 2001)

Górski, Kazimierz, Piłka jest okrągła [The Ball is Round] (Kazimierz Górski, 2004)

Green, Geoffrey, Soccer: the World Game – a Popular History (Pan, 1956; first edition Phoenix House, 1953)

Griffin, Nicholas, Caucasus: A Journey to the Land between Christianity and Islam (University of Chicago Press, 2001)

Grigoryan, Alexander, Iz istorii armyanskogo futbola: ot Bosfora do Kaspiya [A History of Armenian Football: from the Bosphorus to the Caspian] (Amaras, 2003)

Gummer, Andrew, You Come with Me – I Get Tickets: On the Football Terraces with the Locals in 15 European Countries (Parrs Wood Press, 2004)

Handler, Andrew, From Goals to Guns: The Golden Age of Football in Hungary 1950–56 (Columbia University Press, 1994)

Hidegkuti, Nándor, Óbudátó Firenzéig [From Óbuda to Florence] (Sport, 1965)

Hoffman, David E., The Oligarchs: Wealth and Power in the New Russia (Public Affairs, 2002)

Johnston, Harry, The Rocky Road to Wembley (Sportsman's Book Club, 1954)

Jones, Ken, Jules Rimet Still Gleaming: England at the World Cup (Virgin, 2003)

Judah, Tim, The Serbs: History, Myth and the Destruction of Yugoslavia (Yale Nota Bene 2000)

Klebnikov, Paul, Godfather of the Kremlin: The Decline of Russia in the Age of Gangster Capitalism (Harcourt, 2000)

Kucherenko, Oleg, Sto let rossiyskomu futbolu [One Hundred Years of Russian Football] (Russian Football Union, 1997)

Kuper, Simon, Football Against the Enemy (Orion, 1994)

Lebedev, Lev, Rossyiskiy futbol za sto let [Russian Football for 100 Years] (Russian Football Union, 1997)

Lendvai, Paul, The Hungarians: 1000 Years of Victory in Defeat (translated Ann Major, Hurst & Co, 2003; first published as Die Ungarn, Ein Jahrtausend in Niederlagen, Bertelsmann, 1999)

Lomax, Bill, Hungary 1956 (Allison and Busby, 1976)

MacMillan, Margaret, *Peacemakers: Six Months that Changed the World* (John Murray, 2001)

McNally, Raymond T. and Radu Florescu, *In Search of Dracula* (Robson, 1995)

Meisl, Willy, *Soccer Revolution* (Sportsmans Book Club, 1956)

Miller, David, *Cup Magic* (Sidgwick and Jackson, 1981)

Motson, John and John Rowlinson, *The European Cup 1955–1980* (Queen Anne, 1980)

Nilin, Alexander, *Streltsov: Chelovek bez loktey* [*Streltsov: A Man Without Elbows*] (Molodaya Gvardia, 2002)

Politkovskaya, Anna, *Putin's Russia* (Harvill Press, 2004)

Puskás, Ferenc, *Captain of Hungary* (Cassell, 1955)

Redgate, A.E., *The Armenians* (Blackwell, 1998)

Sandbrook, Dominic, *Never Had it so Good: A History of Britain from Suez to the Beatles* (Little, Brown, 2005)

Satter, David, *Darkness at Down: The Rise of the Russian Criminal State* (Yale University Press, 2003)

Sebes, Gusztáv, *Örömök és csalódások* [*Joys and Disappointments*] (Gondolat, 1981)

Shilton, Peter, *Peter Shilton: The Autobiography* (Orion, 2004)

Shirley, Simon and Susannah Wight, *The World Cup: A Definitive History and Guide* (Janus, 2002)

Silber, Laura and Allan Little, *The Death of Yugoslavia* (Penguin and BBC, 1995)

Starostin, Nikolay, *Futbol skvoz' gody* [*Football Through the Years*] (Sovetskaya Rossiya, 1989)

Taubman, William, *Khruschev: The Man, His Era* (Free Press 2003)

Taylor, Rogan and Klara Jamrich (eds), *Puskas on Puskas: The Life and Times of a Footballing Legend* (Robson, 1998)

Végh, Antal, *Gyógyíthatatlan?* [*Incurable?*] (Lapkiadó-Vállalat-Ország-Világ, 1986)

   Miért beteg a magyar futball? [*Why is Hungarian Football Sick?*] (Magvető, 1974)

Vochin, Andrei, *Super Steaua* (Media PRO, 1999)

West, Rebecca, *Black Lamb and Grey Falcon: A Journey Through Yugoslavia* (Macmillan, 1942)

Wilson, Andrew, *The Ukrainians: Unexpected Nation* (Yale Nota
  Bene, 2002)
Winner, David, *Brilliant Orange: The Neurotic Genius of Dutch Football*
  (Bloomsbury, 2000)
  Those Feet: A Sensual History of English Football (Bloomsbury,
  2005)

Yearbooks

Goldblatt, David, *The World Football Yearbook* (Dorling-Kindersley)
Hammond, Mike, *The European Football Yearbook* (Sports Projects)

Magazines and newspapers (UK unless stated)

Aftonbladet (Sweden)
Champions
Daily Telegraph
Delo (Slovenia)
Ekipa (Slovenia)
Financial Times
FourFourTwo
France Football (France)
Gazeta Sporturilor (Romania)
Guardian
Independent
Independent on Sunday
Konsomolskaya Pravda (Russia)
Match (Bulgaria)
Observer
Prosport (Romania)
Przeglad Sportowy (Poland)
Rabotnichesko delo (Bulgaria)
Slobodna Bosna (Bosnia-Hercegovina)
Sovetsky Sport (Russia)
Sport (Serbia-Montenegro)
Sport Express (Russia)
Tempo (Serbia-Montenegro)

The Times
Voetball International (Netherlands)
World Soccer

Websites

Tamás Krauss's essay 'Soccer and Racism in Hungary or: What's the Ajax-Fradi Conflict All About?' at http://eszmelet. tripod.com/angoll/krauszang1.html

The unofficial transcripts of the International Criminal Tribunal for the Former Yugoslavia (ICTY) for the case Milošević 'Kosovo, Croatia, Bosnia Herzegovina' (IT–02–54), as archived at http://mitglied.ly-cos.de/desarea/Dez092002.html

On hooligan and ultra groups:
www.badblueboys.hr
www.hooligans.de
www.oaza.co.yu/sport/delije/prica-e.htm
www.ultrasworld.com

Statistics and news services:
Milos Radulović's remarkable searchable European cups archive at: http://galeb.etf.bg.ac.yu/~mirad/
www.rsssf.com
www.soccerassociation.com
www.soccerbase.com
www.uefa.com

INDEX

INDEX

Ministry of the Interior, Ukraine, 19
Ministry of Internal Affairs, Bulgaria, 186
Ministry of Justice, Azerbaijan, 260
Mirković, Zoran, 157–8
Mirzoev, Ramiz, 261, 262, 263
Misimović, Zvjezdan, 180
Miskolc, 96
Mitev, Yordan, 195
Mitkov, Vassil, 194
Miu, Iulian, 227
Mkhedrioni, 234, 235
MKS, 282
Molde, 295
Moldova, 10
Möller, Andreas, 197
Montana, 198
Montgomery, Jim, 43
Moore, Bobby, 48
Morlock, Max, 82
Morocco, 46
Morozov, Yury, 31
Mortenson, Stan, 78
Moscow, 10, 16, 33, 34, 71, 86, 237, 241, 245, 265, 270, 271, 285, 291, 294, 295
    Council, 284, 286, 287
    Metro, 280
Moscow Chelsea Supporters Club, 303
Moscow Manchester United Supporters Club, 303
Mostar, 168, 179–80
Mostovoi, Alexander, 289, 290
Moulin, Stéphane, 219, 220
Mount Ararat, 242
Mount Vitosha, 199
Moutinho, 300
Mretebi, 236
MSI (Media Sports Investments), 297
MTK, 73–4, 87, 89, 90, 92, 94–5
Mtskheta, 229, 231
Muharemović, Dželaludin, 175–6
Mukachevo, 39
Mulalić, Edis, 168
Mulina, Siniša, 180
Munich, 44, 59
Mura, 138, 141
Musaev, Fuad, 256–7, 257–8, 259, 260, 261
Musemić, Husred, 171
Musiał, Adam, 47
Muslin, Slavoljub, 115–16
Mutu, Adrian, 158, 159, 218
Muzurović, Fuad, 171–2, 173, 174, 176, 177–8

Muzorović, Mirza, 173
Mykhailychenko, Oleksiy, 15, 22–3

Nadj, Albert, 158
Naftex Bourgas, 200
Naftohaz Ukrayiny, 40
Nagorno-Karabakh, 248
Nagy, Imre, 71, 85, 86, 88
Najdoski, Ilija, 107
Nantes, 294
Naples, 106
Nastase, Adrian, 222
National Bucharest, 220, 221, 222, 226, 228
National Anti-Doping Commission, Romania, 217
Neaga, Adrian, 218
Nedelchev, Stoyou, 194
Neeskens, Johan, 128
Neftchi, 256, 258, 259, 260, 261
Neftyanik, 35–6
Népstadion, 79, 92 (see also Ferenc Puskás Stadium)
Netherlands see Holland/Netherlands
Newcastle, 263
Niculescu, Claudiu, 228
Nieto, Lopez, 20
Nigeria, 48, 196
Nikel, Norilsk, 298
Nikoghosyan, Armen, 252
Nikolić, Dejan, 117
Nikolov, Plamen, 186, 189
Nilin, Alexander, 267, 277
Nitu, Gheorghe, 217
NK Bežigrad, 145
NKVD, 11
NK Zagreb, 176
Northern Ireland, 207, 255
Norway, 59
Nottingham Forest, 186
Nova Ljubljanska Bank, 163
Novi Sad, 3, 100
Novruzov, Sudzhethan, 257
Novy Arbat, 303
NSBiH (Bosnian Football Federation), 171, 179
Nydotless Nyíregyháza, 96
Nyilasi, Tibor, 76, 84, 89
NZS (Slovenian Football Federation), 130, 131, 132, 133, 134, 138, 139

Obilić, 105, 112–14, 115
Obilić, Miloš, 113
Oblak, Brane, 128, 129, 130–1, 135, 136, 140, 141, 162